D1345908

GRAMPIAN WAYS

The Bedford memorial bridge in Glen Tilt.

GRAMPIAN WAYS

Journey over the Mounth

Robert Smith

With 44 photographs taken by the author

MELVEN

PRESS
PERTH 1980

Published by
The Melven Press,
176 High Street, Perth, Scotland

ISBN 0 906664 01 2

Acknowledgements are due to Aberdeen University Press for permission to quote from John Milne's poem *Singing Willie*.

Our thanks are due to John Bartholomew, Duncan Street, Edinburgh, for preparing the maps.

Printed and bound in Great Britain by
Morrison & Gibb Ltd., London and Edinburgh

To Sheila, who shared the miles, and
Mandy, who first led the way.

Contents

Illustrations

Maps

Note:
There is a Bawdy Meg and a Baudy Meg—different spelling.
Cairn-a-*Mount* is the peak on the Cairn-a-*Mounth* road.
There is also Tolmount and Tolmounth.
A number of similar words have different spellings: i.e.
Craig and Creag.

Introduction

The Blue Hill marks the eastern rim of the Grampians, a chain of mountains strung like a jagged necklace across the breast of Scotland. There is a broken indicator on top of the cairn, with marker lines reaching out to the nearest peaks. They carry names like Gowl Hill and Finella Hill, Cairn-mon-Earn and Kerloch, Clochnaben and Mount Battock. The remaining fragmented lettering on the indicator points to the mighty Cairngorms.

In the late 18th century, a geographical delineation of Scotland divided the country into three parts, with the middle section containing "many great ranges of mountains." "The most southerly ridge, called the Grampian Hills," said the writer, "extends from Aberdeenshire in a south-west direction, terminating in the great mountain of Ben Lomond, or rather in the mountainous district of Cowal." It is clear enough where the Grampians begin; no one is certain where they end. The limits of the range have been as elastic as the whims of cartographers, so that the word "Grampian" has become an uncertain scrawl on many maps. If it is measured by the passes that cut across its scree-scarred roof, the range runs from the Causey Mounth on the east to the Drumochter Pass, which is roughly the central point of Drumalban, a backbone mountain ridge extending from Ben Hope in Sutherland to Ben Lomond in Stirlingshire.

The name itself has uncertain origins. It was said to have come from the Gaelic "gruaim," meaning gloominess, and "beinn," a mountain, and that the Grampians were called the gloomy mountains "on account of the clouds which often cover them." The historian Hector Boece is also blamed for fostering the word by confusing the words "Graupius" and "Grampius." Whatever the answer, the word "Grampian" stuck, bringing a slow erosion and finally the virtual disappearance of the ancient name of the mountain chain—the Mounth. The word is from the Gaelic "monadh," meaning a mountain or moorland, but it ceased to apply to the Grampians as a whole and came to denote individual passes such as the Causey Mounth. When you speak to an older generation of folk on Deeside about the old hill routes they still talk about the Mounth, pronouncing it Munth. This was the old spelling, and Aberdeen's first trade charter from William the Lion in the 13th century referred to "north of the Munth." Going even farther back, records mention Hungus, King of the Picts, crossing a mountainous district called "the Moneth."

The Mounth was the main gateway to the south and through it ran a whole series of passes, twisting their tortuous way by moorland and loch to the towns and market places of the Mearns and Angus, to the Falkirk Tryst and Paldy's Fair, and south again to the Borders and England. Saints and missionaries carried their message of Christianity over its snow-whitened peaks, coming down from its heights to build their chapels in the valleys. Drovers herded their cattle along the rough and dusty tracks in great cross-country treks that began far to the north and west to Skye. Bandits plundered the unwary traveller using the passes and pillaging armies fought their way across them.

John Barbour, Archdeacon of Aberdeen from 1357 until his death in 1395, made frequent references to the Mounth in his epic, *The Bruce*. After the Battle of Loudoun Hill, King Robert "passit north beyond the Month," and Barbour also told how the outlawed king and his friends "dreand in the Month thar pyne" (endured in the Mounth their suffering). The Month, in one edition of *The Bruce*, was said to be "the mountain which is called the Mound, which stretches from the western to the eastern sea".

Sir James Balfour of Denmylne, who was Lord Lyon King

of Arms to both Charles I and Charles II, drew up a list of "The Chief passages from the River Tay to the River Dee over the Mountains." The list, published about 1630, is not complete, but it is a useful starting point for tracing the line of the Mounth passes. Of the more important passes, the Elsick Mounth can be disregarded, since its actual path is a matter of conjecture rather than fact. It was the route taken by the Romans when they advanced from Kair in Fordoun, crossed the lower Grampians, forded the River Dee at Tilbouries, west of Aberdeen, and pressed north to the Moray Firth. The only reminders of this ancient route are the Roman marching camps at Normandykes, across the Tilbouries ford, and at Raedykes in the Mearns. Two other minor passes led from the Cairn-a-Mounth to Glenbervie and Glenfarquhar—the Stock Mounth, listed by Sir James as "ye Passage from Glenberby to Straquhan one Deesyde," and the Builg Mounth, which linked the main route with Paldy Fair near Glenfarquhar Lodge.

Four of the major passes remain as effective road links; the modern A9 by the Drumochter Pass, the Cairnwell, the Cairn-a-Mounth and the Slug Road. The number is increased to five if the Causey Mounth, or what is left of it, is taken into account.

This then, is the background to what follows. To each track or group of paths where appropriate, is devoted a chapter and my impressions given from years of walking in all weathers and seasons. The hills have always given me pleasure and this partly inspired the book—with a hope that others may be motivated to see and find their own way along these well trodden tracks.

Robert Smith,
Aberdeen, 1979.

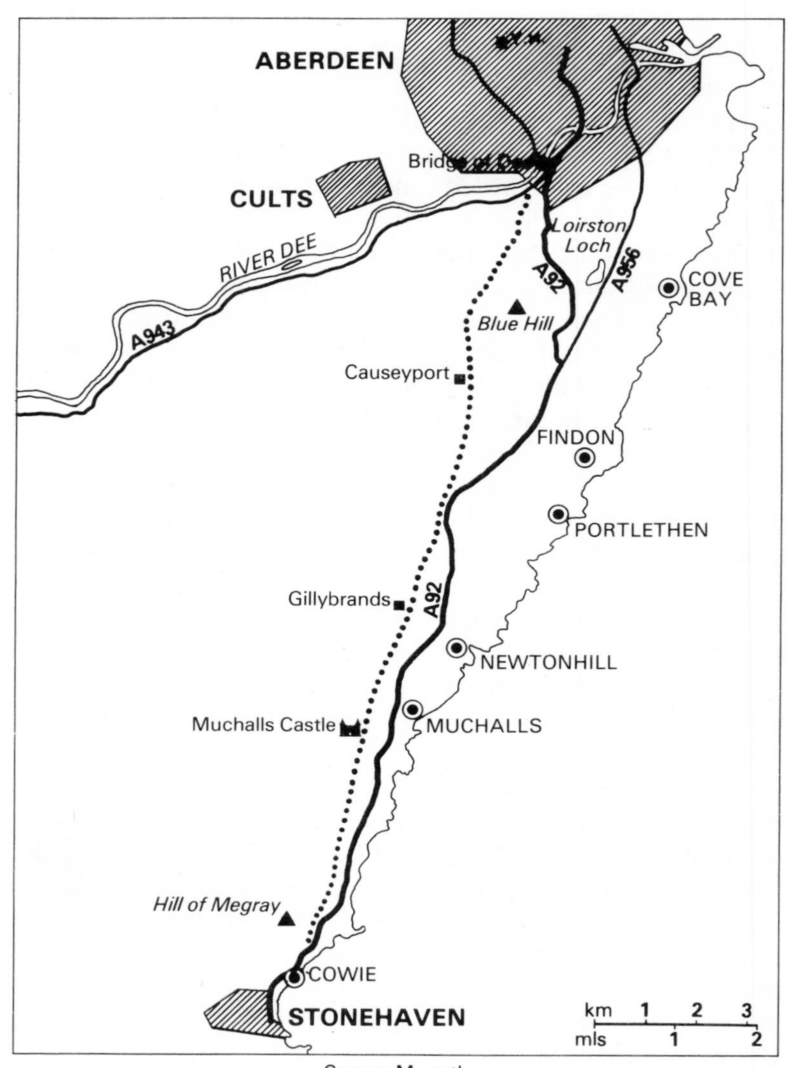

Causey Mounth

1

Causey Mounth

The Blue Hill lies south of Aberdeen, almost two miles from the Bridge of Don and less than a mile from the city's main road link with the south. It is not much of a hill. Even in the broom-bright days of summer it is no longer the week-end mecca that it once was. The paths to the top of the hill have almost disappeared. The cairn on the summit is crumbling away and the old kissing-gate on the road below it is rusted and decaying. Nevertheless, it has its own small place in the story of the north-east of Scotland, for it sits between past and present. To the east is the A92, carrying a tide of traffic that has made the city one of the major oil centres of the world. To the west, running parallel to it and largely swallowed up by modern road development, is the ancient pass known as the Causey Mounth, now a tarmacadam tailpiece to history. It might well have been here that Robert Burns, on his way south, stopped to look back on Aberdeen and remark that it was a lazy town. Now he would see only its oil-rich opulence, the great sweep of its bay busy with supply boats shuttling back and forth to the oil fields, its roads full of the roar and rumble of road-freighters bringing a new wealth to the city.

The Causey Mounth was also known as the Cowie or Cowy Mounth, taking the name from the vanished village of Cowie and the castle at its southern end. Mount Cowie is shown in Gordon of Straloch's map of 1654. John Hardyng, who was sent to Scotland during the reign of James I to obtain certain deeds which were supposed to confirm the superiority of England, wrote in his "Chronicle"—

Than to Monrosse and to Barvye
And so through the Meernes to Cowy as I wene,

Then 11 myles of moor pass to Aberdyne
Betwyxt Dee and Done a goodly cytee,
A marchaunt towne and universytee.

The pass was also known simply as the Mounth, although here the word applied more generally to the area through which it passed than to the road itself. In this sense, one writer described the Mounth as being cut ten miles in breadth and "traversed by a very rugged road which, before the era of turnpikes, was the principal highway leading from Stonehaven to Aberdeen."

The Causey Mounth bore no resemblance to its modern successor. One account described it as a "morass," and both carriages and pedestrians would have found it impassable in winter had it not been for the "causeys" which gave it its name. There were two main stretches of causeway, one about three-quarters of a Scotch mile in length, the other about a quarter of a mile. The punishment they took from traffic and weather was formidable and in 1634 Aberdeen Town Council successfully petitioned the Privy Council of Scotland for permission to exact a toll on the Causey Mounth to pay for its maintenance. "The Calsies in Cowymonth ar now so worn and decayed as there will be no possibilitie of passage in this approaching winter," they warned, going on to say of the work that there was "none within the kingdome more important and necessar." The toll was not the complete answer, for twenty-four years later, in 1658, a Captain Franks who visited the north of Scotland passed over the Mounth and declared, "Causeys uncartable, pavements unpracticable." They were, he said, daubed all over with dingy dirt and the fields were ten times worse, being spread over with miry clay and "encumbered with bogs that will bury a horse."

The upkeep of the Causey Mounth was always a problem, for as far back as 1384 an Aberdeen burgess, John Crab, made provision for an annual sum of money to be paid through his son Paul for the maintenance of the road. The Crabs were owners of the estate of Kincorth, on the south bank of the

River Dee at Aberdeen, and the name is still retained in the housing estate there. The word "Kincorth" is said to mean the head or end of the stony place and it was here that my journey over the first of the Mounth passes began, at a spot where travellers forded the river on their way to and from Aberdeen. It was at one time known as the "Foords," and to-day there is still a stretch of fishing there called the "Pot and Ford," while a hostel on the north bank carries the name "Deeford." The Pot Burn, which gave the popular fishing stretch on the river half its name, is now known as Ruthrieston Burn. It is an insignificant stream, buried in the granite of the Ruthrieston district of Aberdeen, but it was tumbling down into the Dee more than eight centuries ago when Ruadri, a Celtic Mormaer of Mar, had a "motte and bailey" stronghold on the edge of the Foords. In later years, cattle and horse dealers came over the Mounth to the trysts at "Ruadri's toun."

The Pot Burn was not always as tranquil as it is today, for it had to be forded by travellers going along the north bank of the river from the Bridge of Dee, and in 1541 the magistrates decided to build a wooden bridge across it. This was replaced in 1693-94 by a pack-bridge, decorated with heraldic panels and inscriptions. The Old Pack Bridge is still there, sitting a little forlornly in a cluster of trees where the burn meets the Dee, but some of its character has gone, for in 1923 the bridge was moved a short distance from its original site and rebuilt with parapets. No heavily-laden pack-horse would be able to cross it now. The Pack Brig was built more than a decade after the completion of the Bridge of Dee and the Foords gradually slipped into disuse. The crossing, one of thirteen on the Dee listed by Sir James Balfour between Braemar and the estuary, has given faithful service. William the Lion probably used it when he visited the city, as did his son, Alexander II, travelling north in 1221 to spend Christmas in the burgh with his sister, Princess Isabella.

Oure the Mownth theyne passyd he sene,
And held hys Yhule in Abbyrdene.

Old pack bridge over the River Dee at Aberdeen.

The old Bridge of Dee still carries the bulk of traffic to and from the city, despite the modern alternative of the King George VI Bridge a little to the east. There was once a chapel on the north-east corner of the old bridge, where travellers could pray before setting out over the unfriendly miles of the Causey Mounth. Now there are traffic lights, hooting horns and impatient motorists.

The path from the Foords can still be followed along the south bank of the River Dee. West of the Bridge of Dee, from the pleasant little garden which lies below the traffic-riddled road, it runs through a jungle of nettles and weeds bordering the back-gardens of houses on Leggart Terrace, the street which opens out on to the South Deeside Road. It disappears at the Leggart Burn, which was once forded by wayfarers on their way over the Causey Mounth, and it is at the bridge over the burn by the old Poldown Mill that the road climbs away from the city, rising between the Blue Hill and Cran Hill. On the way it passes the farm of Tollohill, which stands where Montrose's soldiers looked down on the town before the Battle of the Bridge of Dee.

History rolls back the years as you travel up from Tollohill to the crossroads at Banchory-Devenick Post Office and look straight and clear down the Causey road. Along this once-dusty highway came Edward III and his army after the ravaging of Aberdeen in 1336. Cromwell's Roundheads marched along the route in 1651 and in 1716 the remnants of a shattered Jacobite army struggled north over the Causey Mounth in the face of bitter winter weather while the Old Pretender slipped away to exile from Montrose. And if you look hard enough you may even see Dugald Dalgetty of Drumthwacket come riding down the causeway, his head-piece burnished bright, rich with its plume of feathers, a case of pistols slung across his military saddle and a double-edged sword at his side. Although Sir Walter Scott was a rare visitor to Aberdeen, he was so struck by the wild, bleak landscape through which the Causey Mounth passed that he immortalised it in *A Legend of Montrose* as the Moor of Drumthwacket, the patrimony of Captain Dalgetty, a soldier of fortune who had taken his "gentle bluid and designation of Drumthwacket" to serve under Gustavus Adolphus in the German wars.

The Moor of Drumthwacket was thought to be the Moor of Drumforskie, about two miles from the Bridge of Dee, which one writer a century ago described as "a most unsightly object to travellers" before it was cultivated. Part of it can still be seen under its present name of Hare Moss, which lies to the west of the Causey, about a mile south of the Blue Hill and only a field's length from the present road. Hare Moss is a small and soggy reminder of what the whole countryside was like along the Causey Mounth at one time and looking at it one wonders why Sir Dugald ever wanted to return to it. This was a barren, treeless landscape, and at the end of the 18th century it was said that Aberdeenshire, for miles backward from the coast, was "perfectly destitute of trees." Kincardine was no exception.

When Dr Samuel Johnson made his famous journey to the Western Islands in 1773 with James Boswell he described the country on the road from Montrose as "naked." There was another Boswell who came to this part of the country and made his mark on it. South-west from Hare Moss, at the Hill of Auchlee, set back from a side road that crosses the old Mounth pass, a familiar landmark provides a striking memorial to John Irvine-Boswell, the laird of Kincausie, who sought to turn this uncompromising moorland into wealth-producing farmland. White wisps of cotton sedge and the gaunt fingers of stunted trees lead you through the heather and bog which surround the massive stone tower known as Boswell's Monument. Boswell was born in 1785 and died in 1860 and the tower was built by his widow, Margaret. The wording on a granite plaque on the side of it reads, "He lived to transform the natural barrenness of the estate into luxuriant fertility."

The heavy iron door of the tower, facing south, swings open on forty-three winding stone steps which lead to a small and perilous platform beneath the crown topping the monument. Through its narrow arched windows I could see across the countryside to where the ancient causeway had pushed its way through the Mearns. The word "Kincausie" was itself a reminder of the old days, for it means "head of the causey." The writing was on the wall for the Mounth road two years after John Irvine-Boswell was born, for it was in 1787 that the first mail coach ran between Edinburgh and Aberdeen and by the end of the century plans were under way for a new road. Long before that, in 1760, the growing use of wheeled traffic made Aberdeen Town Council decide to remove the toll gate on the Causey Mounth "in order to straight and widen the king's highway." The paying of tolls was done at the Causey Port, or Gate, and the price of a "foot passenger" was 2d. A horseman had to pay the same price as ten sheep, 2d, and a cow or an ox cost 4d. A cartload went up to 2s. Scots. The actual site of the Gate is uncertain, but a fairly clear indication is given in the 18th century *View of the Diocese of Aberdeen*, quoting from Macfarlane's *Geographical Collections*. "To the north of Auchorties one and a half mile is the Caulsay Port, with a large caulsay which passes throw a large moss, and the port was built and the caulsay laid MD.C.LXXXIV by the city of Aberdeen; and the said town setts in tack the said port to a man who gathered up from every horse that passes throw the port eight pennies Scots; at the north end, the said Caulsay passes throw the Grampian hills, which goe straight to the sea, and there is a large highway passes from Aberdeen to Edinburgh along this caulsay." The date, 1684, is an error. There is a Causeywend shown in James Robertson's "Topographical and Military Map" of the Counties of Aberdeen, Banff and Kincardine in 1822. The name Causeyport is retained in the farm of Causeyport, south of Hare Moss and Duff's Hill, while there are Causeyport Cottages on the opposite side of the road.

The three-and-a-half mile stretch of road from Poldown Mills, on the South Deeside Road, to a road coming west from Hillside on the A92 is one of the two stretches of the Causey Mounth still in use by traffic. Beyond this it continues as a farm road to Craighead. From Craighead, what remained of the old track thrust towards Old Bourtreebush and I had to push through a wilderness of waist-high grass and weeds and over a spreading barrier of whin and bog. There is a right of way from Bourtreebush to Berryhill House, an imposing red-brick mansion which looks down the second stretch of the Causey Mounth still used by traffic. The tarmacadam surface disappears when it reaches the side road from Cammachmore and south of this becomes a dirt road passing two or three modern bungalows and the gate leading to Elsick House, home of the Duke of Fife, son of the late Princess Maud and the Earl of Southesk.

Thomas Kirke, in his tour of Scotland in 1677, wrote of Elsick as "Elsip." "We called at the Laird of Elsip's house," he recorded, "but he was not at home." Elsick House at one time belonged to the family of Bannerman and the laird at the time of Kirke's visit was Sir Alexander Bannerman, who had been created a baronet by Charles II for his loyalty during the Civil Wars. Kirke, who went over the Causey Mounth to

Aberdeen from 'Stonehive,' described how he and his companions took a footman with them as a guide from Dundee, "it being the custom in these parts to travel upon hired horses." "They send a footman along with them to bring them back again; this footman serves as a guide all the way, and when you alight, he takes care of the horse: they will undertake to run down the best horse you can buy in seven or eight days; they run by the horse's side all the way, and travel thirty and forty miles a day with ease: you may have a horse and a guide for twopence a mile."

Below the entrance to Elsick House the track dips down towards the curiously-named Gillybrands Farm. This was the site of an inn in the old days of the Mounth and Taylor and Skinner's map of the roads of Scotland in 1775 shows it as Jeally Brans Inn. Despite the modern spelling, the name has been carried down a couple of hundred years to both the farm and the farmer. "They just ca' me 'Jeally'," he says. From "Jeally's" place the road rises up to Windyedge Farm. Stand there on a cold day, with the cutting edge of a snell Nor'-easter whistling across the fields, and you will think it well-named.

I stopped to talk to the farmer, wondering if he was often troubled with people poking through his farmyard in search of a lost highway, but apparently not. "There was only one chap I remember," he recalled. "He said that Mary Queen of Scots came past here and he was going to make a film of it. It was a terrible day of rain and the road was an awful state of mud. This chap took one look and said, 'I'm not going down that road even if Mary Queen of Scots is standing at the bottom of it.' I never saw him again." I left the farmer musing on how his chance of fame had been sucked away in north-east rain and glaur and made my way south to St Ternan's, passing the farm of Pheepsie—"Fepe," as Taylor and Skinner called the burn nearby—just before reaching it. This old Episcopal church, tucked away in the trees of the Cookney road, is almost the end of the Causey Mounth as a distinct and identifiable road. Mountgatehead, about a mile farther south, was where the

A farm track alone marks the former Causey Mounth at Gillybrands—once an inn.

causies or calseys came to an end, although the road continued to Stonehaven.

Between St Ternan's Chapel and Mountgatehead is Muchalls Castle. The Causey road, cutting through an area of land known as the Whinward Plantation, covers part of the present road to the castle. Alexander Burnett of Crathes began building Muchalls Castle in 1619 and it was completed by his son, Sir Thomas, in 1627. There is a room said to be haunted by a Green Lady, a daughter of one of the lairds, who was drowned while going down a secret passage to the sea to meet a smuggling friend. The guide said the Green Lady hadn't been seen for some time, but remarked casually that the Yellow Lady had been spotted once or twice. The latter gets her name from the yellow dress she wears, but whatever the colour, not many castles can boast of two female spectres haunting their interiors.

The Causey followed a line across the Burn of Muchalls to Auquorthies, the Limpet Mill and Logie, and on to the Hill of Megray, scene of the "Raid of Stanehyve" in 1639, when the Royalist forces of Viscount Aboyne were defeated by the Covenanters. From Megray Hill, looking across the main railway track from Aberdeen, you can see the last of the Causey Mounth. The old highway doesn't end with a flourish. Instead, it creeps almost ashamedly along the rear wall of the grounds of Cowie House, on the outskirts of Stonehaven, unseen and unused, a tangle of overgrown grass and weeds. The ancient burgh of Cowie once stood here, stretching from the Hill of Megray to the Mains of Cowie, a farm beyond Cowie House. The farm itself is on the site of the White House Inn, once the main hostelry between Aberdeen and Edinburgh.

There is no trace of the ancient burgh of Cowie, but on the cliff-tops opposite Megray Hill a number of stone blocks half-hidden in the grass provide the last remaining link with the Castle of Cowie, the key to the Causey or Cowie Mounth.

These stone blocks are all that remain of Cowie Castle.

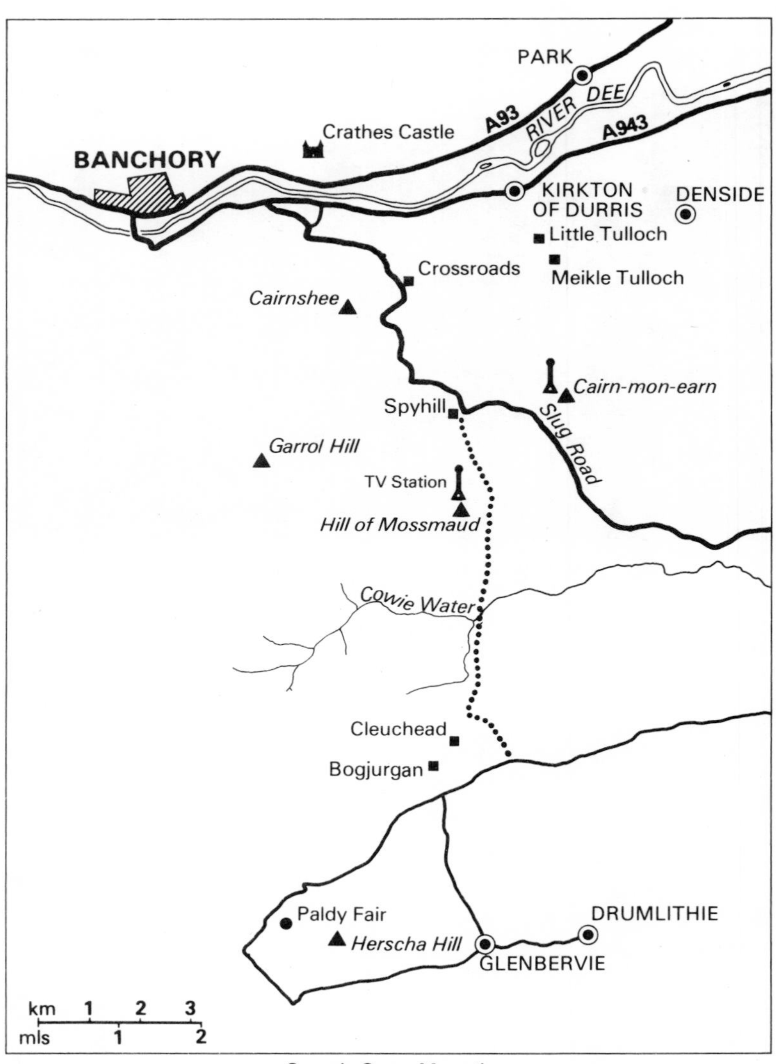

Cryne's Corse Mounth

2

Cryne's Corse Mounth

The citizens of Aberdeen who watched the solemn procession ride by called them the Apostles of the Covenant. Three were ministers, the Rev. David Dickson, of Irvine, the Rev. Alexander Henderson, of Leuchars, and the Rev. Andrew Cant, of Pitsligo. The others, ill-matched with this brooding trio of clerics, were nobles, among them the young Earl of Montrose and Sir Thomas Burnett of Leys. The year was 1638 and their purpose was to convert the City Fathers to the National Covenant. They had an unhappy start, rejecting the magistrates' offer of the traditional Cup of Bon-Accord until the Council subscribed to the Covenant, with the result that the wine was given to the poor and on Sunday the church doors were shut in the commissioners' faces. The Covenanters held their service in the courtyard of the Earl Marischal's house in the Castlegate and, as the Aberdeen chronicler John Spalding put it, "diverse people flocked in within the said close to hear thir preachers and see this noveltie". The visitors left Aberdeen on July 23, hoping for better things in the presbyteries of Buchan, and after returning to the city five days later departed south. The douce townsfolk marked their departure with a piece of street doggerel—

From Dickson, Henderson and Cant,
Apostles of the Covenant,
Good Lord deliver us!

The paths of three of the men in that oddly-assorted party were to cross in curious ways during the years that followed. Montrose, abandoning the Covenanting cause for the Royal standard, was given the King's Commission as Lieutenant-

General and set off with his wild Highland brigade on a military rampage that became known as the "Year of Miracles." His campaign led him by the Causey Mounth to the gates of Dunnottar Castle, where his army burned "the barneyairds of Dunnottar, housses, cornes, and all," while his old ally, Andrew Cant, watched the destruction from behind the castle walls. The reek, he told the Earl Marischal, would be "a sweet-smelling savour in the nostrils of the Lord." Cant became a leading minister in the town whose cup of friendship he had refused. "He was not very wellcome to all," said John Spalding sourly. Unlike Montrose, Burnett of Leys remained faithful to the Covenant but, weary of the excesses of power shown by its leaders, withdrew to his castle on the Dee. He was, in Spalding's words, "ane great Covenanter," and it is one of the enigmas of the time that he remained so friendly with James Graham, the young Earl, even giving him the hospitality of his castle home when he rode down the old Cryne's Corse pass from the Mearns to the Dee on his way to attack the Covenanters in Aberdeen.

The ancient Grampian pass called the Cryne's Corse (Cross) Mounth was well-known to Montrose. That was the way he came to Deeside in the fateful autumn of 1644, when he set his forces loose on Aberdeen. On the north side of the Dee, as well as the route to Aberdeen, roads went north to Huntly by the old Candyglirach and Cullerlie routes, but on the south side of the river a track struck west to a crossing at Balbridie, where you can still see the old toll-house, a neat white building with a milestone beneath its window telling you that you are sixteen miles from Aberdeen. Once across the river at this point the road went by the Mill of Hirn, Monymusk, Huntly and the north.

The Hirn road lies between Crathes Castle and a marshy area of land north of the farm of Lochtown of Leys, a mile from Banchory. The farm takes its name from the loch that was there until the middle of last century. Six centuries ago a stronghold stood on a crannog island in the middle of this vanished stretch of water. It was the home of Sir Alexander de

Burnard, who, like Irvine of Drum, was granted land in recognition of his services to Robert the Bruce. The lands of Killenachclerach or Killenachclerocht, the Candyglirach of to-day, were included in the grant and the loch became known as the Loch of Leys. The Burnett family abandoned their island home in the 16th century and moved into Crathes Castle. The Castle, like Drum Castle, is in the care of the National Trust for Scotland.

Crathes Castle.

John Buchan's *Montrose* says that prior to the ravaging of Aberdeen the Royalist troops crossed the River Dee "about mid-way between Banchory and the Mills of Drum," and it is possible that this was at Balbridie. In his journeyings over the Mounth, however, the Marquis generally crossed the Dee farther east, and Spalding has a number of references to them fording it at "the Milnes of Drum." The precise location of the ford has never been established, although it is known that there were two ferries, the West boat and the East boat, near the Mills of Drum. The West boat was used until a bridge was built in 1862; now it, in turn, has given way to a more modern structure. The East boat was near the Church of Durris, and here we come nearer to marking the spot where Montrose and his wild Irishers went splashing through the waters of the Dee as they came down from the Mounth.

Many of the river crossings connected with the Mounth routes were at or near a church, chapel or hospice, and it is probable that the Cryne's Corse pass emerged not far from the Church of Durris, perhaps where the "East boat" ferry plied its trade. It is certainly in line with the old pass and links directly with the Candyglirach road on the north bank of the Dee. There is one more clue. Castles as well as churches commanded the major routes, and about two miles below Durris Bridge, a stone's throw from the South Deeside Road, you can walk to the river's edge and stand where Edward I of England, the Hammer of the Scots, spent a night in his "manour among the mountains" on July 13th, 1296.

There is not much to see to-day of the great "manour", the motte and bailey Castle of Durris; no more than a wooded knoll overlooking the Dee, almost opposite Park House, on the north bank. Even so, you can conjure up in your mind's eye the awesome spectacle of 30,000 men-at-arms and 5000 mail-clad knights marshalling at the Castlehill, a mighty force strung along the riverbank, ready to advance on Aberdeen the following day. From Aberdeen, Edward moved up Deeside to the Peel of Lumphanan and from there marched north to Elgin. He returned by Kincardine O'Neil, fording the Dee there on his way over the Cairn-a-Mounth to the south.

I left the Dee valley and made my way south to Cairn-mon-earn, a familiar hill overlooking the Slug Road. The Slug Road, or part of it, is one of three Mounth roads still in use as traffic routes from Deeside to the south. It is not the most romantic of names and has its origin in the Gaelic word "slochd," meaning pass. Little is known of its history before the coming of turnpikes in the 18th century and it is used now as a short-cut to and from the Mearns, as well as being a pleasant Sunday run for motorists. Less than a mile up the

Slug a side road goes to Tilquhillie Castle, which sits a little incongruously in the middle of a clutter of farm buildings. The Marquis of Montrose would have kept a watchful eye on this 16th century fortalice when he went over the Mounth, for it was garrisoned by Covenanters.

About two miles from Balbridie is the hamlet of Cross-roads and to the right the fields slope up to the wooded summit of Cairnshee, which probably takes its name from the cairn there. Whatever mystic rites are associated with stone circles, Cairnshee had its own midsummer ritual many years ago, when local folk gathered there to build a monster fire, seen for miles around. There was nothing sinister in this annual ceremony. Alexander Hogg, a native of the parish, left ten shillings yearly to the herdsmen around the hill so that they could make a midsummer fire as a "memorial" to the fact that he himself once herded cattle there. Less than a mile further is the farm of Blairydryne, on the road branching west just before crossing the Sheeoch. It was along this road that King James V came, travelling incognito, making his way to Durris from the Cairn-a-Mounth, past Mulloch Hill, the Hill of the Nine Stanes, relics of the Bronze Age. The king, seeking refuge from a storm, stopped at Blairydryne and the farmer, Monane Hogg, was lavish in his hospitality. The king rewarded him by making him laird of his land and granting the property to him and his descendants.

Crossing the Burn of Sheeoch, I went uphill past the smiddy of Lochton. The pass over the hills leaves the Slug Road below Cairn-mon-earn, just beyond the farm of Spyhill. Uphill from Spyhill, where the Slug takes a sharp bend, a cottage marks the start of the road to the IBA television mast, perched 1060 ft above sea level and itself towering 1000 ft above its hill-top site, beaming out its programmes to the north and south-west towards Dundee. The Independent Television Authority describe it as "exposed and difficult of access," but the surfaced road to the station was luxury travel compared to the remains of the Crynes Corse Pass that lay beyond.

A chill wind tugged at the coat-tails of summer as I toiled up the hill, glancing back to the distant heights of Benachie and the Hill of Fare. To the north-west, Scolty Tower could be seen above Banchory and away to the west Clochnaben brushed the curtain of cloud that moved in ominously over the woods of Fetteresso. On the right was Mongour (1232 feet) and on the left Craigbeg (1054 feet), Crynes Corse Pass pushing between them to the south. It crosses a small stream running down to the Slug Road and rising from a chalybeate spring on Mongour. Red Beard's Well, it is called, and it takes its name from the leader of a robber band who hid in a cave on Craigbeg and waited for unwary travellers crossing the Mounth. They would have had small pickings on this bleak September day.

The old Mounth pass branches off to the left before you reach the TV mast, but the easier way is to loop round the track in front of the station and rejoin the pass below it. Twin cables arcing down from the top of the mast point the way and as I looked up and back the clouds scudding across the sky gave the fleeting impression that the whole mass of metal was about to fall on my head. Plodding downhill, I couldn't help wondering what Scottish patriot William Wallace would have thought if he had come upon this towering structure nearly 700 years before. This desolate hill-top site takes its place in modern history as a booster station for the joys of commercial television, not to mention the tedium of Party political broadcasts. Six or seven centuries ago the politicians and patriots would have put over their message in a more direct way.

Wallace crossed the Cryne's Cross Mounth when he descended on Deeside on his way to launch his attack on Aberdeen. The facts about Wallace's assault on the city are obscure. It was on that trip that he is said to have captured Dunnottar Castle and wiped out its English garrison. Edward of England also crossed the pass in 1296. "Our the Month that tyrand past," reported Andrew of Wyntoun. His "Chronicles," giving an account of what "langschankys

Edwarde did in Scotlande," said that—

Castell baith and wallit toune,
He tuke all in possessioune,
And stuffit thaim with Inglismen.

The origin of the name Cryne's Corse or Cross has never been clearly established; one theory was that it was named after a well-known Aberdeen family called Cryne. It is interesting, therefore, to note that Wyntoun mentioned a Corse Cryne in his "Chronicles," although this particular place was in the south of Scotland. He was writing about a march made by King David II through the Lammermuir Hills from Cockburnspath in the east to Soutra, a route followed by many warring monarchs, including Edward I. This Corse Cryne was also called Crossecarne, and, curiously, Sir James Balfour of Denmylne lists the Deeside Mounth route as Craigincrosse, not Cryne's Cross. "Craigincrosse monthe layes from ye churche of S. Paladius wulgarly called pade kirke in ye Mearns to ye Mylles of Drum." The "pade kirk" is a reminder that the drovers, too, went over the Cryne's Cross pass, driving their cattle to Paldy Fair, near Auchenblae. The fair, named after St Palladius, was held on the Hill of Herscha.

These were the twists and turns of fate that floated on the wind as I made my way down from Craigbeg, hugging the eastern slope of the Hill of Mossmaud on an ancient track that had once been a path to power for ambitious and ruthless men. This was how they had come and gone, past the bleak face of the Stony Muir and along the edge of the wood to where the track drops sharply down to the Cowie Water. The track follows the line of telephone poles to the Cowie, crossing a forest road a little way down. You can turn right here and follow the forest road, detouring round the west section of the forest and coming out at the Cowie Water, but it is a longer walk. The direct way is due south until you cross the East and West Dumer Burns.

On the way down I could see at the other side of the

valley the main forest road through Fetteresso, cleaving a path uphill to the Braes of Glenbervie. But before I reached this track I had to pick my way across rough and boggy ground at the Dumer Burns to another forest road running east to west. The Mounth road is to the right; to the left the road goes past a Forestry Commission picnic site to Mergie House and the Slug Road. Whether the picnic site is much used I do not know, but there are no signs on it, or on the Slug, indicating that it is there.

Certainly, one well-known visitor to the forest was less than welcome. The stane Hoose o' Mergie, a forbidding mansion set in the trees a short distance from the Slug Road, dates back to the 17th century, and Robert Burns had a fleeting association with it when he poached the Cowie Water and was caught in the act by the laird of Mergie. Burns is said to have thrown away his rod and hot-footed out of it. Later, with typical contempt for the gentry, he penned the lines—

> "You're fish are scarce, your water's sma',
> There's my rod—and Rab's awa'!"

The Bard may have thought that he had some claim to the local fishing rights, for one of his ancestors, Walter Burnes, is believed to have been a tenant of the House of Mergie. Heading towards the Cowie Water, I was struck by the thought that Rab had, perhaps, followed the same route, tramping up the Mounth while he shaped in his mind the lines with which to cock a snook at Mergie's laird. It was more than a mere fanciful notion, for on the other side of the hill lay the land of the Burneses.

The road to the Cowie is flanked on the north side by two older paths, one on the east appearing to be the original path, where the stream was forded, the other leading to a wooden footbridge, now demolished. Between them is a sturdy concrete bridge that takes you over to a forest road running parallel to a tributary of the Cowie. There was an inn on the north side of the water at one time, and on the south side are the ruins of an old "Bread and Cheese" house known as Lady's Leys.

I left the silent stones of the old "Bread and Cheese" house and pushed on up the hill. Beyond a sand quarry on the left, the main track was joined by a fairly wide path on the right. About half a mile along it a smaller, unused path cut off south towards the Glenbervie ridge.

This was the old Mounth route, branching off at a spot marked on the Ordnance Survey map as Luncheon Well. Fetteresso Forest is peppered with old wells, as is Drumtochty to the west, and one wonders how they came to get names like Luncheon Well, Mary's Well and Clerks Well? There was no well to drink from on the day I went over the Mounth, for a drought-ridden summer had left them dry and uninviting, the burns a meagre trickle in their dried-up beds. So, thirsty from the long trek through the woodland that now lay behind me, I made my way up the last stretch of forest track to the gate at the top of the hill. Below lay a bare strip of moorland and beyond it the little farms lying snugly in their carefully-cultivated fields. To the right were the rooftops of Bogjurgan, where William Burnes, the great grand-uncle of Robert Burns, farmed, and his son and grandson after him.

Time has cast a deceiving cloak over the Braes of Glenbervie since the first Burnes struggled to carve a sparse living from its unyielding acres. There were no motor roads weaving their way through the Mearns a century or more ago; nothing but rough tracks beckoning the reluctant traveller towards the Mounth. A small farm was no more than a clay bigging, with an earthen floor, one window and one door, and a solitary lum throwing up its peat smoke to a dour sky which, to use the Bard's own words, would have brought the "brattle o' winter war" to the Glenbervie hills.

I went over the gate and down the last stretch of the Mounth track, leaving Fetteresso Forest behind, until I came to the farm of Cleuchead, which has a hilltop view that many a jaded city dweller would envy. The tenant of Cleuchead, a young farm worker who had been there for only a few months, was probably taken aback to find a stranger at his back door. He himself had never been up the hill to the forest and thought that the track petered out in one of the fields. We talked about Burns and Bogjurgan, but not many people came up that way looking for links with the past, although now and again a passing motorist stopped at the road-end and asked if Rabbie had lived there. But there are reminders enough of Burns's ancestry in the names of farms scattered about this corner of the Mearns; Hawkhill and West Kinmonth, Elfhill and Inches, and Clochnahill, near the Stonehaven-Laurencekirk road, where William Burnes, father of the poet, was born in 1721.

About half a mile west of Bogjurgan, set well back off the road, is the farm of Brawliemuir, where Robert Burnes, Burns's grandfather, was born and brought up. It is, by old standards, an imposing building, but it was built to last and not to look at. If you should catch a glimpse of its sturdy walls from the roadside, or walk up the farm track to see it at closer range, it may strike a chord in your memory . . .

"The land climbed red and clay and a rough stone road went wandering up to the biggings of Blawearie. Out of the World and into Blawearie they said in Kinraddie, and faith! it was coarse land and lonely up there on the brae, fifty-six acres of it, forbye the moor that went on with the brae high above Blawearie, up to a great flat hill-top . . .".

Brawliemuir and Blawearie, one real and one fictional, bring together the names of Scotland's poet and a writer whose novels of the land and its people were to make a lasting impression on Scottish literature. The land of the Burneses and the land of Lewis Grassic Gibbon are one and the same, and when the BBC set out to make a film of "Sunset Song" they searched long and hard to find a croft which would recreate authentically the Blawearie of Gibbon's novel. They found it at Brawliemuir.

Lewis Grassic Gibbon, born at the turn of the century at the farm of Hill of Seggat in Aberdeenshire, was brought up at Bloomfield in Arbuthnott and spent his childhood days roaming the hills and moors of the Mearns, the memories of which were to provide the background for the first two novels of his *Scots Quair.* His second book in the trilogy was about the weavers who lived and worked between Drumlithie and Carmount, in the shadow of the Mounth. The opening sentence of *Cloud Howe* sets the scene—"The borough of Seggat stands under the Mounth, in the Mearns Howe . . . if you climbed up the Kaimes of a winter morn and looked to the east and you held your breath, you would maybe hear the sough of the sea, sighing and listening up through the dawn, or see a shower of sparks as a train came skirling through the woods from Stonehaven."

Not everything has changed. I remembered those words when I came down from the Mounth to Cleuchead and, looking east, saw the grey glimmer of the sea in the distance, and later, heading towards the coast road, watched the Aberdeen to London express "skirling through the woods from Stonehaven." Only the sparks were missing.

Up there, on the Braes of Glenbervie, I was thinking mostly about Burns, for this was the fatherland of the poet, and there are a number of references to the Burneses and the father of Robert Burns in Gibbon's works. Old Hairy Hogg, the Provost of Seggat, claimed descent from the Burneses. As for Seggat, it was an amalgam of places and people and its equivalent would be hard to find to-day, which is just as well, for Gibbon thrust it into an unenviable place in literature in a pungent, four-line verse—

"Oh, Seggat it's a dirty hole,
A kirk without a steeple
A midden heap at ilka door
And damned uncivil people."

The folk of Seggat were "folk who walked in the whistle of the storms from the Mounth," and it is clear that the Mounth was never very far from Gibbon's thoughts. There are frequent mentions of it in *Cloud Howe*. "Then the rooks came cawing and wheeling in by, and they both looked up from Seggat to the Mounth, rain drumming upon it far in the heuchs, cattle, tail-switching, dots in the heath."

Here again Gibbon's lines come potently alive when you stand on the Braes of Glenbervie on a crisp winter morning and see it through his eyes, with "the hoar blanching on post and hedge, riming the dykes," while far up in the Mounth "the veilings of mist drape the hills." There is more to Lewis Grassic Gibbon's interest in the Mounth than a clever play with words. He had what almost amounted to an obsession with the hills and moors, with the primitive people who once inhabited them, and with the relics of those far-off days. "And sometimes you'd raise your head and look up when the sun grew still on the peaks of the Mounth, by the glens and haughs you had searched for flints, and think of the men of ancient times." Chris and Robert, walking the hills, came upon a line of ancient stones and visualised the time when hunters roamed the hills, naked and bright, in a Golden Age. Through them, Gibbon was perhaps expressing his own yearning for a return to the values of such an age. *Cloud Howe* ends where it began, with the Mounth. "She could see the peaks of the Mounth wheel one by one into the line of the flow of the light, dun and sun-riding, they rode down the Howe."

So, like Chris, I came down from the Mounth, leaving behind the hills and forest trails. The Cleuchead farm track joins the Stonehaven-Auchenblae road and beyond Bogjurgan a road to the left runs to Glenbervie. Here, and in the village of Drumlithie, just over a mile away, I was to find two final links with Robert Burns and Lewis Grassic Gibbon. The old kirkyard of Glenbervie lies back off the main road, above the Bervie Water. It is not the sort of place you would visit on a dark night. The wind groans through the trees and around its faded tombstones and you become like Burns's Tam o' Shanter, "glowering round wi' prudent cares, lest bogles catch him unawares."

The effect is heightened by the way the ground dips down

to the river, so that the gravestones are tiered upwards towards the ruins of the old church. The walls of this building are smothered in ivy, inside and out, almost as if nature was gradually drawing it into its maw, and when you look through the heavily-rusted bars on the side window or the opening on its barred door you instinctively draw back. Light filters through to show dimly the creeping ivy trailers clawing their way to the floor, while at the back can be seen an ancient tomb. This is the tomb of the Douglases, for long the lairds of the parish.

On the downhill slope of the kirkyard is a stone shelter that is a little out of place, having been built in 1968 to house two tombstones whose inscriptions have more or less disappeared. Beneath them, a plaque tells their story. One is the gravestone of James Burnes and his wife, Margaret Falconer, the poet's great-grandparents, the tenants of Brawliemuir; the other is that of Burns's great grand-uncle, William Burnes, and his wife, Christian Fotheringham, who were tenants of Bogjurgan.

Burns enthusiasts made a pilgrimage to Glenbervie Kirkyard in September, 1968, to dedicate the shelter. Now, having made my own pilgrimage, I went west to Drumlithie before setting out on the last stage of my Mounth journey. Drumlithie is one of those back-of-beyond villages that has retained its character over the years, and even the sight of neatly-packaged council houses on its outskirts fails to destroy the impression that progress has washed over it and left little change.

Two centuries ago it was a weaving community and you can still see, built on to the ends of the older houses, the rooms where the weavers worked their looms. But there is one landmark that identifies its past as clearly as if the Drumlithie folk had erected a memorial to that long-dead industry; a tall, slim tower standing at the end of a row of houses once occupied by weavers. For Drumlithie is the "Skite" of Lewis Grassic Gibbon's *Sunset Song*, and the tower is the one of which Gibbon wrote: "Every time it came on to rain the Drumlithie folk ran out and took in their steeple, that proud they were of the thing."

The Mearns novelist must have left a sour taste in the mouths of Drumlithie inhabitants when he wrote of their village: "Some called it Skite to torment the folk and they'd get fell angry at that in Skite. No more than a rickle of houses it was, white with sunshine below its steeple that made of Skite the laugh of the Howe, for feint the kirk was near it." Whether they are still angry at this slander on their steeple I do not know, but there was a wary look in the eye of one of the older residents when I asked him why it had been built.

"For the weavers," he said, and then, in more expansive mood, explained that they once worked in the houses round about the steeple. The bell, he explained, was "tae waukin them," but when I mentioned Lewis Grassic Gibbon he declared, frowning, "I dinna ken anything about that," and, calling his dog, strode off. Well, maybe it was still a sore point, but at least the steeple bell has not been completely silenced. It still rings out at local weddings and on Hogmanay. So that was Skite. I set off back the way I came, and as I left the village the clouds opened up and it began to rain. I looked back over my shoulder. The steeple was still there. No one had taken it in.

The last miles took me past the kirkyard road and Glenbervie House. The house stands on the site of an earlier building where Edward I rested when he marched over Crynes Corse Mounth to Deeside in 1296. Once again I was in the wake of old Mounth history.

From here I made my way by the Mill of Glenbervie to the high ground overlooking Auchenblae. The sun was breaking through again and the golfers were out on the nine-hole course. Opposite the golf course, a side road leads to Glen Farquhar and on the right of it was the Hill of Herscha, the site of Paldy Fair. The Fair of St Palladius, named after the patron saint of Fordoun parish, was a well-known and important cattle fair, drawing drovers from the north by the Cryne's Cross Mounth and the Cairn-a-Mounth as well as by the Stock

The weaver's tower in Drumlithie which featured in *Sunset Song*.

Mounth from Strachan to Glenbervie. This is really where the Cryne's Cross pass (or Craigincrosse, as Sir James Balfour called it) begins and ends, within sight of the church "wulgarly called Pade Kirke."

I stood on Herscha Hill looking across the patchwork fields where a few small herds grazed peacefully on the land that once saw as many as 3000 head of cattle gathered for the Paldy Tryst. Here, suddenly, the years folded back to a time when the vintners' tents stretched over the hill, fires blazing behind them and broth pots swinging on their tripods, smiling lasses ladling out a gill or half-mutchkin to the hungry drovers; when blind fiddlers and pipers scraped and skirled a tune and legless beggars pleaded for a coin or a crust of bread. There was John Milne, the poet of Livet Glen, reciting his own verse, Singing Willie, who carried a tasselled and gnarled walking stick, and Robbie Stracathro, playing a tune on his tin whistle. Robbie took life as it came and on one occasion, when he was asked if he had got his dinner, he replied—

> Wi' bits o' beef
> An' sups o' kail,
> An' bits o' bread,
> An' drops o' ale;
> Fat aething, fat ither
> I've made a dinner o't.

Charles A. Mollyson, author of *The Parish of Fordoun*, gave a vivid impression of Paldy Fair as he remembered it over forty years before his book was published in 1893. He remembered dealers in cattle, sheep and horses gathering from every parish in the county, from Forfarshire and from "across the hills from the upper regions of Deeside," among them "the rough tykes" of Tarland, who had a reputation for using their fists. There were shoemakers, saddlers and other craftsmen, who turned up to collect their accounts, and young men who had come to get jobs at the harvest. There were also, even in those days, a 19th century version of the cateran who through the years had raided droves on their way to the trysts. John Duncan of Auchenblae was one of them. He had stolen two oxen and a cow from George Burnett, of Mulloch, and three oxen from William Taylor in Knock. He was caught and tried at Stonehaven in July, 1700, and on 2nd August was hanged on a gibbet at the Gallowhill.

The "Nolt" Market at Paldy went back many centuries and

when it came to an end a bright daub of colour was lost to the Mearns. It was still and quiet on Herscha Hill. Away to the west were the wooded hills of Strath Finella, where, as Lewis Grassic Gibbon put it, "Finella's carles builded the Kaimes," and beyond that, by the Clatterin' Brig, the Cairn-a-Mounth began its long climb back to Deeside.

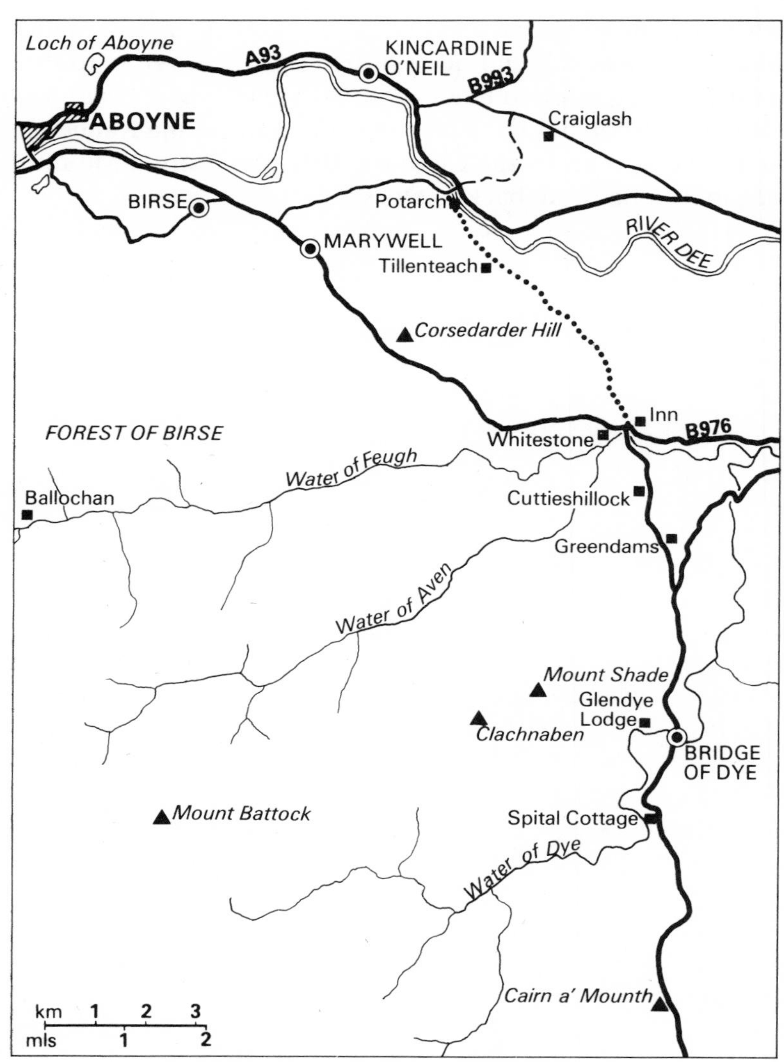

Cairn-a-Mounth — by Potarch and Whitestone

3

Cairn-a-Mounth (1)

He was rycht wa', and tuk the flycht,
And owre the Mownth thai chast hym than
Til the Wod of Lunfanan.
This Makduff was thare mast felle,
And on that chas than mast crwele.

The ghost of Macbeth sighs around the windy slopes of Perkhill, about a mile from the village of Lumphanan, and from the cluster of trees surrounding the cairn where he is said to be buried you can look across the Dee valley to the peaks of Clochnaben and Mount Shade, guarding one of the great north routes through the Grampians. This was the way that the doomed king came, over the Cairn-a-Mounth and across the ford on the Dee to Kincardine O'Neil, then north by Auchlossan to the Peel of Lumphanan, where he met his death at the hand of Macduff, the "mast crwele" of Malcolm Canmore's followers. Seventeen years before, in 1040, Malcolm's father, Duncan I, had gone north by another Mounth route, the Firmounth Pass, and had been murdered by Macbeth in Moray. There is not much to remind you of these events. You tramp through the muddy courtyard of Perkhill farm and up the hill to Macbeth's Cairn, looking for something that will bridge the centuries but knowing that the king was never buried there and that his grave is in Iona.

The ancient Mounth road over which Macbeth "tuk the flicht" after Birnam Wood is one of the few Grampian passes that have survived the centuries. The little village of Lumphanan, whose only concession to the high drama of its past is an inn called the MacBeth Arms, is also the home of the Peel

Macbeth's cairn at Lumphanan with Clochnaben in the distance.

of Lumphanan, an early medieval earthwork of considerable importance, guarding the route to the north. Even more important, however, was the village of Kincardine O'Neil, three miles to the south as the crow flies.

For centuries this small community on the main Deeside road has held its place at the crossroads of history. Strategically placed on the northern edge of the Mounth, it was a vital halting place for travellers heading north by the old route through Lumphanan, Cushnie, Alford and Huntly. To-day there is little evidence that it was once a busy, bustling township offering rest and hospitality to the weary traveller. The traffic of the 20th century is east to west, for Kincardine O'Neil is very much a whistle stop for motorists pouring up Deeside during the summer months. The village has little to attract the tourist. It lacks the holiday air of its upstream neighbours and it cannot boast the Royal tag of Ballater and Braemar. But the hospitality remains. I remember sitting in the public bar of the Gordon Arms supping "tattie" soup and eating an enormous dish of "stovies" beside a blazing log fire.

Kincardine O'Neil's tradition for hospitality goes back to

the days when a cottar named Cochran entertained King James V and his party on their way south from Aberdeen. The crofter and his wife gave their Royal guests a warm welcome, with the result that they were granted the property. Cochran's Croft can still be seen on the east side of the village, although, unfortunately, the present occupiers have removed the name from the building. Another Royal visitor, Edward I, passing through the village in 1296, obviously thought that hospitality meant cleaning out the village larder. As an old rhyme put it—

O' followers he haed a flock,
Left neither capon, hen nor cock,
Na, nor butter, bread nor cheese,
Else my informant tells me lees,
An' worst o' a' I'm wae to tell,
They left them neither meat nor ale.

Edward and his army travelled north by the Cryne's Cross Pass to Aberdeen and from there to Elgin. From Elgin he went "to Kyndroken (Kildrummy) castell belongyng to the Erle of Marre," and on his way south stopped at Kincardine O'Neil—"the hospitall of Kyncarden in Marnes." Nearly seven centuries later the remains of that "hospitall" provide a unique link with the past. The old church at Kincardine O'Neil, now a ruin by the roadside in the centre of the village, dates back to the 13th century, when a chapel and hospice for travellers going and coming over the Cairn-a-Mounth was built by Alan Durward, whose father, Thomas the Durward, built a bridge over the Dee for Mounth wayfarers.

The ford road can still be seen running down the west side of the old church to the river, while the ferry crossed farther upstream. The Rev. Robert Miller, in the 1843 *Statistical Account of Aberdeenshire*, wrote, "At the place where the ferry-boat now passes the Dee, between Kincardine O'Neil and the lands of Balnacraig, in the parish of Aboyne, a wooden bridge was erected by Durward of Coull in the fourteenth century, but of which all traces have long since disappeared." Drovers coming down from the north by

Alford and Lumphanan rested their herds at Bartle or Barthol Muir, about a quarter of a mile north of the village, before fording the Dee and following the Balnacraig road to Potarch, from where they went over the Shooting Greens to Whitestone. The ford was at one time called Cochran's Ford, after Cochran's Croft, and both ford and ferry were still in use half a century ago. The boat-house and "Ferry Cottage" were on the south side of the river and one resident I spoke to could remember when you whistled across the water for the ferryman.

There was another crossing at Inchbare, where the Brig of Potarch was later built, and drovers also used the old Torphins road, traces of which can still be found by Craiglash and Sluie, running down to Potarch. Here we are back in the age of Macbeth, for on Craiglash Hill we have a reminder of his "black and midnight hags." It is a ghoulish coincidence that Macbeth met his death at a place where witchcraft was said to be rife in the 16th century. While following the Craiglash path I came upon a great stone, or, to be precise, two halves of it, which catapulted me back through the centuries. This was the Warlock's Stone, "the gryt stane of Craigleauch," where a Deeside coven met before they were hauled off to be burned and hanged in Aberdeen.

Not many years ago the green at Potarch was a mecca for week-end trippers from Aberdeen. Campers and caravanners made the place look like an old-time fair and the authorities became concerned about health hazards and banned overnight stays. But the trippers were following an old tradition, for Potarch was the scene of one of the many markets held on Deeside at one time. Before the Potarch market got under way at the beginning of last century it was held at Marywell, a few miles west on the ancient Corsedarder road from Aboyne to Whitestone.

There was also a market on Barthol Muir at Kincardine O'Neil, where the drovers rested their cattle on their way south. They came from far and wide for the Barthol fair, crowding the main street of the village, spilling into the kirk-

The Warlock's stone on Craiglash hill.

yard, carrying creels and baggage, tethering their horses to the side of the church or letting them run loose among the graves. They erected tents and booths and even "exposed their wares upon the graves of the dead." They were there for pleasure as well as profit, for as one recorder solemnly put it, "greater indecencies followed at night."

From Potarch the next stage on the Mounth route is from the hotel over the Shooting Greens to Whitestone, which was another halting point for drovers. About a mile from the Brig of Potarch another small bridge takes you over the Burn of Cattie and past the farm of Tillyteach, and it was here that Duncan Deans, a local tailor, had an experience that sent him hurrying home "drookit, dowie and disjaskit." This Feugh-side fairy tale was first published towards the end of last century in David Grant's *Lays and Legends of the North*. It tells how Duncan, who had been working at the Haugh o' Sluie, called in at Potarch Hotel on the way home to pick up a coat which "Potty" wanted altering. He was normally a sober man, seldom seen "waur o' drink," but that night it was twelve o'clock before he set off over the Shooting Greens.

Fan he crossed the burn o' Cattie,
Passed the fairm o' Tullentech,
Clam a mile o' brae, or near it,
Then he did began to pech.

The poem goes on to tell how Duncan went into a "dwaum," his heart thumping like a flail, his head dizzy, his legs turning as "dwaible as an autumn salmon's tail."

Darkness closed in on him and he awakened to a strange, unearthly light, seeing above him a dome of sapphire, "hung wi' lamps o' gowden sheen," while underneath him was a carpet velvet-soft and emerald green. Pygmy lords and pygmy ladies strutted through the hall and at the end sat the fairy king and queen. The fairy folk danced and sung and Duncan watched "an ancient mannie, seemingly a hunner auld," chasing one of the belles round the room until she hid behind a couch and the exhausted centenarian "fell a-greetin".

"Look ahin' the sofa, mannie!"
Duncan cried wi' a' his micht;
Then a thoosand angry glances
Pierced him like a glint o' light.

Duncan was seized, pinched and prodded by a hundred hands, "shak'n, showdit, thrashed an' thumpit," till he thought his bones had crumbled into powder. "Gweed receive my soul!" he cried, and the fairy palace vanished. Instead of a velvet carpet, the tailor found himself lying in a hollow near the Shooting Greens, with the morning breaking and a wetting mist soaking him to the skin.

"Owre the hill he hitch't and hirplet,
Tulzied hame an' wan to bed,
Whaur he lay a month or langer,
Ere he waxed anither thread."

I left Potarch behind and went up the brae on a day that was not unlike that on which Duncan had climbed out of his "dreepin' lair" and fled to the comfort of his bed. Thin wisps of mist and cloud lay in the hollows of the hills and the Dee raged over its banks on the tail-end of a storm that had flooded the roads and left great lochans of rain-water in the surrounding fields. But even in this sort of dreich and dispiriting weather Deeside retained its charm; from the Shooting Greens car park, near Muckle Ord, where the Forestry Commission has opened its trails to the public, I could look west up the valley and see the countryside mellowing into the gold and russet tints of autumn.

From there the road ran downhill to Feughside Inn and Whitestone, which was a halting place for drovers going over the Cairn-a-Mounth. Below me were the open fields where the Feugh comes winding in from the west and the Water of Aven joins it at the end of its tumbling journey from remote Loch Tennet, in the shadow of Mount Battack. Beyond this meeting place of the rivers I could see, on the left, a tiny stretch of the Mounth road showing through the forest. On the right was the wart-like hump of Clochnaben.

The road to the right was an alternative route for Cairn-a-Mounth travellers going north or south by Aboyne. Bonty, as it was originally known, was swallowed up by the creation of Charleston of Aboyne as a Burgh of Barony in 1676. With its ford and ferry, it was the gateway to the Corsedarder Pass, which linked up with the Cairn-a-Mounth at Whitestone.

Aboyne is a pleasant, tidy village which has always projected an air of cultured charm, refusing to be tainted too much by tourism and reluctant to abandon its obeisance to the Deeside lairds. Every year, at the Aboyne Games, the bagpipes skirl, the banners unfurl, and you instinctively look around for a flurry of forelock-touching. Perhaps it has something to do with the fact that the burgh of barony has its roots deep in the history of the Gordon family and that it is called Charleston of Aboyne after Charles Gordon, 1st Earl of Aboyne. But even Aboyne is changing. Hundreds of holidaymakers are disgorged from cars and touring buses during the summer and the village has become a dormitory for Aberdeen commuters.

Aboyne got its charter in 1676, but Bonty retained its name in the ferry, the Boat of Bonty, which operated until the early 19th century. The river crossing has gone, replaced by the Bridge of Aboyne, which was rebuilt in 1871, and the only remaining link with the name is the Boat Inn, which stands on the site of the old ford. Across the river, the road went east by Birse and Corsedarder to join the Cairn-a-Mounth at Whitestone. Robert Dinnie, the Birse writer, said in 1865 that the remains of a road passing Birse Church, Allancreich, and Marywell were believed to be those of one made by King Kenneth III for the purpose of driving deer over the Cairn-a-Mounth to Fettercairn. The road was at one time known as the "Deer's Road," and there is a farm, about a mile and a half from Aboyne Bridge, called Deerhillock. At one time a hostelry stood there.

Dinnie linked the Deer's Road with the Deer's Dyke at the south end of the Cairn-a-Mounth and it was later, at the tail-end of my journey, that I climbed above the Clatterin' Brig to look for this earthen embankment enclosing a King's hunting park. Hollinshed, in his history of King Kenneth, mentioned the deer park—"It chanced hereupon that within a short time after he (King Kenneth) had been at Fordune, a towne in Merns, to visit the relicks of Paladius, which remain there, he turned a little out of the waie to lodge at the castell of Fettercairn, where, as then, there was a forest full of all manner of wild beasts that were to be had in any part of Albion." It could well have been that after that visit he decided to enlarge the "stock" at the Kincardine hunting park by driving deer down from Mar over the ancient Mounth pass.

The road from Aboyne goes down the hill to the hamlet of Marywell, which Robert Dinnie described as "the metropolis of the parish." This high-sounding title was bestowed on it because at the beginning of the 19th century there were some twenty houses at Marywell, which until 1860 also boasted an inn. The hostelry did a brisk business from drovers and cattle dealers on their way to the Cairn-a-Mounth, as did Janet Smith's Ale-house at Berry's Loch, about a mile to the south. Janet kept her pub open for folk going to kirk on the Sabbath, which only proves that she was a good deal ahead of her time. Many ale-houses were sited near or next to churchyards, which is said to date back to the time when James II decreed that butts be set up adjacent to churchyards so that the men could practise archery every Sunday. For teetotal travellers there was a roadside spring at Marywell, and the hamlet is said to have got its name from the fact that Mary Queen of Scots drunk at it on her way north before the Battle of Corrichie in 1562. Queen Victoria's horses were watered at the well on her way from Fettercairn to Balmoral in 1861. She called it Mary's Well. "We got out at a very small village (where the horses had some water, for it was a terribly long stage) and walked a little way along the road," she wrote in her Journal.

About a mile south of Marywell is Corsedarder Hill, where, by the roadside, there is a stone, only 4 ft high, split in half and held together by six rusting metal bands, giving its name to the Corsedarder Pass. This is the Corsedarder or Dardanus Stone, commemorating a Pictish king who reigned nearly 2000 years ago.

The Corsedarder Pass runs down to join up with the Forest of Birse road on its way to Whitestone, meeting up with the main Mounth route over the Shooting Greens from Potarch, and ready for the long climb over the Cairn-a-Mounth. Whichever route you take is a matter of choice, although the Potarch to Whitestone road is probably the more attractive, but one Jacobite fighter showed that it was wiser to avoid the more familiar road to Deeside. Viscount Dundee, riding north to raise the clans for King James in 1689, crossed the Grampians by the Cairn-a-Mounth Pass and rested his Jacobite followers somewhere near the Feughside Inn. He was followed the next day by Government troops led by General Hugh Mackay, who, after crossing the Mounth, reached Kincardine O'Neil to find the Jacobeans gone. Dundee had slipped over the Corsedarder Pass and forded the

The Corsedarder or Dardanus stone near Marywell.

Dee at Bonty. The two forces finally met several months later at the Battle of Killiecrankie in July, 1689, when the Jacobites won the day but paid the price of Viscount Dundee's life.

Where the Corsedarder and Potarch roads meet, the Feugh, joined by the Water of Aven, does a sort of U-turn before winding on to the Haugh of Strachan, and on the day I saw it it was in angry mood, rampaging past the Mill of Clinter and Little Ennochie and under the bridge that takes you up the Cairn-a-Mounth by Cuttieshillock. Farther north, roads were flooded and the Banchory-Torphins road had been closed by the police, while to the west the Gairnshiel road was cut off. The rain had come down in a never-ending torrent; we were paying the price of a long, dry summer.

There were echoes of nearly a century and a half ago in the reports of the storm, for sudden spates are not unknown on the River Dee and its tributaries, and it looked for a time as if we were facing a repeat of the Muckle Spate of 'Twenty-nine. During that watery holocaust in 1829 the River Dee rose to 27 feet above its normal level at Banchory. Bridges were washed away and haystacks, cattle, pigs, sheep and poultry, as well as trees and household goods, were swept downstream to come bobbing up in the waters of Aberdeen harbour.

The Feugh "cam' rairin' doon fae Birse" to join the turmoil, and the Mill of Clinter and Ennochie farm were among its victims, while from the south-west the Aven thundered down with a motley collection of spinning wheels, tables, chairs, girnels, washing tubs, horses, pigs—and smuggled whisky kegs. The events of that August day in 1829 are vividly and hilariously recorded in David Grant's poem, "The Muckle Spate o' 'Twenty-nine," which relates how the souter at Dalbreck lost "a dizzen harn sarks," and Fytie, the farmer at Whitestone, got out of his bed at night to find that "twa muckle rucks o' fairnyear's aits" had vanished. Then there was the Ennochie hen . . .

"At Ennochie a cluckin' hen
Wis sittin' in a kist,
Baith it an' her were sweelt awa'
Afore the creature wist."

What happened to the hen no one will ever know, but it was last seen passing Heugh-head, "as canty as you like," before it disappeared near the Burn o' Frusk sitting on the back of a "droonit stirk." There was a good deal of speculation on whether—

"Gin she were carri't to the sea
Afore her ark gaed wrang,
An' maybe spairt by Davie Jones
To bring her cleekin' oot,
Gin she was rear them like a hen
Or like a water coot?"

Willie Wilson lost his coo, Tam M'Rory's breeding sow went sailing down the Burn o' Cammie, and the dyster of Dalsack lost his shop and his bowies and pots, but there is always someone who makes a profit out of disaster. Johnny

Hoss, a cadger from Bogendreep, who lost his sheltie, cairtie and creels, turned his losses to good account by getting a "begging paper" drawn up and then "beggit Banchory, Birse an' Stra'an" until his pouch was full of siller. After that, he crept slyly "o'er the Cairn o' Month" to the Mearns, where he married and lived "a much respectit man."

There were others who went over the Cairn-a-Mounth to escape the flood. Meg Mill, who was known as "Birlin' Meg," heard the spate splashing against her kailyard and thought it was the kelpie. Fearful that she would be hurled away "to Satan's fiery den," she waited till daylight broke and headed uphill to the safety of Clochnaben.

There has never been, as our Feughside poet told us, "anither spate like auchteen twenty-nine," and the flooding I saw probably had little resemblance to that watery disaster, but as I passed the road to Dalbreck I had a sneaking desire to call in and ask if they had lost any "harn sarks." The Dalbreck road is opposite Cuttieshillock, which had one of the oldest inns in the north, and about a mile farther on there are two fords. The torrent of water rushing over them had brought traffic to a snail's crawl and I stopped to watch a Banchory taxi make an amphibious crossing. There were youngsters inside and a notice on the rear window said "School Bus." They would never have travelled in such high-and-dry comfort in 1829. Beyond the fords an AA box marked the junction of the Cuttieshillock road with the road from Strachan. From there it was a steady uphill climb to the high and windy acres of the Cairn-a-Mounth summit.

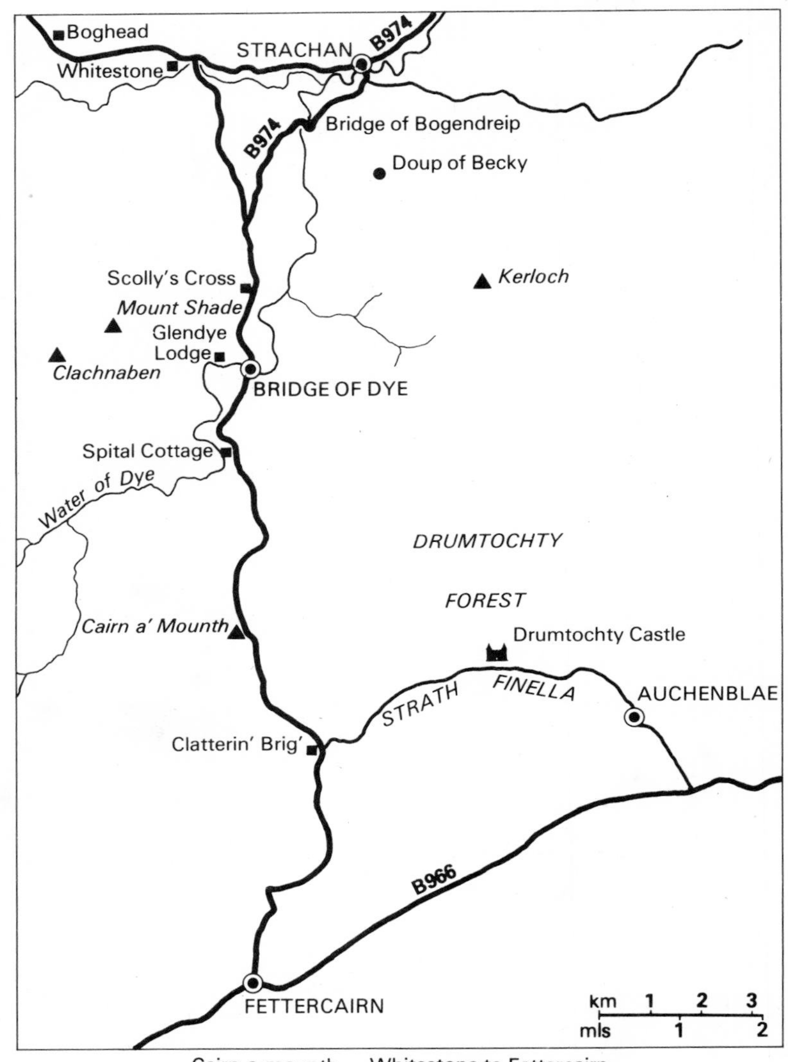

Cairn-a-mounth — Whitestone to Fettercairn

4

Cairn-a-Mounth (2)

"Noo, faur ye gyaun?" quo' Cammie's herd,
Quo' Meg, "To Clochnaben;
Rin, laddie, rin, an' leave yer beasts,
The world's at an en'!"

Birlin' Meg, fleeing over the Cairn-a-Mounth from the Muckle Spate, thought that the sins of men had brought a second flood, and it is easy to see why she looked upon Clochnaben as a 19th century Noah's Ark. Its mighty tor, 95 ft high and lying a few yards west of the mountain's 1900 ft summit, dominates the countryside for miles around, and when you stand on this great rock, looking down on the Feugh valley and seeing the old Mounth road trailing south to Fettercairn and the Howe of the Mearns, you can survey the Lilliputian world below and feel its problems slip into perspective. You are nearer the angels. Meg Mill thought so, anyway. She believed that the day had come when "fouk in toons" would leave their homes and worldly gear and flee to the mountains. Up there, away from the raging torrents, she could nurse the hope that "the angels micht rax doon for us."

The mountain lies about a mile south-west of 1662 ft Mount Shade and the two peaks are separated by a deep gorge which, seen from the Feugh valley, gives the impression of a giant wedge hacked from the landscape by some superhuman force. It is known as the Devil's bite. Although the word Clochnaben is the generally accepted one, the correct spelling is Clachnaben, and it takes this name from the Gaelic words meaning the stone of the mountain.

There are a number of routes to the "Cloch," the main ones

The Tor on Clochnaben.

being from the Bridge of Dye, almost directly east of Clochnaben, or from Greendams to the north-east. I took the latter path, following the Burn of Greendams until I could cross it and have the great snout of rock in front of me. Up there, a bitterly cold wind whined and whispered around the tor, but on the south side it was calm and still. Behind me, away to the north, was the Mither Tap and to the east the skyscrapers of Aberdeen and the horizon-line of the sea. Nearer at hand was Glendye Lodge and the Cairn road, thrusting out of the woodlands to the heights ahead.

Clochnaben is a good place from which to contemplate the past. It has stood sentinel over the Cairn-a-Mounth's rich and turbulent history for many centuries, back over 900 years to Macbeth's ill-fated flight over the Mounth to Lumphanan; back even before that, to a time when the flint people came to the valley of the Dee. It saw the Hammer of the Scots lead his invading troops across its desolate moors and through its forests, and it frowned down on the bandits who robbed and murdered travellers making their way along its danger-fraught miles.

Travellers there were in plenty, for the Cairn-a-Mounth was, and still is, a main road artery linking Edinburgh to the north. They came up from the Lothians to Fettercairn, over the Mounth road to the Feugh at Whitestones, and on to the ford of Inchbare at Potarch. Once over the Dee, they rested at the hospice at Kincardine O'Neil before heading north and west to Kildrummy, or on by Alford and Huntly to Keith and the Moray Firth.

The Cairn-a-Mounth was also one of the most important routes for the great cattle treks which brought the drovers and their herds from the north to the cattle trysts at Brechin, Falkirk and Perth. Their route took them across the Don by the Boat of Forbes at Alford and over the Dee at Kincardine O'Neil or Potarch. The northern stretch of the Cairn-a-Mounth was also the gateway to drovers from the Fair at Old Rayne, who travelled south to the Mill of Hirn, crossed the Dee by ford at Banchory, and made their way by the Mill of Cammie to Strachan, then over the Mounth by the Brig o' Bogendreep.

The 1843 Statistical Account of Kincardine mentions "a considerable transit on this route during summer in droving cattle from the fairs in Garioch and Buchan to the southern markets." The old cattle treks have had little recognition in the history books of the north-east. Practically the only thing that marks them are the disappearing traces of the drove roads that can still be seen in certain parts of the countryside. Yet they were remarkable feats of endurance, and some idea of the immense scale of old-time droving can be found in contemporary reports of roads blocked by hundreds of cattle gathering for the Trysts. It is ironic that our film and television screens satiate us with endless tales of the cattle drives of the old American west; no one, as far as I know, has thought fit to do the same for the drovers of old Scotland.

The old route from the Cairn-a-Mounth to the north was traced in David Grant's "Tammie Tod's Trip to Elgin i' the Days o' Langsyne." Tammie, turning his back on "auld Dramslockit," set off on the trip despite the fact that "ninety miles—mayhap a hunner—lie atween's an' Elgin toon."

Ower the Cairn o' Month gaed Tammie,
Through Glendye, an' past Fytestane,
Through Kincardine, an' past Auchlossan,
Ere the first daylicht hed gaen.

He met up with a couper, Geordie Lowrie, and they went "owre the hill an' doon through Cushnie," on past the Kirk o' Tullynessle, and up the hichts and doon on Clatt. He and Geordie, after having a drink, mounted their horses—"moniments o' skin an' bane"—and Tammie was thrown from his steed, breaking his nose and collar-bone. He did the last stretch to Elgin in "a twa-han' barrow."

Although the road "past Fytestane" to the water splashes was the main Mounth route, to-day the road from Strachan by the Brig o' Bogendreep carries the heavier share of the traffic. The two meet and go on to Glendye Lodge, where the Water of Dye cuts across the road under one of the oldest bridges on Deeside. The Bridge of Dye has been buffeted by nearly 300 winters and it looks as sturdy to-day as it did when it was built by Sir Alexander Fraser of Durris in 1681. Sir Alexander's son, Sir Peter, petitioning Parliament for the imposition of a perpetual toll in 1685, said that when the Water of Dye was in spate it was a great torrent and "Damnefies the bridge exceedingly." Damnefied or not, it has defied the worst that the Cairn-a-Mounth can throw at it, even the Muckle Spate of 1829, when "horses, pigs, an' kye were droon't i' Dye" and other, less solid structures shuddered and crumbled under the storm. "Timmer" brigs keeled over like matchsticks in the 'Twenty-nine spate.

> An' Fytie's Brig, the lady's Brig,
> An' mony brigs forbye,
> That spate sent rumblin' doon the Feugh,
> Or doon the A' an an' Dye.

In the year that the bridge was built an Act of Parliament, giving permission for an initial toll, made reference to it being subject to "great and sudden Innundations and danger of being spoyled by storms." The bridge, it said, stood upon "one of the most impetuous waters within the Kingdom." The tolls, however, were not entirely successful. Before the bridge was built, travellers crossed the Dye by a ford, and after it was built they continued to do so rather than pay up the eight pennies Scots demanded for "each horse with a Burden." If you had an ox, a cow or four sheep, it cost you more—four pennies for each.

There were more hazards on the Cairn road than those offered by the impetuous waters of the Dye, and the Ford of Dye, near the bridge, is a reminder that the route from Whitestone to Fettercairn offered ripe pickings for the robber bands who lurked along its wild and lonely miles. In "The Statistical Account of Kincardineshire" in 1843, the Rev. David Scott Ferguson, minister at Strachan, told of how "a Highlander passing to the south" in the late 17th century ran into trouble. He had stopped at the smithy at the Ford to have his horse shoed, watched, unknown to him, by the chief of a gang who was in the shop at the time. The Highlander took an old pistol out of his pocket and began cleaning it, remarking that the night was dark, the road dangerous, and that he had a trifle of money he wouldn't like to part with. He said if his pistol "widna fell it might maybe fleg." He was scarcely on his way when the gang chief caught up with him, flourishing a cudgel which he thought was match enough for a rusty old pistol. The Highlander drew another pistol from under his plaid, shot the robber dead, "and proceeded in safety across the Cairn."

Travellers who sought safety at the Spitalburn, about a mile south of the Brig o' Dye, were likely to regret their choice of haven. It was here, where the Dye is joined by the Spital Burn, that a "Spital" or hospice once catered for people going over the Mounth, and when it ceased to exist a public-house took its place. This ancient hostelry was a haunt of the Cairn-a-Mounth thieves, but in time the intimation was made in Strachan church: "The Cairn o' Mount road is quite safe now. There's honest folk at the Spital."

It would probably surprise our forefathers that the Cairn-a-Mounth is in use at all. Many years ago, the Commissioners of Highland Roads and Bridges carried out a survey of the road and reported with something like awe that it rose "not less than eight or nine inches in one yard." It was, they said, becoming "totally unfit for the purposes of civil life." There are still times when that is true, but not often.

The Cairn on the Mounth is a disappointment, looking a little like an enormous rubbish heap. Below it on the south side there is a large lay-by from which you can view the countryside. But there were no sightseers when I was there; I was alone with my ghosts. Hidden in the mist were the green fields of the Mearns, a sharp contrast to the peat-brown acres around the Cairn. Lewis Grassic Gibbon, the young James Mitchell as he was then, had seen it in a different mood, on a day when "the heat was caught in the cup of the Howe and little currents of wind had come filtering down through the Grampian passes."

Here, as on the Braes of Glenbervie, I found that Gibbon's prose came easily to mind, reflecting his fascination with what he called "our dour hill-lands" and summing up so crisply and vividly the kind of mental soliloquy that is kindled by the solitude of the mountains. "This is the land," he wrote "unstirred and greatly untouched by men, unknowing ploughing or crops or the coming of the scythe." The people who go over the Cairn-a-Mounth to-day, running effortlessly up its steep slopes in their sleek, modern cars, giving a passing glance at both its beauty and its barrenness are not likely to absorb greatly one or the other. Gibbon himself was aware of our failure to comprehend what we have on our doorstep.

When he came through the Glen of Drumtochty, cycling past the broom and whins and the little burn that "sparkled and spun so coolly," he was unable to appreciate fully what he saw. "I would never apprehend its full darkly colourful beauty until I had gone back to England, far from it, down in the smooth pastures of Hertfordshire some night I would remember it and itch to write of it."

I could see the strip of road he had come pushing up on his bike. "I climbed up the top of Cairn o' Mount with my bicycle and sat and lunched and looked about me; and found it very still, the land of Scotland taking a brief siesta in that midday hour." Gibbon, in his essay on "The Land," thought of the hills— "so summer-hazed, so immobile and essentially unchanging"—and pondered on "what master of the cultivated lands will pass in what strange mechanical contrivance" a century later. He wrote the essay after a visit to the Mearns in the late summer of 1933, two years before his death, and in less than half a century the strange mechanical contrivances have wiped out the way of life that he knew.

He left a message to the future traveller on the Mounth. "I send him my love and the hope that he'll sometime climb up Cairn o' Mount and sit where I'm sitting now, and stray in summer thought—into the sun-hazed mists of the future, into the lives and wistful desirings of forgotten men who begat him." There may have been a personal conceit in the thought that I was among those he had written that message for, but, having mused on those "forgotten men" as I stood on the summit of the Mounth, I thought it a good time to come down from the heights and into the friendly embrace of the Mearns valley. Two miles on lay the Clatterin' Brig.

The Clatterin' brig.

The Green Castle guarded the Cairn-a-Mounth when it was the principal crossing from Strathmore into Mar— "the great line of communication across the Grampians."—and Kincardine Castle succeeded it as the key to the vital pass. The Green Castle is a mile south of the Clatterin' Brig and Kincardine Castle a mile beyond that, reached by a side road leading to the Mill of Kincardine.

The Castle of Kincardine has deep roots in the county to which it gave its name and it is a pity that human neglect has all but obliterated this cornerstone of Mearns history. King Edward stayed there during his first campaign in Scotland in 1296, when he received the abdication of John Balliol. Henry Gough's "Itinerary of King Edward the First" traces the route of the Hammer of the Scots in that fateful summer. He travelled from Farnell to Montrose on July 7—"the Saturdaie to Monorous, castell and a good toune, and ther abidde Sundaie, Mundaie and Tuesdaie; and ther cam to hym Kynge John of Scotlande to his mercy and did render quietly the realm of Scotland." The quiet handing-over of the realm of Scotland actually took place at Stracathro on July 10. The following day he was at "Kynge Carden (in the Mearns), a faiour manour," and on Thursday he was moving across "the montaigne of Glowberwy (Glenbervie)" and over the Cryne's Cross Pass to the "manour amonge the mountaignes" at Durris, or the Dounes as it was called. Saturday saw him in the "cite of Dabberden, a faire castelle, and a good towne upon the see, and taried ther v daies." The following month he returned to Kincardine Castle by the Cairn-a-Mounth.

Robert the Bruce was also a visitor to Kincardine-in-the-Mearns, and the castle and its park are said to have been enlarged by him, but there is little to remind us of any of these events. The thickly-wooded knoll on the farmlands of the Castleton of Kincardine hides its past from prying eyes. The great walls of the castle lie underneath a tangle of undergrowth, lichen-covered and carpeted with moss, tree trunks bursting through the stonework. Strange to think that monarchs like Bruce and Mary Queen of Scots looked out across fields that still bear names like King's Park and Chancellor's Park. Down at the end of the road youngsters at the local school were playing tag in the playground and I wondered if they would grow up with any knowledge of the heritage on their doorstep.

The last lap of my Cairn-a-Mounth journey took me to Fettercairn, which has an old-world charm marred by the massively incongruous arch spanning the main street. It was built in 1864 to commemorate the visit three years earlier of Queen Victoria and Prince Albert, who stayed at the local inn, the Ramsay Arms. The royal visitors had come over the Mounth by Mount Keen and Glen Mark and spent the night at the hostelry, incognito. There were no complaints about the service; they had "a very nice, clean, good dinner," recorded her Majesty.

Dwarfed by the Victoria arch, but a good deal more in character, is the old market cross in the village square. Dating back to 1670, it is believed to be the cross of the burgh of

The Royal arch at Fettercairn.

Kincardine, long since vanished. It is a perfect centre-piece to a community that lets the world go rushing by while it holds fast to a way of life that is becoming increasingly rare in the rural backwaters of Scotland. The impression I got of a sleepy little village wasn't far removed from that of Queen Victoria over a century ago, when she walked through the whole village and noted, with surprise, "Not a creature moved." She must have been even more surprised when she got back to the inn and suddenly saw six men march up with fifes and drums, go down the street and back again, and "not a creature taking any notice of them." "Grant and Brown were out; but had no idea what it could be. Albert asked the little maid, and the answer was, 'It's just a band,' and that it walked about in this way twice a week. How odd!" That evening a guest arrived and wanted to go to the dining room, "the commercial travellers' room," and not unnaturally was a bit annoyed at being told that he couldn't. When he asked what was the matter, Grant told him, "It's a wedding party from Aberdeen."

The Royal party left next morning, going the way I had come, by the "Cairnie Month," as the Queen called it, and over the Corsedarder road from Whitestone. My route went the other way, by Balbegno and the vitrified fort of Green Cairn to where the waters of the North Esk go tumbling under Gannochy Bridge on their way to the sea,

John Taylor, the Water Poet, returning from his visit to Deeside and the north in 1618, travelled south from "Stroboggy" (Strathbogie) by the Cairn-a-Mount and Brechin was on his route to Edinburgh. "So over Carny mount to Brechin," he wrote, "where a wench that was born deaf and dumb came into my chamber at midnight (I being asleep) and she opening the bed, would feign have lodged with me." Taylor thought that either his travels had tamed him or her beauty failed to move him, for he found that her main attraction was that her breath was as sweet as sugar-candy. His hostess told him next morning that the girl had "changed her maidenhead for the price of a bastard not long before." The Water Poet, starting out of his sleep and thinking that the Devil was there, thrust his "dumb beast" out of his room and staked up his door with a great chair.

For me, there were no such temptations. For the moment, my route lay away from Brechin, following the sign at Gannochy Bridge that pointed the way to Tarfside, where the Fungle and Firmounth passes come down through the hills to Glenesk.

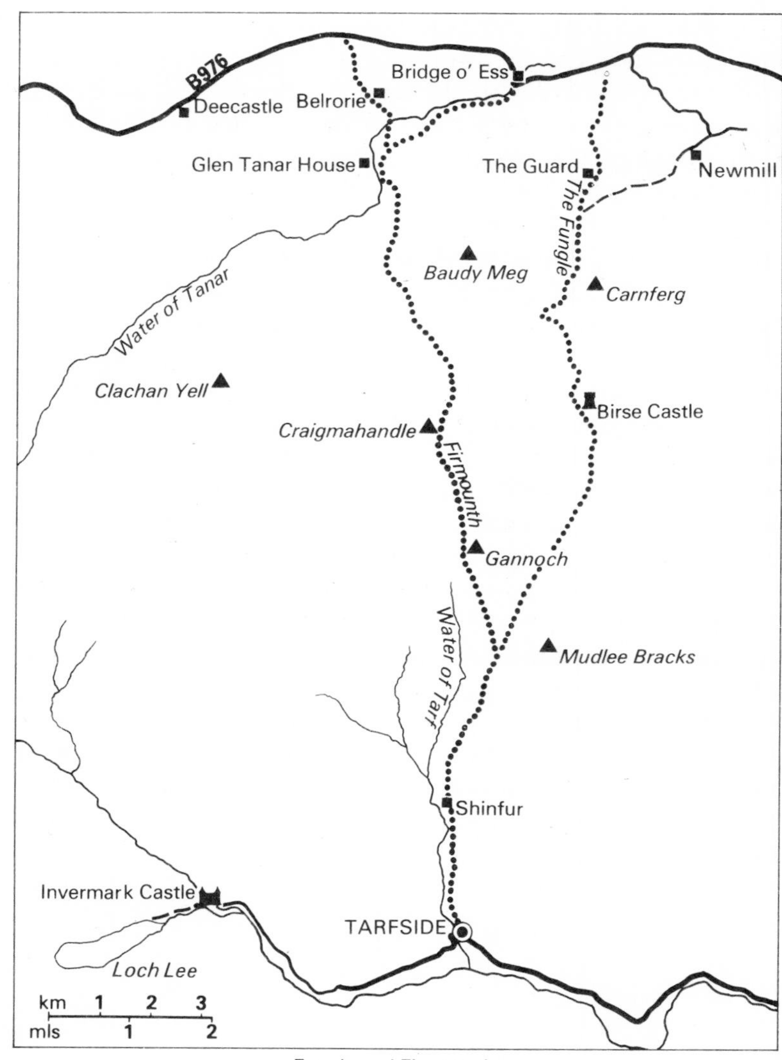

Fungle and Firmounth

5

Fungle

The wind was bitter and the hills unfriendly. Winter was licking its lips in anticipation of the months ahead and as I went through the Fungle I looked up and saw a great skein of geese go by. They were followed ten minutes later by another flight, their long, wavering lines opening and closing until they finally disappeared in the distant hills. The signs of a new season were all about. Dead bracken carpeted the moorland and the first cap of snow lay on the high peaks. The mountain hare was flecked with the early white of its winter coat. But among all these tokens of change there was nothing that matched the sight of these migrant geese winging south at the end of a journey that began limitless miles away in some remote and hostile region in the Arctic wastes. They were heading over the Mounth towards the Angus glens and as I watched them I thought of Violet Jacob's poem. "The Wild Geese" tells of a "hameless loon" who, on asking the roarin' norlan' wind what it had seen as it came blowing down from the land of his exile, hears about the siller tides running up the Firth of Forth and the roving gulls above the Tay, but is moved to tears by the image of the geese "far abune the Angus straths," their "cryin' voices" trailing behind them on the air.

On the day that I went through the Fungle the same norlan' wind was blowing over the Mounth. It was October, when the drovers went through the Grampian passes for the last of their trysts. Before long, the burns would freeze up and the snow would rise knee-high on the shivering slopes of Tampie and Mulnabracks. The leaves were dying on the trees around Birsemore Loch, where Queen Mary enjoyed a picnic tea at Lady Cowdray's cottage while her loyal subjects went puffing up the brae between Craigendinnie and Birsemore Hill. This corner of Deeside, where the Allt Dinnie comes tumbling down to the Dee opposite Aboyne, had a special place in the affections of King George V's queen, and it was one shared by many ordinary folk. Its popularity was at its peak between the two world wars, but even to-day the Fungle still has its week-end influx of visitors. They seldom penetrate beyond the point known as the Guard, about a mile from Birsemore, where the path levels off into a long screen of trees, thinning out farther south and opening on to the hills of Birse.

There is a saying, "It's as auld as the hills of Birse," but the quotation may have nothing to do with the landscape, for one theory is that it originated with a family called Hill, who set up a record in longevity in Birse many years ago. They were certainly long-livers in this part of Deeside, and according to the 18th century "View of the Diocese of Aberdeen" it may have been something to do with the air. "Dee has the advantage of Don in its air," declared the writer, "which is extremely fresh and pure (as particularly in Durris, Brass, and Braemar) by means of its heather and woods; so it is observed that the people who lived along it are very healthy and long-lived." It is interesting to note that Birse is given as "Brass." Robert Dinnie, father of the famous Donald Dinnie, said in his "Account of the Parish of Birse" in 1865 that the most ancient name was Preis, signifying a wooded country. It was afterwards spelled Prese, Brasse, Brass and sometimes Birs, Birss and now Birse.

The name Fungle is neither as old as the hills o' Birse nor as old as the name of Birse. Its meaning and origin are uncertain, but the Mounth road through the mountains to Glenesk was at one time known as the Cateran Road, indicating that the Fungle, like most of the Mounth passes, not only had its share of cattle traffic but was also plagued by cattle thieves. Alexander Smith, in his *New History of Aberdeenshire* in 1875, mentioned the "Cattrin road" running across the Cainach (presumably Gannoch Hill half-way to Glenesk) from Aboyne. He thought that the road, which he described as "a mere bridle track," got its name from the word Cathtrian; Cath- battle, and trian, a road—the battle road. He believed that there had been "many fatal encounters arising out of cattle-lifting raids."

The entry to the Fungle is just over a mile west of Newmill at Birsemore Loch. From an open space used as an unofficial car park you can cross the Allt Dinnie by a wooden bridge and follow the line of the burn uphill, with the woodland opening up on the left to Birsemore Hill. It is a hard, steady slog up through the trees, and if Glenesk seems a long way away you have the sustaining thought that, according to Robert Dinnie, fifty miles on foot was regarded as "nothing extra for a Birse peasant to perform in one day." He was writing about things as they were in the 18th century, a hundred years before his time, but when Sir William Cunliffe Brookes, a wealthy banker who became laird of Glentanar, arrived on the Deeside scene last century he obviously thought that the first leg of the journey was wearying enough. At the top of the hill he built the "Rest and Be Thankful," satisfying his passion for monuments and memorials as well as providing a viewpoint known to hundreds of visitors to the Fungle over the years.

I went on up the hill to the cottage that stands on the Guard. The track goes past the cottage to a gate a short distance inside the wood. Dinnie, in his history of Birse, said that there was a road south across the mountains by the parish of Lochlee, but it could not be much recommended, for it was "very steep and almost impassable, excepting for riders or foot passengers." Even for a "foot passenger" the going beyond the gate was rough, gorse stabbing at my legs and thighs and broom rising shoulder-high, the path narrowing and disappearing. I finally broke clear of the wood where the old track joined an estate road from Newmill.

The Fungle, passing an imposing shooting lodge continues south until you start the descent to the Feugh valley, near the point where the river twists right and goes east through the Forest of Birse. The road from Finzean follows the course of the Water of Feugh to Ballochan farm, where the old Mounth road takes over and runs in line with it to its source on the slopes of 2259 ft-high Mulnabracks. Coming from Birsemore, the road I was on swung left to a triangle of woodland on the edge of which stood the Castle of Birse.

> High on the bonny hills o' Birse
> Stands good Sir Thomas' tower,
> And far an' wide the oak tree spreads
> That shades his lady's bower.

Birse Castle.

The present castle is not the one mentioned in the verse, but it was built much in the style of the original 16th century fortalice, which was the home of Sir Thomas Gordon of Cluny. Abandoned at the beginning of the 18th century, it was taken over by the men who gave their name to the Cateran Road. They rode out from the castle on their shaggy ponies, their plaids wrapped about them against the chill night air, urging their mounts into the hills in search of cattle moving over the Mounth. Tough and ruthless, armed to the teeth, they preyed on the herds which straggled in long, bellowing lines towards the markets in the south. "Those wild, scurrilous people," Sir James Balfour called them.

The caterans were said to be from the Grant and Cattanach clans, and Dinnie tells the story of a Duncan Grant who fought with Prince Charles at Culloden and was hunted in the Forest of Birse by Redcoats after the battle. Culloden was fought in mid-April, but Dinnie, undeterred by such historical niceties, says that Grant was tracked down to a house in Birse "in the winter season on a very stormy night, the ground being covered with snow." Perhaps it was later in the year. Grant, at any rate, rose from his bed, opened the door, and stepped out among the soldiers. He was "a man without shoes on his feet, or a rag on his body, excepting the shirt, and that of no very great dimensions," and the Redcoats suspected nothing.

The bold Duncan, however, bolted from under their noses and got away. He hotfooted it "across the Grampian mountains to the southward, forded the water of Tarf at Shanfurr, passed the Baillies, and crossed Rowanhill, forded the North Esk River, and landed at Gleneffock on the south side of the parish of Lochlee, a distance of twelve miles from his residence in the Forest of Birse." Whatever else he did, Duncan Grant must have been the first man to cross the Mounth in his bare feet, wearing nothing but a nightshirt.

I was to follow Duncan's route by Shinfur and the Rowanhill, but in the meantime the Fungle path took me away from the castle, south across the open ground where the path could be seen climbing uphill on the last stage of the trek to Tampie. Heavy rain had made the ground a morass, but beyond Ballochan I joined the track as it came round from the farm. Away ahead, a group of tiny figures could be seen climbing towards Mulnabracks, and when I looked back I could see four other walkers plodding on behind me. We kept pace and distance for the next mile or so and I watched them vanishing and reappearing as the contours of the hill swallowed them up and pitched them back into sight farther along the road. Then I saw another figure, high on the ridge of Cock Hill to the east, a 'keeper with his dog, keeping a watchful eye on us. He went over the brow of the hill and I moved on, passing a wayside stone with the letters JRK cut in it; a rough memorial, no doubt, to some earlier walker in the hills.

From the memorial stone the track narrowed into a patchy hill path that struggled hopelessly upwards through a thickening carpet of dead heather until it gave up the fight and lost itself in the undergrowth. The sky was heavy with the threat of rain and the mountain streams were in full spate, throwing great torrents of water down towards the valley. I went on and up towards the hollow, over 1900 feet high, that lies between Mulnabracks and Tampie, marking my route by the climbers who were still pushing on ahead of me.

Finally, I was up on top, looking back through the grey day towards the Feugh and the flatter lands of Birse. Mulnabracks was on my left, still over 1000 feet above me. The Firmounth lay somewhere on the right, over the brow of Tampie, but the clouds drifting down from the hill discouraged any thought of a short-cut. The ground in front was scarred by great peat hags and I picked my way across this unfriendly terrain until I came upon the hill-walkers who had led the way up Mulnabracks. They were members of the Boys' Brigade, out on an expedition for the Duke of Edinburgh award. They had come over the Fungle from Aboyne and were going on to Invermark.

There were two leaders, looking not much older than the boys themselves, but they knew their hills and showed me a cairn where the Fungle track picked itself out of the moors again and continued to Tarfside. Back on solid ground, I went round the shoulder of Tampie until I saw a signpost pointing the way north to the Firmounth. Here, two old Mounth roads had come together. As I sat down in the shelter of a gun butt to eat my lunch the rearguard caught up with me. They were a couple with their children, ill-clad for the day and glad that the worst part of their journey was over. I watched them hurry downhill towards Tarfside, where a car was waiting to take them home.

Sign at the junction of the Fungle and Firmounth roads. The track goes downhill to Tarfside.

Both the Fungle and Firmounth link Deeside with Glenesk, but it is difficult to decide which road was the oldest or most important and whether one or the other became a minor branch road at the Tampie fork. The Firmounth would appear to have been the easier and more accessible route; the Fungle, under another name, may well have been the older. But for travellers going south the point where the two roads meet meant the end of the worst part of the journey. From there it was a relatively leisurely downhill walk to Tarfside, four miles away. The cloud-shrouded hills of Angus lay ahead and the long glint of the Burn of Kedloch was on my right, running on a line with Mounth road until it joined the Water of Tarf and spilled into the North Esk.

The path skirted the trim cottage at Shinfur, joined the tarred road at the bridge where the Tarf and Tennet meet, and then it was straight ahead and through a strip of wood to Tarfside, a cluster of houses on the main Glenesk road three miles east of Loch Lee. The hills feed their ancient paths into Glenesk from both north and south and watching over them at the head of the glen is the sturdy ruin of Invermark Castle. The tower was built in 1526 to deal with the caterans who came raging over the Mounth from Deeside to plunder the fat cattle grazing in the peaceful glens around the North Esk. Less than a mile on, the hills part for the grey glimmer of Loch Lee, whose waters point the way towards the wild face of Craig Maskeldie and the twin Falls of Unich and Damff, lonely places unexplored by the trippers who flock up Glenesk in the summer week-ends. At the head of the loch you can see the line of a path that goes up by the Shanks of Inchgrundle and across the hills to Clova. The farm of Inchgrundle stands in a woodland corner near the edge of the loch, and it was here that Dr Thomas Guthrie, a Victorian preacher whose oratory made him known throughout Scotland, spent his summers more than a century ago. Queen Victoria, visiting Lord Dalhousie's shooting lodge at Invermark in 1863, walked down to Loch Lee, and she may well have looked across to Inchgrundle and wondered if this fiery leader of the Free Kirk was in residence. He was a philanthropist as well as a preacher, becoming founder of the "ragged schools" in Edinburgh and taking an active interest in the temperance movement. He also found time to raise £100,000 for manses for the Free Church's ministers.

During his stay in Inchgrundle he often held open-air services, his voice ringing out across the water from the old kirkyard at Loch Lee, where his congregation gathered round the grave of Alexander Ross, the dominie-poet of Angus. Ross, a Deeside man, crossed the Mounth to settle at Loch Lee, travelling over the "high hills and fearsome cloughs" which he was to write about so vividly and come to know so well. It was there, in that tiny lochside community, that he wrote "Helenore," a pastoral tale that was to make him famous.

This ruddy-complexioned schoolmaster with the animated face and quick and piercing eye was an intelligent, educated man who gave up well-paid teaching posts and a comfortable life to build a place for himself in what, two and a half centuries ago, was very much the back of beyond. The school was small and the salary low—"not exceeding one hundred merks." He had a piece of good arable ground, running to five or six acres, and kept two horses and two or three cows. He was also allowed, if he wished, to keep one hundred sheep, but there are no records to show that he turned his hand to this. Another of his "perks" was six bolls of oatmeal delivered to him yearly. There must have been an intellectual gulf as wide as the Falls of Unich between Ross and his new neighbours. Born in Kincardine O'Neil in 1699, he had a university background, holding a degree of A.M. from Aberdeen's Marischal College, and he taught at Aboyne and Laurencekirk before marrying Jane Cattanach, a farmer's daughter from Logie-Coldstone, and moving to Loch Lee in 1732. He fitted in well in his adopted home, becoming session clerk, precentor and notary, and he spent fifty-two years of his life in that remote little hamlet nestling between Glenesk and Glen Lee. The core of his contentment may have lain in the lines written by James Beattie, the 18th century Laurencekirk poet, who was Professor of Moral Philosophy at Marischal College.

> Ilka Mearns and Angus bearn,
> Thy tales and sangs by heart shall learn,
> And chiels shall come frae yont the
>   Cairn-a-Mounth, right yousty,
> If Ross will be so kind as share in
>   Their pint at Drousty.

Drousty was the alehouse at Loch Lee.

Ross, the "wild warlock" as Robert Burns called him, was strangely drawn to the hills. He would look up at those tormented cliffs and crags and be caught up in an emotional whirligig. They fascinated and delighted him. His writing reflected not only their immensity and grandeur, but also the lives of the people who lived beneath them, bending before their storms, changing with their seasons, tramping across their weather-worn paths as Ross himself did when he crossed and re-crossed the Mounth in the years that stretched before him. They also gave him his inspiration. Ross's grandson, the Rev. Alexander Thomson, minister of Lintrathen, believed that his grandfather's muse was excited by the "glens, mountains and purling streams," and that it made him write "many pieces of pastoral poetry descriptive of the wild beauties of the place in which he lived."

In 1812, Ross's grandson, in a preface to *Helenore* told something of his grandfather's life and also described the *romantic place* in which he lived. He himself was entranced by Loch Lee, "this beautiful piece of water," and by the high, steep hills enclosing it. Even then, Glenesk and Loch Lee were a magnet for tourists and during the summer the "fashionable people" stayed there for weeks. The tenants found it of "advantageous concern."

Thomson tells of an interesting example of hospitality shown by one of the gentry who came regularly to this corner of Angus. A traveller going over the old Mounth route by Glenmark passed a house at the foot of Mount Keen and, following the path "straight north over the Mount," lost his way when it began to snow. The mist closed in on him and he found it impossible to "distinguish what might be dangerous ground, mossy pits and dreadful precipices," and when he had covered two or three miles in what he thought was a northerly direction discovered that he had landed back at the house at the foot of Mount Keen.

The tenant, Alexander Mill, took him in for the night and he was made to sit down at a table piled high with the best of food, wine and spirits. The traveller protested to his host that he should not have put himself to so much trouble, but Mill said he was acting on the instructions of Sir James Carnegie, of South Esk, who lived there during the summer. Sir James always left "a certain quantity of wine, spirits, tea and sugar for the refreshment of any gentleman who should happen to call; or, as the place was on a pretty much frequented road, should be necessitated from bad weather to stay for a day or a night." No doubt the spirit of hospitality remains, but the storm-bound hiker of to-day would be unlikely to find such a feast awaiting him in the few cottages still to be found in these abandoned glens.

That the Mount Keen path was "a pretty much frequented road" is an indication of the closer links between the folk on either side of the Mounth two centuries ago. The Grampian chain had a relevance to their lives that no longer exists. There was a steady coming and going over the hills, and some of those who went south to the Angus glens decided, like Alexander Ross, to stay there. Others, like John Cameron, of Crathie, were as well known on one side of the Grampians as they were on the other.

During the winter, Loch Lee was usually buried in snow, and the people would pass the time in music and dancing, often gathering together to listen to "the fascinating music of a celebrated performer on the violin." Deeside was noted for its fiddlers in the early 19th century and this "celebrated performer" was John Cameron, who, although spending most of his time at Glenmuick, came over the Mounth every winter, weather permitting, for forty years or more to entertain the folk of Glenesk. He arrived about the beginning of December, but, as Mr Thomson recorded, sometimes "on account of deep snow which rendered it very difficult, and sometimes impossible to travel over the Grampian mountains, his stay was protracted beyond the time when he wished to return home."

Ross himself played the fiddle a little and learned from Cameron that it was the practice in Crathie and Braemar to express not only their mirth but their sorrow by "moving to music." When any member of a family died a musician was immediately sent for, and before the interment, as soon as possible after the death, the whole family except the children gave vent to their sorrow by a kind of dancing. The musician played slow, plaintive music on the bagpipes or violin and the nearest friends of the deceased went on to the floor, took the first dance, and "expressed their grief as well as by their tears."

Ross never forgot his Deeside ties. For over thirty years he regularly went over the hills, and until he reached the age of seventy he always went on foot. When he was eighty he still made an annual visit to his eldest daughter, who lived with her husband and family near Pannanich Wells, at Ballater. He walked at the rate of twenty miles a day and he would arrive at his destination without the slightest sign of fatigue. His wife died in 1779 at the age of eighty-two. He himself died five years later, on May 20th, 1784, in his eighty-sixth year. He had already written what should have been his own epitaph—

> Hence lang, perhaps, lang hence
> may quoted be,
> My homely proverbs lined wi'
> blythsome glee;
> Some readers then may say,
> "Far fa' ye, Ross,"
> When, aiblins, I'll be lang, lang
> dead and gane
> An' few remember there was
> sik a ane.

Alexander Ross is buried in the kirkyard where the mountains cup the loch at the head of the glen, near the spot where the Marquis of Montrose put torch to the chapel three hundred years ago.

The old road through Glenesk leaves the modern road just beyond the farm of Auchronie, cutting over the Hill of Rowan in a direct line to Tarfside, past Westbank and the Maule Monument, erected by Fox Maule, Earl of Dalhouse, in 1866. The Earl, being a fastidious man, looked at both the past and the inevitable future, for the monument was built in memory of seven members of the family already dead and of himself and two others "when it shall please God to call them hence." Here you have a long, sweeping view of the country-side and the hills, looking back to the Mount Keen plateau, where Lord Dalhousie sat on his pony awaiting Queen Victoria in 1861, and north to Tampie and Mulnabracks, where the

Firmounth and Fungle part company on their way to Deeside.

Down at the other end of the glen, the North Esk leaves the valley with a flourish, passing through a gorge of old red sandstone where larch trees droop over great ravines and dark pools lie still and quiet below the narrow path along the riverbank. Here, the Loups of Esk and the Rocks of Solitude are well-known beauty spots. Beyond them the river tumbles under Gannochy Bridge and surges away to the sea, while the road above strikes south to Edzell and the braw town of Brechin.

6

Firmounth

The ripples of the past gently stir the waters of Loch Kinord as you gaze across its waters to "the dark hill-track over grey Culblean." "The lonesomest road that ever was seen," was how the poet Marion Angus described it, and if you listened, she said, you could hear "the tread and the march of the dead." The old drove road winding around the eastern slope of Culblean Hill, four miles from Ballater, looks down to where Kinord and its sister loch, Davan, are strung together like twin pearls across the bare shoulder of the Muir of Dinnet. Loch Davan is a bird sanctuary, a staging post for the migrating geese that come splashing down on their way to winter feeding grounds. There was a time when Loch Kinord offered a sanctuary of a different sort, for the largest of the two islands lying off its shore was once the site of an ancient castle, a halting place for travellers going over the Mounth. The other island was man-made, a crannog island built when the first of the Celtic immigrants came north to put up their forts and earth-houses and settle in the valley of the Dee. For two thousand years, since that tiny lake dwelling was fashioned from stone, earth and timber, this long valley in the shadow of Culblean and Morven has been a corridor for Mounth wayfarers.

The terrain was harsh and uninviting, much of it moss and bogland, with large areas covered by oak forest. Through it ran a criss-cross pattern of "ways" or paths, linking up with main routes on either side of the lochs. One was the road which drovers used coming south from Strathdon, passing the old inn of Boultenstone, which can still be seen on the A97 to Cambus O'May. From Boultenstone they went through the

Birkhill Pass, resting their herds at Badnagoach, on the banks of the Deskry Water, before skirting Morven by Logie-Coldstone until they came in sight of Loch Davan. There they had a choice of routes. The first was directly south on the line of the present Logie-Coldstone-Cambus O'May road, overlooking Davan and Kinord. The second was over Culblean to Tomnakeist and the ford at Tullich, two miles east of Ballater, where they crossed the Dee and went south by the Capel Mounth.

From the Logie-Coldstone road a minor cross-country path led east, above Loch Davan, to Ordie and the farm of Nether Ruthven, where it met another major route from Tarland to Deeside. This "way" ran from Nether Ruthven, across Mullochdhu and down by Birchbank to the Mill of Dinnet, where it fed its traffic across the Dee to the Firmounth Pass.

Mulloch Hill is an ancient and fascinating area. When she was a child my wife's mother spent her holidays at Mulloch and went up to play among the "big stones". These were the blue cairns of Mulloch, which even then were lost in the undergrowth. Tradition has it that Mulloch's Cairn marks the spot where a Danish king was killed.

These ancient "ways" and paths were the threads which made up the violent tapestry of the Battle of Culblean, fought in 1335 when David de Strathbogie, Earl of Atholl, a leading supporter of the Balliol cause, laid siege to Kildrummy Castle. Sir Andrew de Moray, Guardian of Scotland, whose wife, Dame Christian Bruce, aunt of King David II, was in the castle, immediately raised an army in the Lothians and marched north, crossing the Grampians by the Firmounth to Deeside. When the battle was over Earl Davy was dead, slain "by ane aik (oak)." One of his companions, Sir Robert Menzies, found a short-lived refuge on the Castle Island of Kinnord; "in a peill," said Wyntoun.

The word Kinord is a corruption of "ceann na h-airde," the end of the height, and the Rev. J. G. Michie, minister of Dinnet, who wrote a history of the loch in 1877, thought this referred to the ridge of Culblean or Ord. I like to think that it springs from Kinord's connection with the Mounth, for it was certainly "the end of the height" for travellers reaching Deeside after crossing the Grampians. Mr Michie calculated that there had been eleven different spellings of "Kinord," ranging from Canmore, which goes back to the chronicles of of Fordoun and Wyntoun, to Kender, Ceander, Ceanmor and Kinnord, and the cleric plumped for the latter as being closest to the original. The local spelling is Kinord. Whichever is correct, the two lochs sparkling between Culblean and Mulloch have provided a gateway to the north for all manner of men, both kings and commoners, and the ebb and flow of traffic through the Kinord and Davan valley centred on the ford and ferry at Dinnet. At one time there were nearly forty fords on the eighty-five miles of the River Dee, many of them serving local communities, some acting as vital links in the Mounth passes. The ford at Dinnet was important not only because it served a large area of upper Deeside, but also because it was the main crossing of the Dee for the Firmounth Pass, which went through the hills to Glenesk and the markets

The ancient Mulloch track as it is now.

of the south. It was also used by drovers and harvesters heading for Ceann-na-Coille, a mile and a half west of Dinnet on the south road, from where they went over the heather track to Etnach and Mount Keen, making for Glen Mark and Forfarshire.

The Mill of Dinnet, scene of Sir Andrew de Moray's crossing of the Dee in 1335, was the point at which the Boat Road ran down to the river from the old bridge over the Burn of Dinnet, and the ford was sited about half a mile east of the present Bridge of Dinnet, meeting with the south bank in a line with the farm of Cobleheugh. The ferry was farther upstream, close to the site on which the bridge was built in 1861-62 and a footpath connected it to the Firmounth road. There was a public house at the ferry landing on the north bank but it has long since gone. Its modern successor stands on the main Aberdeen-Ballater road, not a stone's throw from where old-time travellers stopped to quench their thirst after their weary trek over the Firmounth hills.

There were two other fords and two ferries between Dinnet and Aboyne. One ford was at Dalwhing, roughly opposite the Bridge of Ess, and the other crossed the river at the old Church of Glentanar, where there was also a ferry listed by Sir James Balfour as being "at Dalcheipe neir Glentanner Kirke." The second ferry was at Waterside, between Heugh-head farm, once an inn, and Ferrar. It is believed that this ferry was the "Boate of Ferrar," which was also mentioned by Sir James. The ford and ferry at Glentanar Kirk linked up with the Firmounth path.

The Mounth road from the Mill of Dinnet went over to the Firmounth by Tillycairn. I rejoined the track a short distance west of Glentanar kirkyard, at Glentanar School, now a pottery, where a signpost says "Firmounth." The school was built in English oast-house style by Sir William Cunliffe Brooks, the laird of Glentanar, who set his own distinctive—but not always popular—architectural seal on the buildings of the estate.

Beside the school there is a large, unsightly drinking well

opposite the Firmounth path. It was built to celebrate the Jubilee of Queen Victoria, "a bright and shining light to her people." The well, an expression of loyalty to her Majesty and gratitude to God, carries a number of inscriptions, including one that appeared to be directed at square pegs in round holes. "Shape thyself for use," it read. "The stone that may fit in the wall is left not in the way."

The Firmounth route is well signposted. A short distance from the main road, past some farm buildings, a second sign turned right and up a track that was rutted and flooded by heavy rain. At the top of the hill a third sign pointed left to the Firmounth and at this junction I came upon an old, weather-beaten granite memorial erected by the indefatigable Sir William Cunliffe Brooks. It carried the barely-readable inscription: "Fir Munth. Ancient PASS over the Grampians. Here crossed the invading armies of Edward I of England A.D. 1296 and 1303. Also the army of Montrose 1645."

There is a strong possibility that Sir William was wrong on all three counts, certainly on two, and there have been plenty of writers and historians at pains to point it out. There is no evidence that Montrose, although a hardened Mounth traveller, ever crossed the Grampians by the Firmounth, although Spalding recorded that the Royalist leader "directed M'Donald (Major M'Donald) into Birse." Edward I clearly never crossed the Firmounth in his 1296 expedition and most authorities on the subject have dismissed the suggestion that he travelled that way in 1303. The Rev. J. G. Michie had other ideas. He said that the English king stayed on Castle Island on Loch Kinord on his journey north in 1296 and, coming down from Kildrummy on his return, "Crossed the Dee at Boat of Dinnet, whence long files of his soldiers wended their way through Glentanar and over the Fir Munth, and so on by Brechin to Dundee." In 1909, P. J. Anderson, Librarian at Aberdeen University, described the association of Glentanar with either Edward or Montrose as "pure myth." He dismissed the Dinnet minister's description with the unkind comment that it was "an excellent example of the old-

Sir William Cunliffe Brooks's memorial on the Firmounth.

fashioned way of writing local history and of the play of Mr Michie's fancy." Anderson mentioned Gough's itinerary and underlined two points. The first was that at Kincardine O'Neil "there was a bridge so far back as 1234," and the second was that the Cairn-a-Mounth "formed, from the eleventh century to the eighteenth, the main road connecting the northern and southern provinces of Scotland." Even so, the Firmounth was still an important pass. Although Gough's map of the 1296 expedition plainly shows the route over the Cairn-a-Mounth, his map and itinerary of the 1303-4 campaign are confusing. The line drawn from Elgin appears to run west of Kildrummy and Kincardine O'Neil and cross the Mounth somewhere in the region of Glentanar or Birse. This, at least, leaves as an open question the possibility that Edward travelled south by the Cabrach to Strathdon and Loch Kinord and went over the Firmounth to Glenesk, from where he made his way to Dundee. From Edward's stone the road went south-east by Belrorie Hill, passing the farm road to Hillhead, until it came to a large, semi-circular granite entrance to one of the estate houses. From here, the dirt-track gave way to a motor road that went downhill to meet the main road through the estate from the Bridge of Ess. Directly below, the Tanar wound its way through the green fields to the Dee and in the distance the sun slanted through a heavy layer of cloud masking the hills. The road over Belrorie Hill was the approach to two main routes through Glentanar at one time. Both crossed the Water of Tanar at Braeloine Bridge, skirted Glentanar House, and parted company on the south side of the house, one climbing uphill as the Firmounth Pass, the other swinging round behind the house to recross the Tanar at Knockieside Bridge and join the road to Mount Keen.

In 1930, the Deeside District Committee of Aberdeen County Council went to court to claim right of way in the Belrorie Road and the one crossing Braeloine Bridge to Knockieside. The settlement resulted in the situation existing to-day, with traffic being allowed to run up Glentanar to the car park behind what were the stables. From there to Mount Keen the road is a right of way for walkers, as is the Firmounth route. What is interesting is that the road from Fasnadarroch by Belrorie to Braeloine was declared a public road for all forms of transport. Fasnadarroch is on the South Deeside Road, a little west of the point where there is a Firmounth sign, and it runs past the junction where the memorial to Edward I was erected. In the petition it was described as the road "leading from South Deeside Road at Fasnadarroch to Snakeswell and thence, skirting Belrorie Wood, to the point west of West Millfield at or near Braeloine Bridge, where the said road joins the public road from Bridge of Ash (Ess) to Glentanner."

The evidence throws a good deal of light on the use of these old roads and on Glentanar itself. Snakeswell, for instance, takes its name from an old well which Cunliffe Brooks built near the Edward stone. The inscription on it reads, "The worm of the still is the deadliest snake on the hill," an obvious allusion to the illicit whisky distilling that went on in Glentanar. Lord Mackay, who gave judgement on the case, said there was "a very considerable traffic in the distilling of whiskey in the low hills and this traffic went by donkey, pony or mule across the Munths to Brechin." He also mentioned the droving traffic to Brechin and the southern markets and to the fact that they "came wondrous distances from the summer feeding at Gairnhead, Coldstone, Tarland, Auchlossan and further away from Dinnet and Castlenewe, Towie and even further." There was also a "considerable body"of travelling farm hands going south to the harvesting and shearing." "Traffic took the most ready routes leading to several well-known and old-established fords, at some of which there were also boats adapted for sheep and cattle," said Lord Mackay. "Such a ford existed at Dinnet near the site of the old Glentanar Church. There was also one at Aboyne and one at Pannanich."

One of the witnesses, 55-year-old James Paterson, remembered going "over that old Roman bridge with the *ceud mile failte* and over by the Chapel there." The Gaelic welcome can still be seen on the drinking well at the north side of Braeloine Bridge. The "Roman" bridge is a single-arch, hump-backed bridge set picturesquely in the trees flanking the river and it still carries the two stones placed at the end of the bridge to block vehicular traffic. Few people would try to take a car over Braeloine, even if the stones were removed. It takes you across the Tanar to a path which runs along the riverbank then swings left between two fields, passing what looks like a toadstool-shaped doocot. This, in fact, is a building that was used to house a turbine which until recently provided electricity for the nearby Chapel of St. Lesmo. The old Mill of Glen Tanar stood not far from the "doocot" and the line of the lade carrying the water from the river can still be seen. The millstone used in the mill lies beside the turbine building.

St. Lesmo's Chapel was another product of the fertile imagination of Cunliffe Brooks. An old bell peeps through an ivory-covered belfry, the windows are stained glass, and later in the year the russet-leafed trees and holly bushes red with berries provide an ideal setting. Two gravestones lie side by side in front of the chapel and behind them a striking Celtic cross. Sir William, the English magnate who came to Deeside and moulded Glentanar into what it is to-day, died in 1900 and is buried in the shadow of one of his own creations, named after the saint who brought Christianity to this part of Scotland 1200 years ago. The second gravestone is that of his wife. At the other end of the chapel are two similar stones, those of the 2nd Baron of Glentanar, who died in 1971, and his wife. His father, the 1st Baron Glentanar, of the Coates family of Paisley, bought the estate in 1905.

The old house of Braeloine once stood on the site of the chapel, forming the centre of the communities of Braeloine and Knockieside. These consisted of the meal mill, several soutars' (shoemakers) shops, a merchant's shop, an inn and fifteen houses. Braeloine is first mentioned in the records in 1638, when John Garden of Bellamore took the feu of the croft of Braeloine, the mill, and the alehouse croft from the Marquess of Huntly. The decline of the Firmounth as a major route south brought the end of this little community on the banks of the Tanar and the last tenant of Braeloine and the mill was a Peter Begg in 1850. Sir William Cunliffe Brooks took over the estate in 1869.

The Firmounth path, after meeting up with the Bridge of Ess road on the south bank of the river, continues towards Glentanar House, which lies on the opposite bank, and finally turns uphill where a signpost indicates the Mounth route. The road climbs away from the Tanar, hugging a stretch of woodland until it breaks to the right and makes for the Burn of Skinna between the Strone and a hill called Baudy Meg. Dropping down to the Burn of Skinna, it crosses it and climbs steeply up through woodland to the face of Craigmahandle. It was there, where the wind flailed a sagging deer fence separating the forest land from the hill country, that I marked off the Mounth landmarks like a storekeeper taking stock. I could see Mount Keen, towering above Glentanar on one side and Glenmark on the other, and, a long way off, the great corrie of Lochnagar, snow still white in its gullies, and I could see the rocky cap of Cairn Leuchan, where a Mounth track came over from Balintober, near Ballater, to make its obeisance at the foot of Mount Keen. I could see, too, the line of the Etnach road, another ancient byway which once carried drovers and travellers from Deeside and the north into the Angus glens.

Turning to the east, I could pick out the wart-like snout of Clochnaben, watchdog of the Cairn-a-Mounth, while below me lay the green and fertile hollow by the Castle of Birse, where the Forest of Birse runs itself out in the grey foothills of the Fungle. This was another Mounth road that was to keep me company over the hills until it met up with the Firmounth and ran straight and clear down to Tarfside in Glenesk. They trailed south from the valley of the Dee, old forgotten paths whose rocky, peat-strewn miles opened up vistas far beyond the straths of the Dee and the Esk. They were passageways to forces that changed and moulded the face and future of the north-east of Scotland, if not of Scotland itself. There was more than the jagged landscape to see from the summit of Craigmahandle; here, too, you were looking back on the contours of history.

Heading towards the Hill of St Colm, treading the spine of the Mounth, I thought of all the other travellers whose journey over the Firmounth had taken them into the pages of history and I remembered that it was the German novelist Theodor Fontane who said that the Grampian country was the land of the old Scottish kings. One king made his mark on this Mounth route by proxy, for while the stone erected by Sir William Cunliffe Brooks to commemorate Edward I's crossing of the Firmounth may have been historically inaccurate, the Hammer of the Scots sent the Prince of Wales, later Edward II, over the Firmounth on the heels of Robert the Bruce, who took to the hills while his Queen sought refuge at Kildrummy Castle under the care of his brother Nigel.

From Craigmahandle the track drops down and then climbs

again sharply to the Hill of St Colm, named after one of the missionaries who brought Christianity to Deeside, and on its flat summit a stone with the letter "B" cut into it can be seen at the side of the path. It appears to be one of Sir William's "calling cards," for a little farther on is St Colm's Well, which the Glentanar laird commemorated by the laying of a circular stone with the inscription "WELL BELOVED." The well was once the scene of an annual pilgrimage on the Saint's Feast Day, October 16th, but the only pilgrims now are the hill walkers who, like myself, stop to drink the cool mountain water.

There is a certain irony in the fact that this token of Christian compassion on a lonely hilltop is only literally a stone's throw from a cairn which is said to stand on the spot where a tinker going over the Firmounth murdered his wife. The cairn is called the Tinker's Cairn and the inscription "W.E. 1814" can be seen on one of the stones. The man was brought before the court at Aberdeen and one of the witnesses was a Tarfside woman at whose house the couple stopped on their way north. The tinker declared that he had never been there, but when the witness said she had given them a drink of milk he unthinkingly exclaimed that it was only whey. The remark sealed his fate.

The path goes on over Gannoch Hill, past another boulder with a "B" on it, and descends again before going up to the peaty plateau of Tampie, where it bears right to a line of crumbling shooting butts. On Tampie, the highest point on the Mounth pass, I could turn full circle and see the whole panorama of the Grampian hills, stretching west to Mount Keen and east to Mount Battock. Below, like some vast amphitheatre, was Tarfside, green and sunlit in the valley of the Esk. I went on down the south shoulder of the hill until I came to the signpost, bordering the rocky path to Shinfur. Erected by the Scottish Rights of Way Society, it indicated the road to Dinnet by the Firmounth, pointing back the way I had come. There was no accompanying sign to show the route through the Fungle, which came looping round between

Tampie and Mulnabracks to join the Firmounth below the sign.

Things might have been different for both the Fungle and the Firmounth if the seed of an idea planted over a century and a half ago had taken root. When the Earl of Aboyne erected a chain or suspension bridge over the River Dee at Aboyne in 1831, replacing a similar one swept away in the great flood of 1829, it was thought that it might link up with a new road going south over the Grampian barrier to Strathmore, In "The Statistical Account of Aberdeenshire" in 1843, the Rev. Robert Milne Miller, minister of Aboyne and Glentanar, noted that there was "an excellent road, either turnpike or Parliamentary, from Huntly to Aboyne" and said that "a continuation of the line southward, through the Grampians, is naturally indicated."

The route was, in fact, surveyed from Aboyne, through the top of the forest of Birse, the lower part of Glenesk, the Clash of Wirren and the parish of Menmuir. The survey showed "a very inviting line as to levels and facility of formation." The new road, said Mr Miller, would join the great Strathmore road at a point near the bridge of Finhaven, about twenty-five miles from Aboyne. He went on to make the point that the expense of the projected road would be less than the cost of the Aboyne bridge and that it would be "a spur given, in a neglected district, to that spirit of improvement which is generally carried on along a new line of road." This brave new highway was more or less following the old Mounth route, for the Fungle and Firmounth paths, as well as another track over Mount Keen to Glen Mark, were feeders for the road to Menmuir by the Clash of Wirren. Curiously, I was to come upon the remains of another unfinished highway south of the Clash of Wirren while going from Glen Mark to Strathmore later in my travels. Nothing came of the Aboyne plan, but I could not help thinking that, if it had, I would not have been tramping across these lonely hills. Instead, I would have been driving south on a modern road that challenged the Cairnwell and the Cairn o' Mount as a main artery for traffic crossing the Grampians.

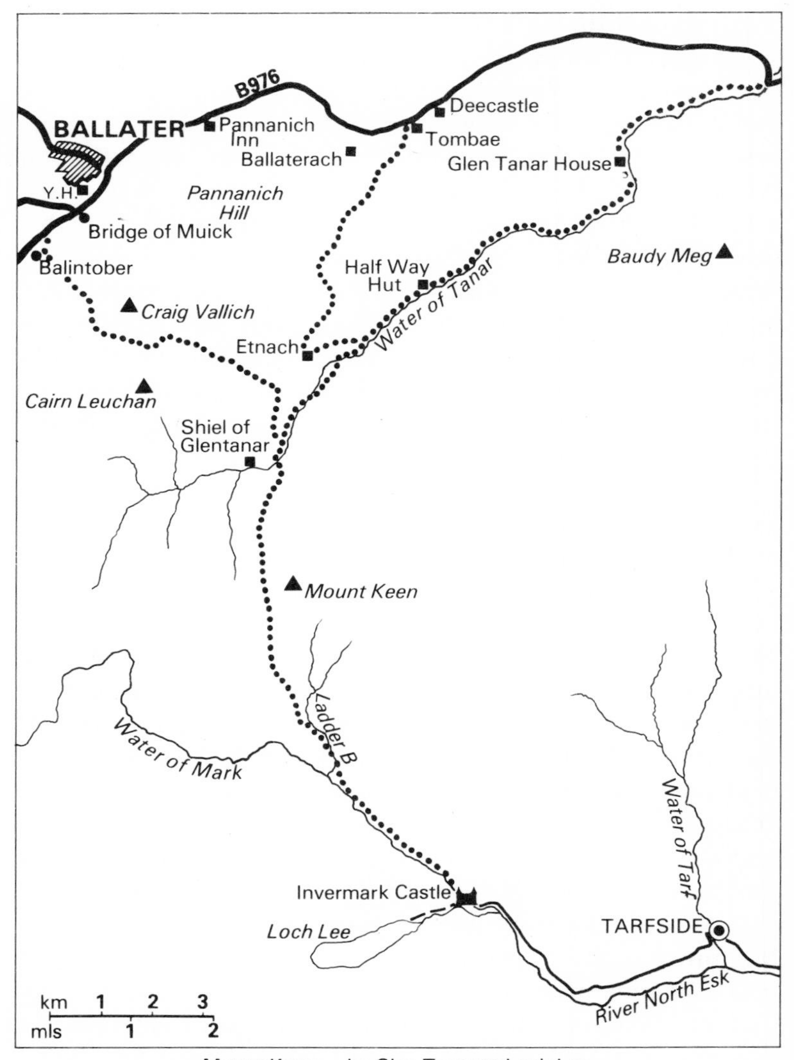

Mount Keen — by Glen Tanar to Loch Lee

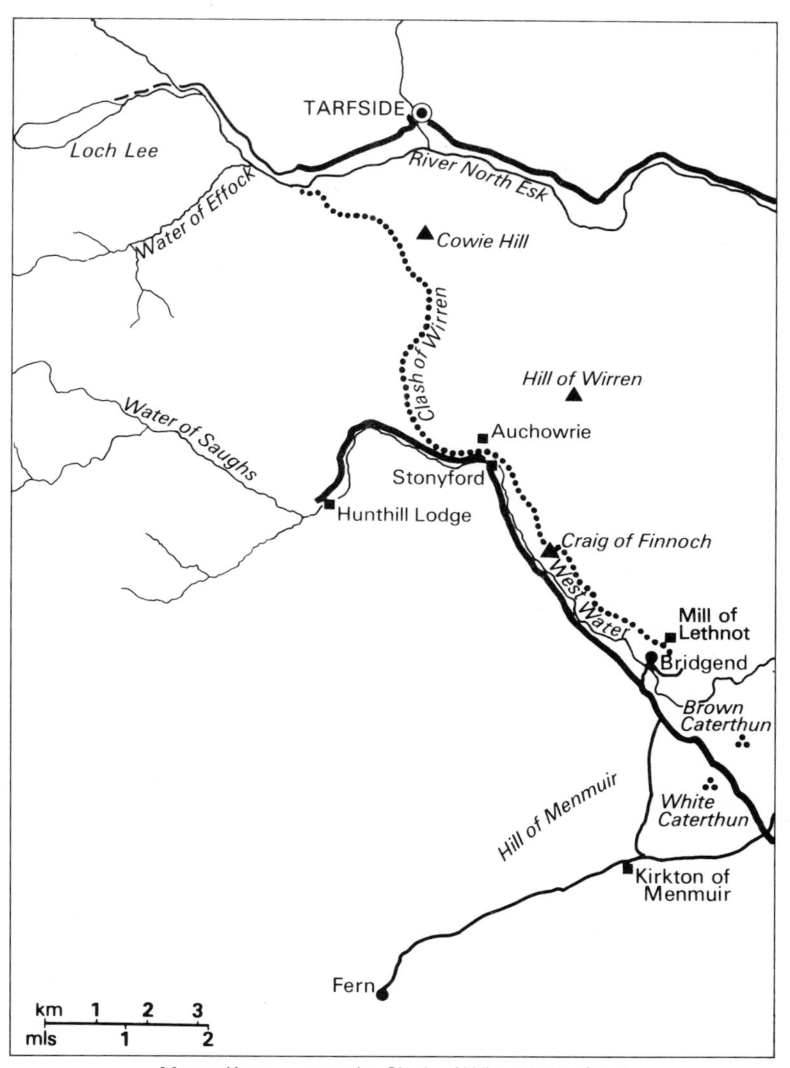

Mount Keen — over the Clash of Wirren to Lethnot

7

Mount Keen

Mount Keen draws the old trails to it like a spider spinning its web. Queen Victoria called it "a curious conical-shaped hill" when she crossed it in 1861. It is 3077 ft high, the most easterly of the Deeside "Munros," and at its feet are the ruins of the old inn of Coirebhruach, which once served thirsty travellers making the giant "leap-frog" from Glentanar into Glenmark. Lord Mackay, in his judgement on the Glentanar right-of-way case of 1930, mentioned four public roads which carried a large volume of traffic from Aberdeenshire to Forfarshire via Coirebhruach. The first was the road from the Bridge of Ess on the South Deeside Road, a mile and a quarter west of Aboyne. This road, which meets the historic road into the glen by Belrorie Hill, ends at a small car park behind Glentanar House.

There are two signs there, one asking motorists to "Ca' Canny doon th' Brae" on their way back to Aboyne, the other pointing walkers to Mount Keen. A hike of about six or seven miles lies ahead, although there is a place for a breather three miles through the woods at the Half-way Hut. Beyond this the trees thin out and give way to the hills and moors and, past a sign indicating a path to Mount Keen "by the Mounth," Etnach can be seen above a sturdy stone bridge spanning the Tanar. Here we meet up with the second road mentioned by Lord Mackay. He called it "the road from Canakyle (now Deecastle)," and, although it is now one of the least well-known of the Mounth paths, at one time it was one of the most important, featuring in Sir James Balfour's list of main passages through the mountains from the River Tay to the River Dee. Sir James gave it as "Monnthe Keine" and drew its

The half-way hut on the road from Glentanar house to Mount Keen.

line "from Innermarkie to Canakyle on Deesyde." There is an old song which goes—

> We'll up the moor of Charleston
> And o'er the water of Dee,
> And hine awa' to Candecaill,
> It's there that we should be.

Canakyle is four miles east of Ballater on the South Deeside Road. The word has had different spellings through the years, among them Kanakyle and Candecaill, but the correct version is believed to be Ceann-na-Coille, meaning Woodhead or Woodend. The name eventually disappeared and the spot became known as Dee Castle, which is still in use to-day. The original Ceann-na-Coille, built by the first Marquis of Huntly, was burned in 1641.

The ford at Dinnet was used by travellers going by Ceann-na-Coille to Mount Keen, following a road that cut deep into the Glentanar hills until it turned down to the Water of

Tanar at Etnach, once a keeper's cottage. Etnach was visited by Queen Victoria when she was returning from her Second Great Expedition. "Eatnoch," she called it, "a very lonely place." Her initial impression of it was soured by the fact that the keeper was away and the only person to welcome her was "a wretched idiot girl."

For anyone following the Mounth route the starting point is Tombae, a little west of Dee Castle. From here the road goes up past the farm of Greystone until it clears the woods and heads uphill towards the Black Moss. Once over the brow of the hill you can see the rocky outline of Cairn Leuchan, below which a path from Balintober leads to Mount Keen, and behind the dark rim of distant mountains and the corrie of Lochnagar. The Etnach path swings left and up over Cairn Nairvie, dropping down into Glentanar on the south side of the hill.

The road from "Innermarkie to Canakyle" has slipped into disuse, and only a scattering of cattle graze on the heather-covered slopes where once great herds of cattle went south to the trysts. From Etnach I got my first view of Mount Keen, the Mounth track a long, grey scar on its face. Then I was at Coirebhruach, looking at the rickle of stones which were all that remained of the old inn. I ate a snack in the lee of the Shiel of Tanna, a shooting lodge not unlike that in the Fungle, which stands a few hundred yards from Coirebhruach. The stable door was open. There were two stalls and on the wall large wooden pegs for hanging harness. There was also the usual writing and one scribbled note said that a George Sutherland had stabled his horse there in 1890. He was back in 1922 "enjoying a picnic," but this time he came by car.

Incredible though it seems, wheeled transport has actually gone up and over the massive bulk of Mount Keen and down the "Ladder" to Glen Mark. "Bicycles have been taken over what is called the 'Ladder' at a height of 2500 feet on Mount Keen," observed Lord Mackay, "but they must, I think have been carried much of the way." He added solemnly, "No other vehicle is proved to have passed except as a reputed freak." William Duncan, a 56-year-old Dinnet man, told Lord Mackay that he "went over the shoulder of Mount Keen with my cycle" to Tarfside. The reason for this feat was a simple one. He wanted to see Loch Lee. He said that droving to the south was a common practice in his own and his father's time. Drovers going north from Brechin would spend a night about Etnach, another night up in Gairnside, and then from there to Strathdon.

A sign near the Coirebhruach ruins pointed the way to Mount Keen, to Aboyne and Dinnet, and over the hills to Ballater by Balintober. This last route was spotlighted by Lord Mackay as the road from Ballater via Glenmuick. For me it began, not at Glenmuick, but at a distillery that lies snugly in the foothills of Easter Balmoral. Queen Victoria's visit to Lochnagar Distillery in September, 1848, placed the Royal seal of respectability on the age-old business of whisky-making, and in many ways it marked the end of a long and violent era of illicit distilling. This was still booming in the first quarter of the nineteenth century and gradually faded out when legal distilling was sanctioned by the Government in 1823. The first man to take advantage of the 1823 Act was a Glenlivet farmer, George Smith, and his example was followed by John Robertson when he founded the distillery on the Balmoral estate. It was bought by John Begg in 1845.

Thirteen years after her visit to the distillery, Queen Victoria set out on her Second Great Expedition. It led her over the Whisky Road, the route along which illicit stills had flourished under the noses of frustrated excisemen and over which the smugglers had driven their ponies south laden with illegal Scotch. The Whisky Road was also one of the old Mounth roads between Deeside and Angus, starting near Ballater and winding over the moors from Glenmuick to Glentanar. From there it climbed 2000 ft over the shoulder of Mount Keen to Glenmark, Glenesk and Brechin. The road from Glenmark and Fettercairn was the last of Lord Mackay's public roads.

The Bridge of Muick, about half a mile from the bridge linking Ballater with the A973, was the meeting place at which Queen Victoria, driving down from Balmoral in her carriage, was greeted by the five ghillies who were to lead the Royal party over the Mounth. At this Muick junction there is a signpost to Balintober. As you climb up the hill the track swings left and rises to a marker post on the ridge below Cairn Leuchan. It may have been the way the slanting sunlight struck the hill against the dark sky, but it looked like some mysterious fairy castle and I left my pack on the ridge and slogged my way to the top. The view was reward enough. Looking back along the track I could see down into the valley of the Muick, with the Birkhall road winding its way towards Lochnagar. Through my binoculars I could follow the familiar path that clears the woods beyond Allt-na-giubhsaich and rises steeply towards the "frowning glories" of that forbidding mountain. I could make out the dark drop of the Black Gully and the twin mounds of the Meikle Pap and Little Pap.

Then, swinging round, I was looking into the face of Mount Keen, the old Mounth track a hairline mark against its massive surface. It was somewhere about here, perhaps on Cairn Leuchan itself, that Queen Victoria stood entranced by what she saw and later wrote "Mount Keen was in great beauty before us." Away to the east were the green fields of Deeside and the waters of Loch Kinord. A young stag broke from the heather as I made my way downhill and on a ridge a mile away a small herd of deer watched my passage with uneasy interest. A hawk hovered overhead; mountain hares, their summer-brown coats changing to winter white, were everywhere. The scenery, as Queen Victoria had said, was grand and wild.

On the marshy land below Cairn Leuchan a path drops down and across the moorland to a ridge above Glentanar. The route is signposted, but it is not easy to follow. The large signpost on the ridge is virtually unreadable, but part of it says "Public Footpath . . . Ballater . . . over shoulder of Mount Keen". The path down into Glentanar is at times also difficult

The path from Etnach (lower left) leading up over Mount Keen to Glen Mark.

to follow, but with care it can be traced down to Coirebhruach and the ford across the Water of Tanar to the base of Mount Keen. The climb up Mount Keen is slow and hard, but when you reach the top you are on the rim of two of the loveliest glens in Scotland; the long sweep of Glentanar on one side, Glenmark on the other. "We came in sight of a new country," wrote Queen Victoria.

John Taylor, Thames waterman, self-styled Water Poet, and author of "The Pennyless Pilgrim," an account of his journey through Scotland in 1618, saw it in a different light. Perhaps he had had a bad start. Travelling north from Brechin, he "did go through a country called Glen Esk, where passing by the side of a hill, so steep as the ridge of a house, where the way was rocky, and not above a yard broad in some places, so fearful and horrid it was to look down into the bottom, for if either horse or man had slipped, he had fallen, without recovery, a good mile downright." Taylor thanked

God when he came to the Laird of Edzell's land, where he "lay at an Irish house," but even here all was not well. His hosts could speak "scarce any English" and during the night he was forced to rise because he was "so stung with Irish musquitoes." This creature, said the Water Poet, "had six legs and lived like a monster on man's flesh."

The next day Taylor went through Glen Mark and over Mount Keen, or "Skene," as he called it. The valley was warm, but by the time he got to the top his teeth "began to dance in my head with cold, like Virginal's jacks (an old keyed instrument), and withal, a most familiar mist embraced me round, that I could not see thrice my length any way: withal, it yielded so friendly a dew, that did moisten through all my clothes." Taylor had found, as he observed, that weather phenomenum, a Scotch mist. He thought that the hill was six miles "up and down," and the way "so uneven, stony, and full of bogs, quagmires, and long heath, that a dog with three legs will out-run a horse with four." It took him four hours to cross it.

The track plunging down into Glen Mark from the plateau on the south side of Mount Keen is known as the Ladder, and the stream running parallel with it is the Ladder Burn. There is an attractive little cottage at the bottom of the Ladder, and it was here that Victoria stopped for lunch—"in a little room of a regular Highland cabin, with its usual 'press bed.' " There were other Mounth travellers on the move when the Royal party was there, "a picturesque group of 'shearers,' chiefly women, the older ones smoking. They were returning from the south to the north, whence they came." On the right the Water of Mark comes down past a great rocky pudding of a hill, the Craig of Doune, south of the Hill of Doune.

Before Queen Victoria set out along the glen she stopped to drink at "a very pure well called the White Well." The well is still there, but it is better known now as the Queen's Well, for straddling it is a massive granite memorial in the shape of a crown, built by Lord Dalhousie to commemorate the visit. A small plaque on one of the stones reminded me that the year of the Second Great Expedition was "the year of her Majesty's great sorrow," for it was not long after that that Prince Albert died. The spring flows into a stone bowl which carries the inscription—

> Rest, traveller, on this lonely green,
> And drink and pray for Scotland's Queen.

The Queen returned to Glen Mark two years later, riding over the Polach and "down that fine wild pass called the Ladder Burn." She stood at the well and thought of the day when she had been there with "my beloved Albert." "We drank with sorrowing hearts," wrote the Queen. Grant, in what appears to have been a sudden sentimental gesture, handed her his flask. It was one that she herself had given him and "out of which we had drunk on that day." It was, as the Queen remarked later, quite a pilgrimage.

I drank to Scotland's Queen and made my way along the glen by the Water of Mark. Ahead lay Loch Lee and the ruined Castle of Invermark, bringing me a reminder that I was still on the Whisky Road.

It is easy to hear the voices of the past when you walk these lonely glens. John R. Allan, that well-known son of the North-east, once lived in the manse at Loch Lee, and in that warm, couthy way of his tried to define how it felt to live in "the quiet of that empty place," out of the world, as he put it, yet never lonely. In *North-east Lowlands of Scotland* he described how the road came up to the gate of his house, went on as a rough track for three miles, and continued as a hill path over the mountains to Deeside. "The drovers had come this way with their cattle from the Highlands; the bands of young men and women had gone this way to the harvest in the low country, carrying their boots round their necks to save the leather, and this way they returned, with their boots worn out but a harvest fee in their pockets."

From Loch Lee I set out on the next stage of my journey along the Whisky Road. The first had taken me from Ballater across the hills to Glentanar and over Mount Keen to

Glenmark and Glenesk. The second was to take me through a wild, haunted glen, full of ghostly tales, which was the whisky smugglers' last mountain barrier before they rode into Brechin to sell their illicit wares and return north with empty kegs and full pockets. On that final stretch of the whisky trail the smuggling bands from the north and Deeside were joined by others from Glen Effnock and the Rowan at Tarfside.

The glen is Glen Lethnot, through which the old hill path runs for some eight miles from Glenesk before reaching the hamlet of Bridgend, four miles west of Edzell. It was also known as the Priest's Road, because it was used by the Episcopal minister of Loch Lee to travel to his second charge at Lethnot. One must admire that reverend gentleman for stepping out through this bleak and inhospitable countryside to take a Sunday service on a winter morning. He had my sympathy, for the first snow of winter was powdering the distant hill-tops when I pressed uphill over the Priest's Road.

The path is marked by a signpost two miles east of Loch Lee. You cross the North Esk by a narrow stone bridge and go through the farm of Dalbrack and over the Burn of Dalbrack to where the track climbs up Cowie Hill. Looking back, I could see Mount Keen like a miniature Fujiyama and the Mounth road, now deep in snow; to the north was the hollow between Tampie and Mulnabracks, where the Firmounth and Fungle paths parted company on their way to Deeside. Then, on the ridge, the Whisky Road plunged down to the Burn of Berryhill, and went sharply up and on to the Clash of Wirren. The name Clash Wirren is from the Gaelic *"clais fhuaran,"* meaning the hollow of springs, which was an inadequate description of the great dip that lay ahead. From the side of the Hill of East Knock, looking north-east, I saw an unexpected and familiar landmark, the top of Clochnaben, peeping up over the far-away hills. So at one glance I encompassed four mountain tops that marked the line of Mounth roads; the Cairn-a-Mounth, the Fungle, the Firmounth and Mount Keen.

Turning south again, there was a choice of routes. The

direct route was down to the farm of Tillybardine, swinging left to follow the West Water on its way to join the North Esk near Stracathro. The alternative route was up over the West Craig, where the cairns tempted me away from the footpath. I took the high road through the heather and was rewarded with an awe-inspiring view of the Angus hills. I could see clear down Glen Lethnot, with the road and river nudging each other past the farm of Auchowrie, which was almost directly below me. There was another road on the opposite side of the West Water, clear enough as it struck south-east from Auchowrie but barely discernible as I followed it round the lower slopes of the Hill of Wirren. This was the last stretch of the Priest's Road between Auchowrie and Bridgend.

Near Auchowrie there is a Scottish Rights of Way Society sign indicating "Public Footpath to Glenesk and Ballater," but in this quiet Angus glen Deeside seemed remote; another world, far, far back along that dipping, winding path over Mount Keen and through Glenmark. Yet two miles south of Auchowrie on the Priest's Road you are walking on the broken dreams of some forgotten visionaries whose plan would have made near-neighbours of two tiny communities separated by the Mounth barrier, Bridgend of Glenmuick, where the Whisky Road began, and Bridgend of Lethnot, where it all but came to an end. The track that the drovers and whisky smugglers took on those two miles from Auchowrie is half buried in heather, narrow and difficult to manoeuvre, but at the Craig of Finnoch there is a remarkable change. Here, suddenly, it widens into what was the start of a major carriage road that was intended to go all the way through the hills to Deeside.

The carriageway began at Clochie, on the Lethnot-Edzell road near Bridgend, and it ran some two miles up the glen before coming to a halt at the Clachan of Finnoch. That was 200 years ago and one can only guess at the thoughts of the folk who lived there, cut off from civilisation, as they watched this great new highway, wide enough to take a horse and carriage, creep towards them along the face of the hill. New horizons would have opened, isolation would have become a thing of the past, and Ballater would have been a pleasant trot over the hills by pony and trap. But their dreams withered and died and in time the clachan, like the road, was itself abandoned. The last resident left his cottage nearly a century ago and now all that remains are the crumbling walls of the cottar houses, the gaping windows of their gable-ends looking up the glen to where the old road threads its way towards Auchowrie.

Across the water from Finnoch I could see the dark shadow of the Burn of Callater curving down from the Hill of Mondurran, which the caterans passed on its west side before the Raid of Saugh. The caterans were attacked and defeated at the Water of Saugh after raiding in Fern, well to the south of Glen Lethnot. The burn comes down to meet its mother-stream at Craigendowie, and it was a mile up this tributary that old Peter Grant lived two centuries ago, on a holding called Westside. If that grand new carriage road had been completed, Peter, or Dubrach as he was called, would have made his last journey in style, as befitted the King's oldest enemy.

Peter Grant took his nickname from the farm of Dubh-bhruach, in Glen Dee, where he was born in 1714, the year before the first Jacobite Rebellion. A weaver and tailor to trade, he took arms with the Jacobites in the '45 Rebellion, winning the rank of sergeant-major. He was captured at Culloden, imprisoned in Carlisle Castle, and escaped to make his way back to Auchindryne, Braemar, in 1746. In later years, his son John went south to farm at Westside in Lethnot, and when he retired "Dubrach" and his wife joined him. In 1814, celebrating his 100th birthday, he was the last surviving "rebel" in Scotland and in 1822, when his story became known to King George IV, he was granted a life pension. He was now 108.

But the years were running out for Dubrach, and in 1823 he had a yearning to return to his native Deeside, so Peter Grant went over the Mounth for the last time. He died on

February 11th 1824, at the age of 110 years, and his tombstone can still be seen in the kirkyard at Braemar. They turned out in their hundreds to bury the oldest rebel. The whisky flowed and the pipes played, and Peter Grant's friend, a youngster of 90, played a pibroch at the graveside. The tune was "Wha widna fecht for Charlie's richt?"

I left old Dubrach and the memory-haunted Clachan of Finnoch and went on to Clochie, down that roadway of forgotten hopes, past the shepherd's cottage at Dikehead, where the windows were boarded up and an old jacket swung a little eerily in the open door. On the right I could see Bridgend and far beyond Clochie the road that went thrusting up the hill to the Caterthuns and on to Brechin. The carriage road goes straight down to the main Lethnot road, but the old Priest's Road crossed the Burn of Drumcairn at the Mill of Lethnot. There is a story that the Devil once made an appearance through the floor of the old mill house and that the Rev. John Row, the Lethnot minister, chased him back through the hole, but it is hard to believe that this lovely little corner was ever troubled by satanic visitations.

John Row had two kirks, one in Lethnot and one across the West Water in Navar. Both are gone, Lethnot a ruin and Navar no more that a belfry tower with ivy roots choking it as it stands in the middle of a circle of trees near the Paphrie Burn. It is not the sort of place you would want to be on a dark night and the old tombstones, faded, moss-covered, leaning grotesquely in the wild grass, add to the doom-ridden atmosphere. This was the burying place of a legless beggar called John Gudefellow, who went around the district on his hands and stumps living off the goodwill or superstition of the local folk. It is also said to be the last resting place of a Lethnot farmer's wife who was carried off by caterans. There was also an Episcopal meeting-house at Clochie, but it was burned down after the 1745 Rebellion, meeting the same fate as the chapel at Rowan in Glenesk. The minister of these two charges gave his name to the Priest's Road.

From Clochie you climb away from the green valley of the

West Water to the breezy heights of the Caterthuns, two ancient hill forts guarding the road that runs from Bridgend to Brechin. The Brown Caterthun is given its description because its turf and stone ramparts distinguish it from the collapsed stone ramparts of the White Caterthun, but both take their names from the Gaelic word "*cathair,*" meaning fort. While each goes back to Pictish times, they are thought to be of different periods and it is believed that the Brown Caterthun was abandoned after its "white" neighbour was built.

The White Caterthun is certainly an incredible structure, and its tremendous size makes it certain that it was a hill-top town rather than a straightforward fortification. You turn full circle round an endless panorama of changing countryside, the kirk steeple of Montrose at your back, and the far-off glint of the North Sea, and facing you the dark hills and hollows of the Mounth. You can imagine the Pictish tribesmen, deciding to halt here, building that great stone crown on the head of the hill, turning it into an impregnable fortress from which they could look at the Lilliputian world below. You can imagine them, too, watching other bolder bands pressing farther on into the unknown, challenging the Mounth, cutting through the wilderness until they crossed the hills and found themselves in the valley of the Dee. They were the first of the Mounth travellers.

I came down from the White Caterthun and set off on the last stage of my journey to Brechin, that braw town lying between the Mounth and the sea, dominated by its Round Tower and Cathedral. I was making for a wayside hamlet that until recently sat on the edge of the busy Aberdeen-Brechin road, but now placidly watches the traffic roaring north and south on the other side of the local golf course, being thrust into the background by modern road development. The name of the hamlet is Trinity and the golf course is built on the Muir of Brechin. This was once the rendezvous for drovers coming over the Mounth, down from Glentanar and Glen Lethnot, over the Cairn-a-Mounth, bound for the great Trinity Tryst.

The roads about Trinity, or Tarnty as they call it locally, were once black with cattle, many of which were sold and moved on to the market at Perth.

If it was the end of the road for the drovers, it was equally so for the whisky smugglers. They had come out of the glens in their sturdy Highland ponies, dodging the gaugers by day, travelling by night, to sell their illicit whisky in the towns and villages of Strathmore. Then, before returning home, they would go riding through the streets of Brechin, beating their cudgels on the empty barrels that had been filled from stills on the banks of cool rivers deep in the Grampian Hills. The folk of Brechin would come to their doors to watch them as they headed out, pointing their ponies the way they had come, back over the Whisky Road.

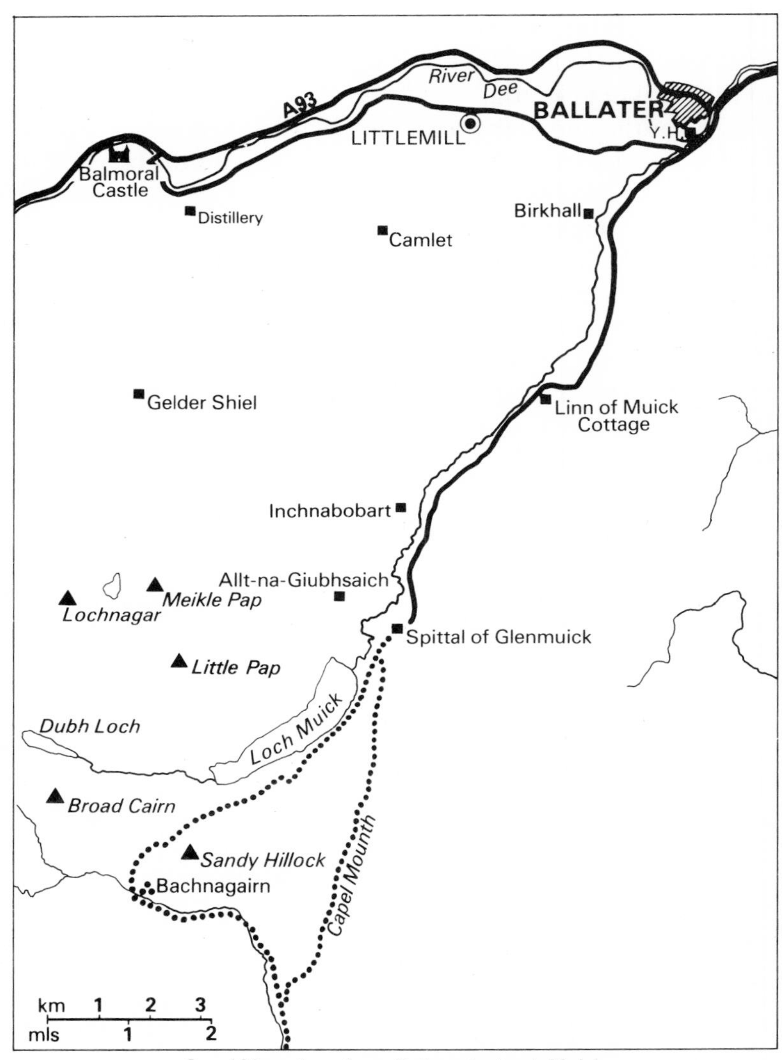

Capel Mounth — from Ballater by Loch Muick

8

Capel Mounth (1)

The little hamlet of Tullich lies less than two miles from the burgh of Ballater, in the lap of Byron's "Morven of snow." From the top of this 2862 feet mountain you can follow the Mounth from Lochnagar to the Blue Hill at Aberdeen. "Such seas of mountains," wrote Queen Victoria when she climbed it in 1859. It was, she said, more magnificent than could be described, and as she looked east to "Aberdeen and the blue sea" she could "even see ships with the naked eye."

The Burn of Tullich rises on Morven and comes down between Creagan Riach and Crannach Hill to the huddle of houses on the main Deeside road, their front doors facing away from the highway as if they had turned their backs on the changes that have made Deeside a mecca for tourists and Ballater a busy, thriving township.

On the old railway line running past the ruined Kirk of Tullich a notice-board carries the information, "In 1831 the population of Kirktown of Tullich was 75—now half a dozen cottages remain." It is a message of despair, a bell tolling for what-might-have-been. Ballater basks in discreet prosperity; Tullich broods on lost opportunity.

It could have been so different. Tullich, rich in a history that goes back through the centuries, should have blossomed while its upstream neighbour, a squalling infant by comparison, decayed and died. Long before Ballater was a gleam in the eyes of late 18th century speculators, Tullich was an important link in the route that took travellers from Donside and the north across the Dee to the Capel Mounth Pass and through Glen Clova to the south. They came by Tarland and over the old drove road on the slopes of Culblean Hill to the ferry at Tullich, from where they struck through Glenmuick to the Capel Mounth. The hamlet was also a stopping-place on the road from Aberdeen to Braemar.

The future of Tullich turned sour in the early 1780s. Ironically, the seeds of its own decline were sown in the promise of new prosperity, and there is a touch of gall in the fact that the source of its downfall stares it in the face as it looks out across the River Dee to Pannanich Hill. It was there, in 1760, that an old woman suffering from scrofula, a disease characterised by suppurating swellings, drank from a spring near Pannanich and bathed her sores in its waters. The "King's Evil," as the disease was known, disappeared and the woman returned to full health. When news of this "miracle" spread Pannanich became the Lourdes of Deeside.

The local laird, Francis Farquharson of Monaltrie, was the man who saw the potential of the wells and cashed in on them. There were four wells, and when the water from them was analysed it was discovered that they were rich in iron. He built an inn that is still there to-day, he installed bath-houses, and he began a boom that brought people flocking to Deeside for "the cure." And Tullich, the little village on the north side of the Dee, suddenly found itself changed overnight from a halting place for travellers to the focal point of a new trade in health-giving waters. The high and the humble converged on Tullich, crossing the Dee to Pannanich by a ferry described in Sir James Balfour's list of passages over the River Dee as the Boat "at Dalmuckeachie, now called ye Kirke of Tulliche." There is a Dalmochie Farm on the south side of the river, a mile west of the inn.

Thomas Pennant, the naturalist and traveller, visited Tullich in 1769. "Refreshed my horses at a hamlet called Tullich," he wrote in his *Tour of Scotland*,[1] "and looking West, saw the great mountain Laghin y gair, which is always covered with snow." Rheumatism, scrofula and "complaints of the gravel" were the illnesses which Pennant said benefited from Pannanich's waters. "During summer great numbers of

[1] Reprinted by Melven Press, 1980.

people afflicted with those disorders resort there to drink the waters; and for their reception, several commodious houses have already been built." The fashionable members of society lived in comfort at Pannanich Inn; the less fortunate, who were probably more in need of a cure, caught the water as it trickled down the side of the hill. In 1793, a surgeon advertised in the *Aberdeen Journal* that he would "attend at the Wells every week," and would call on his convalescing patients scattered in different hamlets "for the benefit of the goat milk."

But the boom became a boomerang for Tullich. The ferry was unable to cope with the hordes of pilgrims who descended on Pannanich and in 1783 a bridge was built over the Dee to the bare moor lying at the foot of Craigendarroch. Before the end of the century the foundation stone of a "centrical kirk on the moor" was laid and the village of Ballater began to take shape. Tullich, a mile and a half east, felt a cold wind of neglect come whistling down the valley, and in 1857 its rejection was complete when its market cross was broken up for road metal.

There was a last, bitter twist to the whole affair. In 1870 Queen Victoria paid a visit to Pannanich Wells and in 1885 she opened a new bridge over the Dee, one of the successors to the first bridge that had carried traffic away from Tullich. There have been four bridges in all and it was almost as if some guardian angel had made a desperate bid to halt the decline of the Royal burgh at the foot of Morven. The first was swept away by flood in 1799, the same fate met the second in 1829, and the third bridge, made of wood, was replaced by the stone structure still standing solidly there today. Queen Victoria named it the Royal Bridge.

If things had been different, this Royal patronage might have given Tullich the sort of popularity now being enjoyed by other Deeside villages. Instead, it vanished; its market, its post office and its inn, known as the Change-house at the Stile of Tullich." Here the weaver, the shoemaker and the tailor had their workshops. The ruins of the old kirk remain, a reminder of the days when people crossed the Dee to worship at Tullich on a Sunday. "In winter," said *View of the Diocese*, "Dee so overflows here that it cannot be ferryed over, so that the poor people of some one of these parishes are frequently without publick worship for some weeks." The folk in Easter Morven area helped to swell the Tullich congregation and when the church closed in 1800 they went over the old kirk road by the Burn of Tullich to the new church on the moor at Ballater. Their route took them by Creagan Riach to the Pass of Ballater, near the back entrance to Monaltrie House.

Tullich had a number of reasons for anticipating growth before the "miracle" of Pannanich. It was important to traffic from Aberdeen as well as on the north-south Mounth route. The old drove road climbed up the slope of Culblean Hill from Lochhead of Davan, passing above the Burn o' Vat and the site of the Battle of Culblean. It crossed the Vat Burn, rounded Cnoc Dubh, crossed the Queen Burn and an old quarry road from Turnerhall, went over a stream called the Rashy Burn and passed above Tomnakeist to the Burn of Tullich. The path can still be followed, although walkers going over Culblean now use the track that starts from the main road east of Tomnakeist.

Another reason for Tullich's stake in the future was the fact that it was the Gateway to the Highlands by the Pass of Ballater. Pennant described it as the eastern entrance to the Highlands. Deeside Field Club, on the other hand, placed the "gateway" farther east when they erected a stone near the Mill of Dinnet which said "You are now in the Highlands." One local entrepreneur had his own ideas on the subject when he put up a notice urging motorists to buy their petrol as they entered the Highlands east of Aboyne.

The Pass is a good deal less forbidding than it was two centuries ago. When Pennant passed through it the whole bottom was covered with "the tremendous ruins of the precipices that bound the road." "Here the wind rages with great fury during winter, and catching up the snow in eddies, whirls it about with such impetuosity, as makes it dangerous for man or beast to be out at that time. Rain also pours down sometimes in deluges, and carries with it stone and gravel from the hills in such quantity that I have seen the effect of these spates, as they are called, lie cross the roads, as the avelenches, or snow-falls, do those of the Alps."

Workmen were pruning the bare trees around Tullich kirkyard when I was there. There was a wintry bite in the air and it reminded me of a cold Sunday morning when another piece of Tullich folklore was born. The congregation was waiting for the minister to appear and some started to stamp their feet to keep themselves warm. The waiting went on and a fiddle was produced, then a keg of whisky from the local inn, and the foot-stamping turned into a reel—the famous Reel o' Tullich. I could imagine how they felt, but I resisted the attempt to stamp my own feet, for there was a fearsome postscript to this sacrilegious affair. It is said that when the minister finally turned up he cursed his erring flock so soundly that not one of the revellers lived to see the end of the year.

It was near the kirkyard that I came upon what appeared to be another slice of Deeside mythology, for it was here that I saw the White Deer of Tullich. I was walking up the old railway line when I first spotted it, but it leapt over the fence and vanished. When I finally tracked it down it was grazing contentedly with the cattle at Eastfield. I learned later that it had been roaming the farmlands of Eastfield for five years, but there were arguments over whether the animal, a hind, was natural or albino. The general belief is that it was a fallow. The deer was born at Eastfield, its mother giving birth to its calf after coming down from the hills to the farm. The hind suckled it, weaned it, and then left it among a herd of Friesian-cross cows. The young deer stayed with the herd, although in summer it wandered away from its adopted home. Perhaps in years to come the legend of the White Deer of Tullich will take its place with that of the Reel and the miracles of Pannanich and Tullich.

There was no Dalmuickeachie ferry to take me over the

Dee as I went on my way to the Capel Mounth, so I went over the bridge at Cambus o'May and through the woods to Tomdarroch, turning right to Pannanich and up the high road that looks down on the magnificent sweep of the Dee valley and across the river to Tullich. The first of the famous wells is just off the road before you come to the inn, a stone trough which was fighting a losing battle against the weeds. I couldn't help thinking of the writer who said in 1825 that "none of them is very inviting" and of the visitors who would "drink of a morning seven or eight quarts without feeling the least uneasiness." They must really have been iron men! One of the inscriptions on the trough read—

> Drink weary traveller in the land,
> And on they journey fare,
> 'Tis sent by God's all-giving hand
> And stored by human care.

There was little sign of human care when I saw it, and it is perhaps just as well that there is no notice drawing attention to the well. Other faded lettering included the words "Victoria 1837—1897."

From Pannanich the road runs steeply downhill to the base of wooded Craig Coillich, opposite the Royal Bridge. A short distance downstream you can still see under the water the supporting stones of the wooden bridge which stood there until 1885. Upstream, on the south side, a path runs down to the river at the spot where a ford was in use before any of the bridges made an appearance, and on the north side there is another reminder of this in the name of one of the houses on the riverbank, Ford House.

The ford was used by drovers coming down from Speyside to Tomintoul and Corgarff, where they crossed the River Don and struck south to Glengairn and Crathie by the old drove roads through hills and, after the mid-18th century, by the military road which is now the A939 from Deeside to Cock Bridge and the Lecht. From Ballater they headed for Glenmuick and the Capel Mounth, and there are tales of how local folk would buy a side of beef from the drovers as they went through the village. It was probably the sort of "perk" they picked up at various points on their route, explaining away the loss of a cow by the hazards encountered on their trek south.

On the South Deeside Road the A973 runs west for about half a mile to Bridgend Cottages, where it turns right over the Bridge of Muick to Balmoral, while the Glenmuick road branches south-west to Loch Muick and the Capel Mounth. The Muick, one of the longest tributaries of the River Dee, runs peacefully on and I followed its rippling path towards the Mounth and the dark gullies of Lochnagar, passing ruined St Nathalan's Chapel, built by the Mackenzies of Glenmuick, and the side road leading down to the river and across to the Mill of Sterin. There was a ford at the Mill at one time and it was probably here that Queen Victoria crossed the Muick on her many journeys up the glen. Her diary recorded that she changed horses near Birkhall, which is only a short distance from the Mill.

Less than a mile on is the Linn of Muick, a tumbling, frothing Niagara in miniature which, in its setting of pine-covered rock, can be beautiful in summer but cold and forbidding when winter puts its icy hand on the Muick glen. It is a popular spot for tourists and Pennant's travel notes show that travellers were stopping to admire it as far back as the 18th century. The pool at the bottom of the falls, he said, was "supposed by the vulgar to be bottomless."

The Linn marks the end of the woodland, for a little way beyond it you cross a cattle grid and step into Mounth country. Here, in days gone by, travellers going south must have huddled into their coats and felt a shiver of apprehension as they gazed on the uncompromising landscape ahead. For the next two and a half miles the road twists and turns through the moorland until it reaches the Spittal of Glenmuick, where the Capel Mounth rises into the hills on its way to Glen Clova in Angus. The Capel was one of the main routes over the Grampians from Upper Deeside but there were other sub-

Loch Muick, Glas-allt shiel marked by woodland in the middle distance.

sidiary tracks linking up with it. While drovers made for the Capel Mounth by way of Ballater, harvesters and other travellers took a short-cut south over the hills from Crathie to join the Mounth pass at the Spittal of Glenmuick.

They had the choice of two glens, Glen Girnock and Glen Gelder. Glen Gelder goes south from Balmoral towards the "back door" of Lochnagar and Glen Girnock starts four miles to the east at the tiny hamlet of Littlemill, on the road that runs from the Bridge of Muick to Balmoral. Strathgirnock is a quiet and lovely glen seldom used even by hill-walkers, but it was important enough to be mentioned in the *View of the Diocese of Aberdeen* as one of the main glens on the south side of the River Dee. "Glengirneiche," it was called. In the days of illicit distilling its remoteness made it an ideal centre for illegal stills and smuggling. There were said to be as many as a dozen whisky bothies in the upper reaches of the glen.

The Gelder pass starts at Easter Balmoral, where there is

also a linking track to the Girnock road and from there to Inchnabobart on the west bank of the River Muick. "Inch Bobbard" is what it was called by Queen Victoria, who came rattling down it in her carriage on a fine September morning in 1849. Easter Balmoral is only a short walk to the gates of Balmoral and the bridge linking the castle to Crathie. At one time the crossing was made by ford and ferry and records show that they were well used by Mounth travellers. One of them was the Marquis of Montrose, who, after his retreat from Dundee, was reunited with Aboyne and the Master of Napier in the Trossachs. Montrose moved north, but by which path is uncertain, although it is clear that he forded the Dee near Balmoral. John Spalding, in his account of "The Troubles," told of how "Oboyne (Aboyne), Neper, Delgatie and Keir cam in to Montrois beyond Die, who was all jouful of utheries. They began to marche, crossis the river of Die at the miln of Crathie. . . ." This was the Milltown of Crathie, where there was "a ferry and a ford over the Dee, communicating with the south country by the Capel Pass and Glen Clova." The mill disappeared at the beginning of last century, but the boat-house was used as an inn for some time after that.

The Gelder pass leads to the Gelder Shiel, the "Ruigh an Bhan Righ" or the Queen's Shiel, which was at one time a popular Royal picnic spot. It was in this solid stone building, fringed by trees on the edge of the Gelder Burn, that Queen Victoria had afternoon tea with the exiled Empress Eugene of France, when she took her guest on a trip through the glen. They enjoyed "some excellent brown trout cooked in oatmeal."

The ponies on that outing were housed in the stables a few yards away, but nowadays the occupants are hill walkers and climbers sheltering from the winds that come howling down from Lochnagar. They are there, as a notice inside the stables indicates, with the permission of the Royal estate, and many a time I have been thankful that such permission was granted. It may not have the elegance of the Royal shiel next door, but even by the light of a guttering candle stuck in an old whisky bottle, and seated on the hard edge of the bunks provided for overnight sleepers, it has seemed like a home from home. There is a broom to sweep away your crumbs, and there was at one time a visitors' book, but some souvenir-hunting caller must have carried it off in his pack. I have never been there on New Year's Eve, but the Hogmanay revels must be something to see. I was there in the second week of January, 1974, and there were two entries—

> 31st December—Saw the New Year in with a bottle of Royal Deeside.
> 1st January—Someone has stolen Lochnagar!

The view of Lochnagar from the Gelder Shiel is vastly more impressive than that from the popular route by Allt-na-guibhsaich, and mountaineers believe that the finest approach to it is by the Gelder, up the Lochnagar Burn to the awe-inspiring corrie between Meikle Pap and the summit. There is a path from the shiel that peters out in the moor, and from there you pick your way across the rough and boggy ground and over a barrier of boulders until you look into the gut of Lochnagar and the dark pool from which it takes its name. For those with higher ambitions, the alternative is straight to the summit by Meall Coire na Saobhaidhe.

But other mountains and other hill tracks lie ahead, and from the Gelder Shiel another path swings you back to the Coire na Ciche road and on to the Capel Mounth.

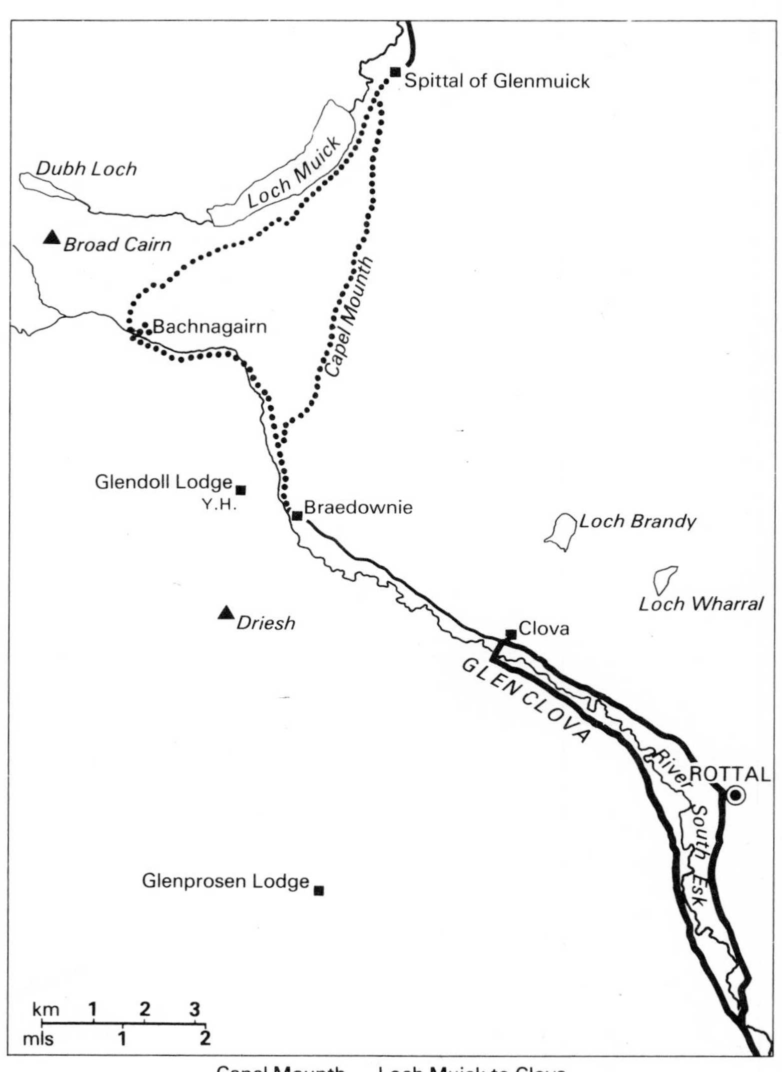

Capel Mounth — Loch Muick to Clova

9

Capel Mounth (2)

The red deer had come down from the high tops. They were foraging for food in the woods at the Spittal of Glenmuick, drifting down the path to Allt-na-guibhsaich. The ice crackled under my feet and the hinds shied away nervously, breaking into a trot. The stags stood their ground, antlers high, watching me warily. This was the time of the year when their vigil relaxed, as if they knew they had less to fear from human interference than the hazards of winter. Before spring came, the weaklings would be dead. One day in late April, in the wood at Lochend, above Loch Muick, I found the body of a young deer lying in the heather not far from the Capel Mounth road, and there were three more on the path at the south end of the loch. It was a saddening sight, and even the most hardened stalker finds it difficult to accept this toll without regret.

You have to see this wild and beautiful mountain country in all its seasonal changes to wholly appreciate it. I watched the flurries of snow high in the corries, drifting in the clear, crisp air. The rich days of autumn were over. The rutting season, when the bellowing of the stags echoed across the hills as they challenged and fought for their hinds, had come and gone. Winter held the landscape in an icy embrace and all around the mountains and the valley of the Muick were deep in snow. It was a scene unfamiliar to the thousands of tourists and trippers who flock to Loch Muick during the summer months. The picnic tables on the banks of the Allt Darrarie looked forlorn and out of place. There was a scattering of cars in the car park, left behind by hardy climbers. The nature centre was deserted.

No nature centres or mountain rescue posts greeted travellers who went over the Mounth in bygone days, but there was a hospice or hospital, as the name Spital of Glenmuick suggests. The hospices were in many places succeeded by hostelries, and this was what happened at Glenmuick early last century. The Spital inn, which stood on the banks of the Allt Darrarie, succeeded an earlier inn near the ford at Inshnabobart and remained in business until the middle of the century. The Inshnabobart inn was known as the "Teetabootie," which meant "Look about you," although what the customers were supposed to have a "teet" or look at is not quite clear. It was sited to serve travellers coming through Strath Girnock from Easter Balmoral, crossing to the Capel route at Inshnabobart, which is an indication that the path from Crathie fed a fair amount of traffic on to the Mounth road. The Capel was one of the main droving routes to the south, as well as being used by sheep herders and harvesters, and no doubt the "teetabootie," as well as its successor at the Spittal, saw many a merry evening in the shadow of old Lochnagar.

From the Spittal a track branches right to Allt-na-giubhsaich and Lochnagar, while the main path goes straight ahead to a fork where a signpost points the way uphill to Glen Clova. The lochside path also takes you to Glen Clova, but by a longer, tortuous route which climbs up towards Broad Cairn and then strikes south-east by Bachnagairn to join the direct route below the Capel Burn. The last time I went over the traditional route was in late May, when the winter snow was melting in the corries. The cars were rumbling into the Spittal car park and the climbers, their eyes on Cac Carn Beag, were kitting themselves up, eager to go.

There was still a covering of snow on Lochnagar, but it wore its mantle gracefully on that warm spring day. Loch Muick was a mirror, throwing back images of the hills around it. It was as if the whole valley had come alive again after its winter hibernation, but, climbing up the hill from Lochend I saw the body of a young deer in the heather, a sobering

Loch Muick at Glas-allt shiel. The path over the loch leads to the Broad Cairn and the Bachnagairn track.

reminder of the season that had gone. Now the snow posts were clear and the cairns pointed the way. On the plateau, heading towards Glen Clova, I could see the track that scaled the hill face above Loch Muick at the Black Burn and ran round to the "junction" at Sandy Hillock. From there you could follow it up the Broad Cairn until it disappeared from sight, or you could cut south to Bachnagairn ro rejoin the Capel before Glen Doll. Farther on the dark cleft of the Dubh Loch track could be seen and above the loch the towering rock face below Broad Cairn.

Although the Capel was an important drovers' road, there is little to show that it was greatly used by the military forces who tramped through other Grampian passes in their incursions into the North. Robert the Bruce is believed to have crossed the Capel Mounth to Tullich, and the Jacobites came the same way after the Battle of Killiecrankie in 1689. Here, too, are the fading echoes of Culloden, for the last time it was used by a military force was shortly after that ill-fated battle. Lord David Ogilvie's regiment went over the Capel Mounth to Culloden in February, 1746, and four days after the battle the tattered remnants of the Angus force returned the same way to Glen Clova, where they were disbanded.

The Jacobites, the drovers, the thravers . . . the Capel Mounth has seen them all, but the strangest company it has ever witnessed was on a May day in 1892, when sixteen cyclists went pedalling along the rough track. They were the first cyclists to cross the Mounth from Glenmuick to Glen Clova, finishing the day at Forfar. Even on foot the Capel is a relatively short trek from the Spittal of Muick to Braedownie, but it is perhaps because of this that you get a real feeling of going "ower the Mounth," heightened by the fact that at both ends of the plateau you look down on magnificent views. On the north side the long shimmer of Loch Muick and the glen itself is below you, while on the south you have a bird's eye view of Glen Clova; Glen Doll, with the broad track to Kilbo and the line of the forest trail to Jock's Road; and, on the right, the path to Bachnagairn. I stood looking at it a long time before going quickly down the hill to the path from the keeper's house at Moulzie, a mile and a half from Braedownie.

The road by Bachnagairn is by far the most spectacular way of crossing the Mounth from Glenmuick. Taking the low road at the fork near Lochend, you follow it as far as the Black Burn, a turbulent stream that runs into Loch Muick about a mile from its upper end. Queen Victoria thought that the hill slope here was "very fine indeed, and deeply furrowed by the torrents, which form glens and corries where birch and alder trees grow close to the water's edge." From the bridge over the Black Burn a track zig-zags steeply up to the plateau overlooking the loch, and as you follow it you look down on Glas-allt-Shiel, the Royal lodge on the north side of Loch Muick. The road meets another rough track coming up from the loch by Corrie Chash, striking south to Bachnagairn near two wooden huts used to house ponies when the Royal Family are out in the hills.

From the main track above Loch Muick I went south across the moor to the land "where water rins and gowans blaw, and Grampian mountains busk their heids wi' snaw." The bald dome of Braid Cairn was on my right and the narrow path dipped towards the trough of the South Esk. I could see the fringe of the Bachnagairn firs, the slope of the hills east of the Tolmount pass, and, away to the left, the dark knuckle of Glen Doll. Bachnagairn is a green gem on the bare neck of the Grampians, a long strip of woodland draping the banks of the river as it leaps down from Loch Esk. About a mile below the loch the South Esk drops about 70 feet or 80 feet, in one great leap, through a ravine that is largely obscured by the overhanging trees, and from there cascades down to the valley over rocks worn smooth and flat by the endless torrent of water.

The descent from the north becomes steep and sharp above the woodland, pitching you down to the small wooden bridge spanning the river. The old county boundary line lay farther back, but I felt that the two or three steps across the bridge had taken me from Deeside to Angus. The lodge that once stood at Bachnagairn was, in fact, owned by Sir Alan Russell Mackenzie, 2nd Baronet in Glenmuick. What is left of it, two fragments of wall and the corner of a fireplace poking through the grass, are about a hundred yards from the bridge, while the ruins of the stables are at the other side of the path.

From the shooting lodge the path goes downhill on a line with the river, bending right to open out into the broad Clova valley above the keeper's house at Moulzie. Whether the laird chose the site because of the setting or simply because it provided quick and easy access to deer haunts in the high places I do not know, but it is certainly an idyllic spot. Dorothea Maria Ogilvy of Clova, an Angus poet who wrote an epic piece about the glen a century ago, dipped into her rich broth of local dialect to draw a vivid picture of the eagle soaring over Bachnagairn, the greedy hawk and the whaap (curlew) above Broad Cairn, and "the prood gorcock chittering on the Sneek o' Barnes.'' The lines went—

> When morning's rosy neb a' tipped wi' gowd
> Is glinting through a siller cloud,
> Fu' grand to see the yammerin yearn
> Rise frae the cleughs o' Bachnagairn,
> And, soarin' high owre heather bells and fern,
> Seek his wild wonnying on the bauld Braidcairn;
> There greedy gleds, whaaps and white hares won,
> Tod, martins, hoody craws and ptarmigan;
> To hear the merry lilt o' rill and fount,
> To feel the wuns blaw frae the Capel Mount.

I went down the long track to the glen, under the beetling brow of Juanjorge and the slopes of Dog Hillock, where an avalanche once killed nearly forty deer, and, crossing the Esk by a wooden bridge lashed to a central stone, headed for the keeper's house at Moulzie. Half a mile beyond that the road joined the Capel Mounth track and a mile farther on the White Water came in from Glen Doll to join the South Esk. The dusty tracks were behind, the tarmacadam road ahead, and before long I was passing the ruin of Clova Castle and unloading my pack at Milton of Clova. This tiny hamlet looks after both your soul and your senses. There is a school on one side of the road, a kirk on the other, and in between them a friendly inn that served me free red wine with my dinner.

Behind the hotel a rough path struggles more than 2000 ft up the hill to Loch Brandy, which lies under the Snub of Clova, a sharp ridge running from the loch to the Corrie of Clova. It is a cold, eerie place, and as I stood on the ridge I thought of the witch's curse which foretold that these cliffs would one day crumble and collapse into the loch. In 1662 a woman called Margaret Adamson was burned as a witch at Milton of Clova, and one wonders if it was she who had thrown out that last dreadful curse as they put the torch to her stake. The more likely answer is that it came from the lips of the creature described as—

> A rummelshackin, runkled randy—
> The weirdest witch o' wild Loch Brandy.

The witch of Loch Brandy was created in the fertile imagination of Dorothea Maria Ogilvy, who wrote a mammoth poem called "Willie Wabster's Wooing and Wedding on the Braes of Angus." It is the story of how Willie, who lived "no far frae Kinnordy yett (gate)" was chased through Glen Clova and Glen Doll by the Loch Brandy witch, who wanted to marry him. The poem is a kind of alcoholic Cook's Tour of the Angus braes, for the reluctant bridegroom was said to be "fair dased and doited" by barley bree. He floats up the Esk in a haze of whisky, cognac, beer and sherry, and his progress can still be followed by the place-names in the poem. Willie, a cattle drover, was riding a "shalt" (Shetland pony) he had found at the Muir of Ord on one of his cattle treks, and this fact itself is a fair indication of the distances covered by the drovers of a century ago. Willie's creator was a niece of the Earl of Airlie and one of the fascinations of the poem is that this high-bred lady could pour out a torrent of broad Scots as if she had been fed on a diet of it since childhood.

Dorothea's poem was published in 1868 and she died in 1895. The witch of wild Loch Brandy has never been seen again and the rocks on the Snub of Clova stand firm. But not everything has changed. There are still "buirdly, brosy chields" in Clova, just as there are "strappin', wiselike lads in Prosen Glen." You can still see the eagle rising over the "cleughs o' Bachnagairn" and feel the winds blow from the Capel Mount. The capercailzie are still there, and the muirhens, the tods, the martins, the hoody craws and the ptarmigan, and as you stand by Loch Brandy and look towards Prosen you might still hear "the gorcock chittering on the Sneck o' Barnes."

The two roads on either side of the Esk meet at Gella Bridge and run on for over a mile to a roadside picnic spot marked "Cullow Market." This was journey's end for many of the drovers who came over the Capel and Tolmount passes, for it was to Cullow that they brought their cattle for sale. Others went on to the Tryst at Falkirk. Below Cullow is Dykehead, and beyond that the gates of Cortachy Castle.

When I stayed at the Milton of Clova hotel my bedroom window faced east. The school was on the left, at the start of the path to Loch Brandy, and directly ahead was the road to "Kirrie." Early in the morning I looked out of the window and saw the mist rising in lazy wreaths over the river. The sun was creeping up over the hills and there was a sense of total isolation. I felt detached from the outside world, the world beyond Cullow and Cortachy, as if I had been cut adrift from the places and people at the end of that ribbon of road. It was only later, when I was thumbing through J. M. Barrie's *Auld Licht Idylls*, that I came upon the line, "The road to Thrums has lost itself miles down the valley. I wonder what they are doing out in the world."

The folk in these lonely glens, cut off for weeks or even months during the winter, must often have wondered what was going on "out in the world," but it may be that nowadays the outside world intrudes too much and too often. When Barrie wrote *Auld Licht Idylls* in 1888 there were already signs that the end of the century would bring an era of change. At one time, the countryside was overrun by itinerant showmen, but, wrote Barrie, "Nowadays the farmers are less willing to give these wanderers a camping place and the people are less easily drawn to the entertainments provided, by fife and drum." One of the travelling shows was "Sam'l Mann's Tumbling-Booth," which had tumblers, jugglers, sword-swallowers, and balancers. You could look at the half-penny peepshow or enjoy "Aunty Magg's Whirligig" for an old pair of boots or a handful or rags. There were also the legless or armless "Waterloo veterans" playing a tune for your pennies and "queer bent old dames" offering lucky bags or telling fortunes. They supplied the uncanny element, said Barrie, but hesitated to call themselves witches, "for there can still be seen near Thrums the pool where these unfortunates used to be drowned, and in the session book of the Glen Quharity kirk can be read an old minute announcing that on a certain Sabbath there was no preaching because the minister was away at the burning of a witch." This was no fanciful notion on Barrie's part, for records do show that the service at Cortachy was scrapped because the minister was up at Milton of Clova watching Margaret Adamson being burned at the stake.

10

The White Mounth

Fecht for Britain? Hoot awa!
For Bonnie Scotland? Imph, man na!
For Lochnagar? Wi' clook and claw!

These lines by the Buchan poet John S. Milne may not be as familiar as Byron's well-known verse, but they mirror more accurately the possessive pride which North-east folk have in that dark, craggy mountain overlooking Loch Muick, on Deeside's Royal estate. The Cairngorms have their Braeriach and their Ben Macdui; Deeside has its Lochnagar. Byron put it eloquently when he handed over to "the minions of luxury" the pleasures of gay landscapes and gardens of roses; he would settle for mountains where cataracts foamed and storm mists gathered. He sighed for the valley of dark Lochnagar, and he was not alone. It has a perpetual fascination that is hard to explain. It may not reach the lofty heights of the Cairngorm summits, but you cannot measure the mood of a mountain in feet and inches.

This is the White Mounth, Mon'Gheill,[1] towering between two of the most important of the Grampian passes, Glen Callater on the west and Glenmuick on the east. The name White Mounth strictly applies to the plateau south of the twin peaks of Cac Carn Beag and Cac Carn Mor. I have often wondered if the person who named these summits got them mixed up, for the highest, rising to 3789 ft and beating its rival by a mere 21 ft, takes its name from the Gaelic word "beag" which means little, while the word "mor" means large or great. There are, in fact, eleven summits on Lochnagar, each

[1] Gaelic—Monadh geal.

Lochnagar in its winter coat, a scene from the Ballater road.

over 3000 ft, but none can claim particular credit for the mountain's reputation as "the most sublime and picturesque of the Caledonian Alps", for it owes much of its magnificence to its great corrie. The corrie at summit level is almost a mile wide and it is this that you see when you catch your first glimpse of Lochnagar when travelling up Deeside.

The mountain takes its name from the loch at the base of the giant corrie. The original name was Beinn-nan-Ciochan, or Benchinnan, the Hill of the Paps, and this is retained in the Meikle Pap and Little Pap. Perhaps it was just as well that it changed, for no one could imagine Byron writing about the dark frowning glories of the Hill of the Paps. Nevertheless, even the word "Lochnagar" has raised a good deal of controversy over the years. Some say it is derived from loch na gaoir, the loch of sobbing or wailing, others that it comes from loch nan gabha, meaning loch of the goats, and there were certainly wild goats roaming its slopes at one time.

Dr William MacGillivray, who was Professor of Natural History at Aberdeen University a century ago, thought that the true name was Lochan-nan-cear, the little lake of hares, from the many mountain hares on Lochnagar. There was, he pointed out, another corrie called Lochan-eun (Loch nan Eun), the lake of the birds, which was a breeding place of gulls.

It could never be said of Lochnagar that it made men speechless. Between Byron and J. C. Milne there stretched a ghostly, and sometimes ghastly, army of versifiers who wanted to immortalise this dour Deeside hill-top. One of them was Alexander Laing, of Aberdeen, who in 1819 tried to out-Byron Byron in *The Caledonian Itinerary*, which was a poetic tour of Deeside, "with historical notes from the Best Authorities". He dipped his pen into ink to write—

> High Loch na Garraidh, behold majestic rise,
> The heath clad summit hid in vaulted skies.

Towards the end of the same century an oddly named couple called Dryas Octopetala and Thomas Twayblade looked into the great corrie of Lochnagar and declared that it was a scene "which for terrific magnificence baffles description". They themselves, however, were not completely baffled, for they then proceeded to describe in vivid detail "the dazzling whiteness of the snow sharply contrasting with the black cuboidal shattered walls of granite, which here and there partially protruded from their winding sheet".

Whether Dryas Octopetala and Thomas Twayblade were pseudonyms I do not know, but they wrote a series of articles for the *Aberdeen Journal*, which in 1880 was reprinted under the title "Our Tour". They appear to have known their Deeside hills, and the account of their ascent of Lochnagar gives a fascinating and amusing glimpse of how our Victorian forbears tackled the hazards of hill-walking a century ago.

They travelled up Glen Muick and, once into the moorland beyond the falls, followed a road to the river, opposite Inshnabobart, where they expected to find a bridge. "Feint a bridge was there", they recorded, but they waded across the river, finding the stones "confoundedly hard and uncompromising", and took the Royal road to "her Majesty's hut". There, at Allt-na-giubhsaich, they set out to climb Lochnagar "in spite of rain, mist, wind and snow".

D.O. and T.T., as they signed their articles, give a rather neat description of the corrie—"the range of precipice which shuts in the leg-of-mutton shaped lochan, called Lochnagar". "The bottom of the Corrie and the Lake we could not see", they wrote. "The clouds of vapour circling in the rifted gullies far below hid both from view". The weather was appalling. They found shelter among "some huge blocks of granite" on "the White Mounts", and as the rain poured down our intrepid travellers carried out "the investigation of a tin of salmon". The leader of the expedition "went ploughing through the snow after his umbrella, which had blown away", and the cook, fed up with waiting for snow to melt and boil to make tea, "seized the pannikin of hot water, threw in tea, sugar, condensed milk, and whisky and stirred the whole vigorously together". The mixture was "comforting".

The climbers made a dash through the snow for a cairn, which from its height (3768 ft) appears to have been Cac Carn Mor, but that was as far as they got. The brolly, which would be a rare sight on the mountains these days, was what finally decided them against the final push. "The gale would not permit the uplifting of an umbrella even on the lee side of the cairn", recorded Dryas and Thomas. "The rain, when you faced it, hit in the face like showers of pease, and we had to wade through the slushy snow knee deep, so we saw no propriety in spending our strength on a farther quarter mile tramp to the peak of Cac Carn Beag, eighteen foot higher".

Whether the White Mounth was much used as a hill pass is uncertain; a journey over its stormy plateau would not have been taken lightly, but it would have provided a quicker access to the Capel Mounth from Braemar, cutting out the detour to Crathie and Glen Gelder or, farther east, to the Bridge of Glenmuick. The route from Braemar is by the Cairnwell road to the farm of Auchallater, two miles from the village, and from there a track follows the Callater Burn for three miles until the path to Lochnagar rises into the hills at Callater Lodge, on the edge of Loch Callater. It goes round by Cairn Taggart and crosses the White Mounth plateau towards Dr MacGillivray's lake of the birds, Loch nan Eun, and from there to Cac Carn Mor.

There is an alternative route to Lochnagar from the north by the Garbh Allt and Ballochbuie, and this was the approach taken by Byron when he ascended the mountain as a boy of fifteen, accompanied by a ghillie. Queen Victoria took the same path by Ballochbuie Forest—"that beautiful wood"—in September, 1848. The Queen and Prince Albert started their climb in thick fog and when they got to the top "the mist drifted in thick clouds so as to hide everything not within one hundred yards of us". It was, she said, cold, wet and cheerless, and the wind was blowing a hurricane. Lochnagar was showing that it was no respecter of rank or social standing.

By far the most popular approach to the White Mounth is by Glenmuick, and it is from the south side that you can best explore the glens and gullies above Loch Muick. Wherever you go you are walking in the footsteps of Queen Victoria. She left numerous reminders of her Balmoral years in the cairns scattered on hill-tops around the estate and in the shiels which still stand unchanged from the days of her "Great Expeditions". She loved the hills, displaying an excitement and enthusiasm that some of her less energetic advisers could scarcely understand. She wished she could travel about on her ponies "and see ALL the wild spots in the Highlands". Deeside reminded her of the Thuringerwald; it seemed, she said, to breathe freedom and peace, making her want to forget the world and its sad turmoils.

Victoria's journeys into the hills covered many of the old Mounth paths, by Balintober to Mount Keen, from Balmoral down to Inchnabobart and Glenmuick, up the Cairnwell pass, through Glen Callater and high into the mountains on the

Monega Pass, and along the old drove roads that ran from Strathdon to Glengairn and Crathie. Her tracks often took her back to that brooding stretch of water south of the Spittal of Glenmuick. If Lochnagar is the heart of this Deeside glen, Loch Muick is its life's blood. Its source is near the Stuic Buttress, west of Lochnagar's main corrie, from where it runs down as the Allt an Dubh-loch to the Dubh Loch and drops almost 800 ft into Loch Muick. There can be few more magnificent settings, with steep hills and ravines hemming it in on either side and the Broad Cairn looming in the distance at its head. The loch is over two miles long and at some points about half a mile broad.

There are the remains of an old boat-house at Lochend and another boat-house, built of stone, stands in the opposite corner. I have never seen a boat on its surface, although the Duke of Edinburgh at one time made use of a motor-boat there during his stay at Balmoral. Queen Victoria often made trips on the loch, her boat pulled by three stout ghillies, a piper playing and the men shouting at the skirl of a reel. It reminded her of Sir Walter Scott's lines in "The Lady of the Lake"—

> "Ever, as on they bore, more loud
> And louder rung the pibroch proud.
> At first the sound, by distance tame,
> Mellow'd along the waters came,
> And, lingering long by cape and bay,
> Wail'd every harsher note away".

The Queen was told that the word "Muich", or Muick, meant "darkness" or "sorrow", but as far as she was concerned it was a misnomer, for she found nothing but happiness there.[1] The focal point of her delight was the "Hut" at Allt-na-giubhsaich, a mile from the north-west corner of the loch. It is still standing to-day, a neat, trim building on the edge of the wood from which the Lochnagar path starts its

[1] Probably Gaelic muic, pig. Cf Beinn na muic Duibh. Hill of the Black Boar (Ben Macdui).

climb to the Meikle Pap. It was the first and most famous of the Royal shiels. "Our little bothie", Victoria called it, but before it became the "humble abode" of the Queen and Prince Albert it was a sod-roofed building with one chimney.

Allt na guibhsach shiel in which Queen Victoria once stayed. It is still owned by the Royal Family.

The lodge at Allt-na-giubhsaich marks the start of a three-and-a-half-mile climb to the summit of Lochnagar. The path follows the stream from which the "Hut" takes its name, and the first stage is towards the ridge running from the Little Pap on the left to Cuidhe Crom, 3552 ft up, and the familiar swell of the Meikle Pap on the right. The peak of Lochnagar skulks behind the ridge, out of sight, but behind you the valley opens out and you can see the cars meandering, toy-like, through the glen to the Spittal of Glenmuick. The path veers right and dips down until you look into another glen, Glen Gelder, away to the shiel where Victoria had tea and brown trout with the exiled Empress Eugene of France. Here you turn left, crossing another path to Glas-allt-Shiel, and head towards "the tempests of dark Lochnagar".

There is a spring called the Foxes' Well up by the Meikle Pap and from there a zig-zag path, "The Ladder", takes you up to the plateau, but before you tackle that final climb it is worth going right to a gap between the ridge and the Meikle Pap. Here you look straight into the face of the eastern corrie and down to the loch at its base, the Black Gully slicing its way up the cliff face on the left. It is probably the most impressive view there is of Lochnagar. There is a plaque at the gap showing the main climbing routes on the cliff, but it was badly damaged the last time I saw it. The slope on the left takes you back to "The Ladder" and the plateau, and from there it is an easy walk round the arc of the corrie to Cac Carn Mor and Cac Carn Beag, where you can "do a Hilary" and climb up the great mass of rock at Cac Carn Beag to the highest point of Lochnagar. There is an indicator erected by the Cairngorm Club in 1924, pointing to all the prominent landmarks in view. At one glance you can take in the hills of Caithness, Ben Nevis, Ben Lomond and the Pentlands. The whole of Scotland is at your feet.

It would be fascinating to know how many thousands of people have made a pilgrimage to this rocky eminence over the years. There is an endless stream of them during the summer months, and on mid-summer's day they come trailing up "The Ladder" to sit at the foot of Cac Carn Beag and watch the dawn break over that vast undulating sea of mountain tops. For many it is an experience that turns sour, for dour old Lochnagar has a habit of chilling both their hopes and vision in a cold curtain of mist. Nor are they always prepared for the mountain's sudden changes of mood; they come, some of them, as if they were out for a casual stroll in the Muick valley. They remind you of Batterbury, one of Queen Victoria's grooms, who accompanied the Queen on her first ascent of Lochnagar. He wrote "ordinary dress, with thin boots and gaiters and seemed anything but happy". Not surprisingly, Queen Victoria notes: "He hardly ever accompanied me after this".

The first time I went up Lochnagar I sat among the rocks at Cac Carn Beag, eating my sandwiches and wondering if this was the "little nook" where the Queen had had her picnic meal. "We got off and walked, and climbed some steep stones, to a place where we found a seat in a little nook, and had some luncheon". Not much later a mist swirled in over the corries, obliterating everything in sight, and I shared the feeling she had when she wrote, "It was cold and wet and cheerless". I waited till the mist had lifted, for there was no ghillie to show me the way down, and it was a long fall from the top of the Black Gully.

The White Mounth plateau gives you the feeling, if not of being on the roof of the world, certainly of looking at it from one of its highest storeys. There are two small lochs west of Cac Carn Beag, the Sandy Loch and Loch nan Eun, which Queen Victoria called "Nan Nian". They lie in the shadow of the Stuic Buttress on the western corrie, which is less imposing than the main corrie, but striking enough in its own way. About two miles to the north, where the Feith an Laoigh[1] begins its downhill course to the Gelder Burn, is the Prince's Stone, marking the spot where Prince Albert spent a night in the open. The summit plateau stretches for almost two miles to the "little sister" of Loch Muick, the Dubh Loch, which feeds the main waters of the Muick, but if you cross the plateau you can cut down by the Glas Allt, joining the path from the Lochnagar route, and follow it to where it goes frothing and tumbling into Loch Muick at the Royal Lodge built by Queen Victoria.

Victoria crossed the White Mounth on her first visit to the Dubh Loch, fording the Glas-allt Burn. The year was 1849 and she had little idea then that nearly twenty years later, with Prince Albert dead, she would be building the Glas-allt Shiel as her "Widow's House", unable to face the memories that the "Hut" at Allt-na-giubhsaich held for her. In those early years at Balmoral she was creating such memories. She was young

[1] Gaelic—Burn of the calves, i.e. recalling an area where summer grazing was practised.

Glas-allt shiel.

and gay and in love with her "dearest Albert", and she had given her heart to her "Paradise" at Balmoral. She was a woman a world away from that stately old lady who later rode round Deeside in her carriage, dreaming perhaps of those forgotten days when she could shake off the stuffiness of court life and escape to the freedom and adventure of the hills.

Nothing subdued her enthusiasm, neither the mists nor moods of wind-ravaged Lochnagar nor the dangers that faced her on many of her outings. On one occasion, returning from a trip over the Capel Mounth, her carriage overturned in the darkness in Glen Girnock. "I had time to reflect whether we should be killed or not", she wrote later, "and thought there were still things I had not settled and wanted to do". The Queen fell with her face on the ground and John Brown came running up crying in despair, "The Lord Almighty have mercy on us! Who did ever see the like of this before! I thought you were all killed!" There were appeals to her to take more care, but she paid little heed. I have often wondered what sort of outcry there would be to-day if the Queen went climbing up Lochnagar on a shaggy Highland pony, with a thick mist obscuring everything within a hundred yards and "the wind blowing a hurricane". Queen Victoria faced such hazards with equanimity. The mist would rise, the wind would drop, and she would come down to Loch Muick when the moon was shining on the water and see poetry in the scene. Everything was always "very fine".

The morning of her trip to the Dubh Loch was "very fine", but the hill paths were rough and the burns and rivers were in spate. They went up from Allt-na-giubhsaich and "rode over the Strone Hill", 2326 ft, An t-Sron, east of the Little Pap and overlooking Loch Muick, where they found "the wind blowing dreadfully hard". Victoria, appropriately, was riding her pony "Lochnagar", but changed it for another mount, and eventually they came to a hollow above the Dubh Loch, where they had lunch. Their return journey took them by Loch Muick, where the Queen went out on a boat, but the wind was so strong that she "begged to land". With her on that occasion was a ghillie called John Gordon, who nursed Prince Albert during his illness in December 1861, and later became Victoria's personal groom. Gordon had a native gift for understatement. He amused Albert by saying that their road over the White Mounth had been "something steep and something rough", and that it had been "the only best". "That", said the Queen, "meant that it was *very* bad".

"We rode home along a sort of sheep path on the side of the lake", wrote Victoria, "which took us three-quarters of an hour. It was very rough and very narrow, for the hill rises abruptly from the lake; we had seven hundred feet above us, and I suppose one hundred feet below". That sheep path is now a broad Land Rover track used, not only by the Royal Family, but by visitors walking around Loch Muick and hill-walkers going farther on to the Dubh Loch. Two and a half miles from Allt-na-giubhsaich it passes the Glas-allt Shiel, where a path loops round through the woods so that passers-by do not pass the front door of the lodge when the Royal

Family is in residence at Balmoral. Out of season, I have dined on its doorstep, and on one occasion, seeking shelter from the wintry blasts in the outbuildings, I found two climbers who had settled in for the night.

Glas-allt, the "shiel of the grey burn", is one of the largest shiels on the Balmoral estate and it has more of a Royal "look" than the others. It is built on an idyllic picnic spot, a tree-covered delta where the rhododendron bushes bloom brightly on the edge of the loch and the burn ripples past the lawn where Victoria and Albert picnicked so many years ago. The Queen is said to have built the Glas-allt Shiel because Allt-na-giubhsaich was a constant and painful reminder of the happiness she had there with her husband, but there was more to it than that. There was a shiel there before the present building was erected in 1868, seven years after the Prince Consort's death, and in an entry in her journal in September, 1852, the Queen wrote, "We came down to the Shiel of Glas-allt, lately built, where there is a charming room for us, commanding a most lovely view". When she first stayed in the new Shiel, she recalled that Albert had "always wanted to build here, in this favourite wild spot, quite in amidst the hills".

The Glas-allt Shiel is best seen from the high ridge across the loch, where the path to Bachnagairn winds its way towards the Broad Cairn. Here, you really are "in amidst the hills", with the whole panorama of Loch Muick and the surrounding mountains stretching before you and, far below, the Royal Shiel nestling in the trees on the lip of the Loch. Sometimes you can see tiny figures moving about the lawn, passing walkers, perhaps, or guests from Balmoral, and your mind strays back through the years to the time when Victoria and Albert strolled there. Or, if there is only one, a solitary figure, you remember the Queen's words, "The sad thought struck me that it was the first widow's house, not built by him or hallowed by his memory".

When snow caps the cone of the Broad Cairn and brushes its wintry fingers across the high plateaux the view from the

Bachnagairn path is magnificent. The hills and loch can be incredibly beautiful in late autumn and early winter, and as the ice crunches under your feet and you go striding along some remote hill path you are apt to put at the back of your mind the thought that in a short span of time this fantasy landscape will turn its Christmas card loveliness into something hostile and dangerous. Queen Victoria never saw the White Mounth in its cruellest season. She watched the first snow fall and wished that it would never stop so that she would "be snowed up and unable to move". To her it meant the end of her stay on Deeside and she "gazed and gazed on God's glorious works" so that she could take away a memory of it when she returned to the dull routine of her Royal round.

She saw the valley and the mountains in "the gorgeous bright October" of Arthur Hugh Clough's poem, which she quoted in her journal to illustrate the kind of beauty which so captivated her in her Highland home. It was a time when "jewels of gold were hung in the hair of the birch tree", but close on its heels was the season of wind and storm, when the snow that signalled her return south would blanket the paths and choke the gullies. Lochnagar would disappear under its leaden winter umbrella and Victoria's "beautiful path" to the wild and rugged Dubh Loch would become an ice sheet that would daunt even the Queen's sturdy Highland ponies.

The road to the Dubh Loch runs from the Glas-allt Shiel through the woods to the head of Loch Muick, where it strikes west uphill towards the gap between the White Mounth and 3314 ft-high Cairn Bannoch. It is a long, rough climb and one place to draw your breath is at the Stullan, where a torrent of water comes gushing down the north slope to cut across your path on its way to the Allt an Dubh burn. Queen Victoria called the waterfall the Spullan, or Spout, which is an apt description of it, and John Campbell, the Marquis of Lorne, must have thought it a romantic spot when he stopped there in 1870. It was there that he proposed to Princess Louise and there is a small cairn near the waterfall to mark the happy occasion. The Stullan takes its water from a small and slightly eerie-looking lochan called Loch Buidhe, hidden from sight above the path.

Beyond the Stullan the path continues its steep climb until it levels out and you come up above the ridge and look down the rocky corridor to the loch. It is striking enough from the distance but as you get nearer the immensity of the great cliff face on the opposite side of the loch dominates and dwarfs everything else in sight. "The loch is only a mile in length", wrote Queen Victoria, "and very wild; the hills, which are very rocky and precipitous, rising perpendicularly from it". This massive expanse of stone, almost as long as the Dubh Loch itself, is between 700 ft and 900 ft high and is known as the Creag an Dubh Loch, the crag of the black loch. Another less precipitous rock face rises to the Eagles Rock on the north side, and it is this hemming in by the cliffs on either side that gives the loch its dark and gloomy appearance.

The path more or less peters out when you reach the loch, but it is easy enough to make your way along its side to the head of the loch where you can stand at the foot of the great crag, near which the stream comes down from its source on the White Mounth. Mountain lochans are cold places at the best of times and it would be a bold man who stripped off for a quick dip in the Dubh Loch, but one visitor is known to have braved its icy waters. He was Queen Victoria's son, the Duke of Edinburgh, who swam into the loch to kill a wounded stag after it had taken to the water to escape its pursuers. I half expected to see a cairn at the edge of the loch to commemorate the event.

The White Mounth has seen many travellers in its time, but there has been nothing to equal, nor is there likely to be, the procession of famous names which descended on Deeside during Queen Victoria's years at Balmoral. They came with varying degrees of reluctance or eagerness, Lords and Ladies, Empresses and Princesses, Ministers of State, Equerries in Waiting, Dukes and Duchesses, clerks and clergymen. The famous John Brown once remarked to the Queen that it was very pleasant to walk with someone who was always so content, and he must have turned a dour and jaundiced eye on those dignitaries who regarded their attendance at Balmoral as something of a penance. Lady Dalhousie visited Balmoral with Gladstone in 1884 and commented bluntly, "I never saw anything more uncomfortable or that I coveted less".

Gladstone, on the other hand, revelled in the wild countryside. At the age of fifty-three he went off on a 25-mile hike into the hills, and on another occasion climbed Lochnagar, covered nineteen miles, and returned "fresh as a lark". Nearly fifteen years later, at the age of sixty-seven, he was still tramping along the hill paths, recording a walk of fifteen miles in just over four hours.

Disraeli was less enthusiastic. He thought the mountains were "graceful", but he was more impressed with the gardens at Balmoral, and Byron would no doubt have put him in the category of those "minions of luxury" who preferred gay landscapes and gardens of roses. In 1850 Sir Edwin Landseer paid his first visit to Balmoral and in the following year painted "The Monarch of the Glen", a romanticised and controversial work that must have owed its origin to Landseer's first sight of a stag on the Deeside hills.

The passing parade of Royalty continued through the years. To-day, Balmoral is still the holiday home of the Royal Family, but their attachment to it is a pale shadow of the link forged by Queen Victoria more than a century ago. There are no more great expeditions over the Mounth roads. There are no trips on Loch Muick with ghillies rowing and pipers playing. The famous still come and go, the Privy Council scurrying up and down from London occasionally on urgent business, giving the impression that they share Disraeli's belief that it is difficult "carrying on the Government of a Country six hundred miles from the metropolis". Prime Ministers still fly in as week-end guests, but the scenario has changed. Gladstone tramped nineteen miles up Lochnagar; Sir Harold Wilson played golf on Balmoral's nine-hole golf course.

When I went up the Capel Mounth and found a pair of

Highland ponies grazing on the hill, tended by soldiers guarding Prince Charles while he was out deer-shooting, I wondered if they were descended from the hardy animals which carried Queen Victoria over the White Mounth to the Glas-allt burn and the Dubh Loch. Did their Royal master have the same affection for them as Victoria had for Lochnagar, which took her up the mountain from Allt-na-giubhsaich, or "dear Fyvie", who was "perfection"? Probably not; there was a four-wheeled monster farther up the hill waiting to whisk the Prince down to the Spittal of Glenmuick and back to Balmoral. But they were a nostalgic reminder of those happy days when a young Queen found peace and contentment in the mountains, following the trail of the old-time travellers across the lonely passes, meeting their challenges, creating in her own way another legend to add to the story of the Mounth. There was a famous occasion when a minister at Crathie Church offered up a prayer that his Queen "may skip like a he-goat upon the mountains". It had a faintly ludicrous ring about it and the Queen, who was said to have been deeply moved and to have buried her face in her hands, may simply have been having a quiet and irreverent chuckle to herself. But the sentiment was honest enough, and it sprung from the knowledge that this was where her heart really lay. I like to think that the ghost of the old Queen is still there, high on the windswept bogland of the Monelpie Moss, where the mists swirl and eddy from the corries of Lochnagar.

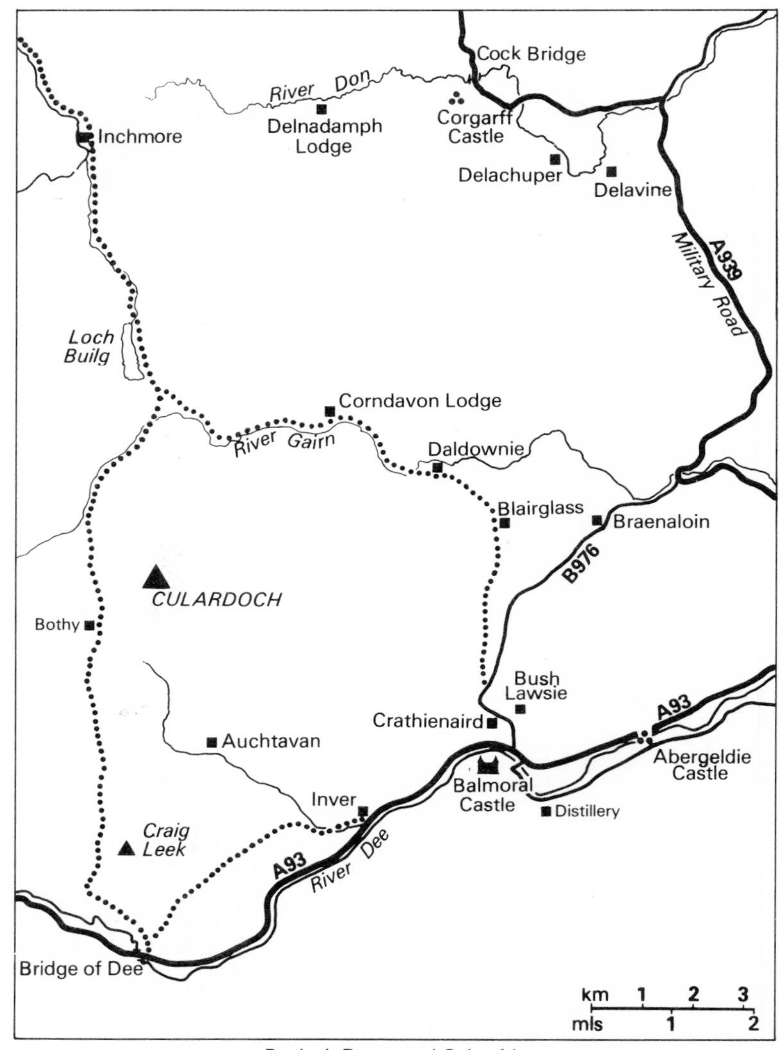

Bealach Dearg and Gairnside

11

Land of Gairn

The land of Gairn stretches from Byron's "Morven of snow" to the great granite tors of Ben Avon, the mountain which the poet John Taylor, saw with "a furred mist upon his snowy head instead of a nightcap". Below these craggy outcrops of rock the River Gairn begins its long sinuous journey to the Dee, twenty miles away, crossing tracks and drove roads which for centuries carried trade and traffic south to Braemar and the Cairnwell Pass, one of the most ancient of the Mounth roads. That vast tract of mountainous country spreading north and south of the Gairn between the Dee and the Don is bounded on the west by the Bealach Dearg, which lies in the lap of Ben Avon, and on the east by the old military road going north from Crathie by Gairnshiel, cutting through "the dark heath" at the foot of Morven. Between them are the lesser-known passes, now largely abandoned and forgotten, rough and untrodden paths threading their way through the hills from Deeside to Strathdon.

The military road, although generally called a Wade road, was, in fact, built in 1753 by Major William Caulfield, General Wade's Inspector of Roads, and the stretch through Glen-gairn formed one tiny segment of a highway that sliced through the heart of Scotland from Perth to Fort George, over 160 miles away. It went north by way of Blairgowrie and the Spittal of Glenshee, following the Cairnwell until it turned east at Braemar and then went north again from Crathie to Gairnshiel, Corgarff, Tomintoul, Grantown and Nairn to the Moray Firth. But not even the Wade military machine could perform miracles, and the planners had to face the fact that beyond Braemar the nearest direct route north was by the

Bealach Dearg, the Red Pass, at Invercauld, up to the head-waters of the River Gairn, on the edge of the Cairngorms. The Bealach Dearg presented too many problems, and it is interesting to note that nearly eighty years later an even more ambitious plan for a major road over this ancient hill route was considered and abandoned. The mountainous terrain was too formidable for Caulfield and the tracks to the east in the Gairn hills were no foundation for a new road system. Caulfield moved along the line of the Dee from Braemar, probing for a gap that would swing him back on course again, and at Crathie he found it. The way north was still bleak and uninviting, but a plan to avoid Glengairn completely by taking the road even farther east to Cromar was contemplated and rejected as too costly.

Four miles from Crathie the road crossed the River Gairn on the great hump of the bridge at Gairnshiel, following the Glas-choille for another four miles until it struck north-west by Delavine and Delachuper to Cock Bridge, a deviation from the line of the present road. Queen Victoria travelled by Delachuper in 1859 during an expedition into the Gairn hills, passing through the "small straggling toun" of Corgarff. "The road was soon left for a mountain one in the hills", she wrote in her "Journal", "above one of the tributary streams of the Don, and was wild and desolate; we passed Dal Choupar and Dal Vown, and, as we ascended, we saw Tornahoish, at a distance to the left. After going along this hill-track, over some poor and tottering bridges, we joined the road by which we had driven to Tornahoish".

Where the old road breaks away from the present A939, you look clear down the flanks of the hills south of the Don to Corgarff. The route is a straight continuation of the Glas-choille road and it is easy to see why Caulfield set his line in that direction in 1753, but the modern road veers away to the right and north to Colnabaichin, leaving its ageing forerunner to its memories. It is still worth stepping into the past to walk the old road three miles to The Cock. I did it on a warm Spring day, when peewits were wheeling and diving in the clear, bright air and pockets of snow hugged the hills as if reluctant to give way to the changing season. The old track dipped and rose like a roller-coaster and away in the distance the Lecht could be seen climbing up from the hotel at Allargue, at the foot of the hill.

There are three houses and three bridges in the valley—the "poor and tottering bridges" crossed by Queen Victoria over a century ago. The first is the best, a miniature edition of all the "Wade" bridges scattered throughout the Highlands. It spans the peat-brown waters of the Burn of Tornahaish as they tumble down from the heights of the Ca' and it is still in remarkably good condition. Half a mile on the old Ca' drove road, coming over the hills from the River Gairn, joins the military road and farther on the farm of Delavine is on the right. Its attractive, white-washed cottage is used as a bothy for shooters, but for most of the time it stands empty.

The second bridge crosses a tributary of the Don beyond Delavine and it was probably the largest of the three, but half-way over the hump it has crumbled into the burn. Even so, what remains is fascinating. The surface has so eroded that the detailed work of the bridge-builder is shown clearly underneath and it is well seen why Wade bridges have survived the ravages of the years. The last bridge is about a mile from the end of the road and it is the smallest and most badly damaged, with barely enough width left on top to cross from one side to the other. Delachuper, pronounced Delahooper, is near it, a cottage that was formerly a youth hostel but was temporarily occupied when I was there. The farm of Ordgarff, like Delavine, was deserted, and from it the track runs on to join the main road on the final steps to Cock Bridge.

From Cock Bridge, Caulfield's road went over the notorious Lecht to Tomintoul and from there to the Moray Firth. This was not the old historic route from Deeside and the south. Before the Lecht became a major route most of the hill paths crossing the Gairn had taken the traffic from the south and funnelled it north-east through Strathdon, meeting up by the Deskry Water and Towie with travellers and drovers

The Wade bridge at Delachuper.

journeying through the Howe of Cromar from the Capel and Firmounth passes.

There are three ways into the Gairn from Deeside. One is the road at Crathie, the other two are about five miles east near Ballater. The first two meet at the Gairnshiel bridge, forming a loop from Ballater to Crathie, and the last is a minor route on the north side of the River Gairn, providing access to what was once a flourishing community at the mouth of Glenfenzie. At one time it offered a route through the hills from Ballater to Strathdon and there are still traces of it at either end. From the pass it goes up past Craggan and the farm of Abergairn, skirting the wood which holds the ruins of Gairn Castle, an ancient hunting seat, and from there running along the slopes of the Craig of Prony parallel with the present road until it comes down to meet it. There are paths to Morven Lodge and to Gairnshiel, but the old road goes on round Lary Hill above the cottage at Laggan and pushes its way, largely hidden and unheeded, to the ruins of Glenfenzie Lodge.

Laggan in Glen Fenzie, where the Lary hill path goes north to join the Glas-choille road.

From there it went to Tornahaish and Strathdon.

Today the main approach to Gairnshiel from the Bridge of Gairn is by the west road, circling Geallaig Hill and passing the ford that separates the farm "touns" north and south of the river. These homesteads, some long since gone, are the heartbeat of the community. They lie in the triangle of land formed by the Glenfenzie burn, the Gairn water and the military road, nudging each other protectively against the encroaching wilderness. Here is Dalfad, where the remains of the MacGregors of Glengairn are buried. It was to Dalfad, the "long haugh," that they came following the proscription of the clan and Rob Roy is said to have visited his Deeside relatives during his wanderings through the country. The MacGregors of Glengairn came out in support of the Stuart cause in both the 1715 and 1745 Rebellions.

Dalphuil, the old schoolhouse, the Teapot Cottage of the Royal children, is on the north side of Gairnshiel Bridge.

Rinloan, on the opposite side, was once an inn and also had a Royal connection. Queen Victoria halted there on her way back to Balmoral after her day's outing to Loch Builg and Corgarff. "There, at the small public-house, we found the carriage, and drove off as soon as we could. We had to drive home very slowly, as the road is not good, and very steep in parts." West of Rinloan, the land of Gairn, as the Queen called it, opens out into a dark desolation of hill and moor where the River Gairn runs to the Dee. Along its banks are the larachs, the ruined homesteads, which once breathed into the valley what little life there was. The holdings scattered frugally west of Rinloan were linked by a road from Braenaloin, about a mile south-west of Gairnshiel.

Near Braenaloin the road passes Renatton, which at one time belonged to Macdonalds claiming descent from the Lords of the Isles. During the '45 Rebellion, John Symon, a tenant of Renatton, showing less enthusiasm for Bonnie Prince Charlie's cause than the MacGregors, was ordered to march with the Jacobites to Tullich or have his house burned down, his corn destroyed and his cattle driven away. Half a mile from Renatton are the ruins of Loinahaun, which Queen Victoria used to visit, and across the river is Tullochmacarrick, reached by a sturdy wooden bridge. The buildings here, like many more in the glen, are abandoned, the windows shattered or boarded up, the door inside the porch padlocked. Behind Tullochmacarrick a path climbs round the west face of Fox Cairn to The Ca'. Time has almost obliterated the Ca' Road; it runs down to a stream called the Allt Coire nam Freumh and from there, crossing to the opposite bank, you follow a rough and ill-defined route to Delavine, two miles from The Cock.

From this path, before it turns away into the hills, you can see Easter Sleach, about a mile west of Tullochmacarrick, a crumbling ruin on the slopes of Tom Odhar. This remote holding was reached by a ford across the Gairn, and it sat on the route of the drove road called the Camus Road, which went north over Tom Odhar and Carn Mor to Ordgarff and Cock

Bridge. From the Fox Cairn path, too, you can look straight down the glen, following the glinting course of the Gairn, to Daldownie, which until 1977 was the last building of any consequence in the glen. Here, indeed, you are "at the back of nowhere".

Queen Victoria passed Daldownie on her expedition in 1859 but she took another route. About a mile north of Balmoral Castle, where the Crathie Burn comes down from Monaltrie Moss to cross the old Military road, the A939, at Bush, a hill track breaks off to the left and heads through woodland to the open moor. Near here, on the opposite side of the road, the farm of Bridgend of Bush clings to the edge of the moorland wastes, its front door facing down over the hollow of the Dee to Balmoral. It was from holdings such as these that the Castle drew many of its servants, particularly its ghillies and 'keepers; men like old John Gordon, Macdonald, Duncan, Grant. Their sons, in turn, followed them. Macdonald was a "Jager" to the Prince of Wales. Grant, the head keeper, "an excellent man, most trustworthy, had six sons, one of whom became a wardrobe man to Leopold. It was Grant who was "on the box" when the Queen's carriage rattled up the brae on its way to Daldownie on that September morning in 1859.

The folk at the Bush would have watched the carriage passing their door with a special interest, for one of their nine sons was on that outing. He had been with the Royal household for ten years and had done well for himself. Only the year before, in 1858, he had been selected by the Queen to become her regular attendant "out of doors everywhere in the Highlands". James and Margaret Brown had reason to be proud. They could never have foreseen that their son, John, had set himself on a course that was to make his name a household word throughout the country and bring a spicy breath of scandal to Court circles.

Over the years, thousands of words have been written about the relationship of John Brown and Queen Victoria. There were stories that after Victoria's death steps were taken to wipe out every memento, every reminder of the ghillie's place in the Royal affections, and even Deeside, the Queen's "dear Paradise", was not immune from the tittle-tattle and gossip-mongering. I was told by a Ballater man of how, as a youth, he had set out one night to search the woods around Crathie for a bust of Brown said to have been dumped there by Royal command. It was never found.

The Bush has changed little outwardly over the years, and there is not much different at Crathienaird, the neighbouring farm where Brown worked as a boy of sixteen before becoming a stable lad at the old Balmoral, tenanted by Sir Robert Gordon. He was plucked out of these humble beginnings to become John Brown, Esquire, a form of address insisted upon by Queen Victoria, and it was an elevation of rank and social standing that would see him lampooned and caricatured in the Press and on the stage.

In an entry in her diary in 1865, Victoria gave a glimpse of the qualities she admired in Brown, as well as an insight into why others disliked him. He had, she said, "all the independence and elevated feelings peculiar to the Highland race", an independence, perhaps, that rested ill with those who looked for subservience and servility. He was "singularly straightforward", which meant that he could be blunt and outspoken, as when he silenced Gladstone with the devastating dismissal, "You've said enough!" He was also "simple-minded, kind-hearted and disinterested", and it may be that these were the qualities resented more than any others, bringing as they did, a breath of fresh Highland air to the hothouses of Windsor and Osborne. To the Queen, Brown was the one lasting link with her early days at Balmoral. Burdened by advancing years, weighed down by the cares of office, she must have looked back on them with nostalgia, remembering the moonlight trips by Loch Muick, the pony treks over the White Mounth, the ride to Inchrory with Brown at her side.

Perhaps, for a moment, some of the old romance returned and she saw again the mist rising on the Deeside hills and heard the chuckling cry of the grouse as the Royal carriage clattered over the Coulchan Burn bridge and climbed up towards the farm of Blairglass. Looking east, she would have picked out the line of the old military road as it pushed its way through the hills and in the distance the hump-backed bridge crossing the Gairn at Gairnshiel. Then she would have been over the brow of the hill, beyond Blairglass, and heading down towards the Gairn, passing the track that comes west from Braenaloin to meet the Bush road just before Daldownie. "Doll Dounie," the Queen called it. On my first visit there there was only a ruin to remind you of the old days, but a year later there was nothing. It had been reduced to a rubble heap of charred timber and stone.

Daldownie mentioned in Queen Victoria's diary. It is now demolished.

About a mile ahead was Corndavon Lodge, a shooting box at the base of the Brown Cow Hill. It was at one time used by Royalty and had obviously been an impressive building, buried in the Gairn wilderness, but one wing was in ruins. The main building was in good order and I could see through the windows that large murals of deer and the hills had been painted on two of the walls. Nearby were the ruins of a number of smaller buildings, probably servants' quarters, but one was still in use by hill-walkers and there were chairs and a table inside.

Farther on I came upon an old wooden footbridge which linked the Builg road with a track on the south side of the Gairn climbing away to the hill of Culardoch. Lumpy Ben A'an was coming nearer and at last I was at Lochan Feurach, one of a number of small lochans leading to Loch Builg. Loch Builg Lodge was on a knoll on the left and to the south the Bealach Dearg. This is a meeting place of old tracks; the Bealach Dearg coming up from Invercauld and the road from Inchrory coming down through Glen Builg, while the Corndavon path cuts in from the east. There is also a track going over Tom a'Chuir to Culardoch and this, with the Culardoch path from the footbridge over the Gairn west of Corndavon, strikes deep into Aberarder.

John Brown's mother, Margaret Leys, was the daughter of a blacksmith at Aberarder, whose remote and windy acres spread up the valley of the Fearder Burn to the hills between Monaltrie Moss and the old Bealach Dearg pass. Through it threads one of the old drove roads from Deeside to Strathdon. To-day, few people tread these ancient ways through the hills. Red deer roam the desolate country where cattle herds once lumbered south from Speyside on their way to the Perth Tryst. There is a sense of total isolation, sharpened by reminders of the depopulation that has eaten into the fabric of life in the upper reaches of the Dee.

The district of Aberarder at one time had a population that, in the early part of last century, sustained a school of 100 pupils. Now the signs of decay are all around; the ruins of Ratlich on the banks of the Fearder Burn; the old mission church, its bell and belfry still intact, its windows shattered and its interior a storehouse for farm fodder; the crumbling walls of holdings along the shallow valley of Felagie. The entrance to Glen Fearder is at the hamlet of Inver, on the main Deeside road, less than a mile west of the Carn na Cuimhne, the rallying point of Clan Farquharson. It was from here that I made my foray into this forgotten pass and it was not a bad starting point, for it was to the Carn na Cuimhne that the clansmen came over the hills when the fiery cross went out. Before they marched off to battle each man placed a stone on the cairn, removing it on his return. The stones that were left told their own story; they were left on the cairn as a memorial to the fallen.

The path goes up by Ballochlaggan, where a laird of Invercauld once hanged eighteen troublesome "bonnet lairds." Below the farm a wooden bridge takes you across the burn and up to the old mission church. Here you are at the junction of routes, the main one coming east from Invercauld by Felagie and turning down to Inver, with a branch striking north at the church by Balnoe and Balmore. Another road runs along the north side of the Felagie valley towards Craig Leek.

The path by Balnoe was yet another drove road through the Gairn hills. It crosses the Fearder Burn below the ruins of Ratlich, climbs through the woods to meet the track from Ballochlaggan, and curves round to break out into open moorland. Where it clears the treeline another path branches to Auchtavan, but the Culardoch path continues and swings left to a choice of two more routes. One goes to ruined farm buildings at the base of Leac Ghorm, the other, higher up, runs along the side of the hill, the two meeting near a deer fence. From there the route runs on the east side of Culardoch until the wart-like head of Ben A'an can be seen above Loch Builg, with the Bealach Dearg on the left coming in to join it on the way north.

On another day I took the Auchtavan path, going deep into Glen Fearder. The shieling there, which has been used by the Queen Mother for many years, sits in the lap of Creag Bhalg. The Gaelic meaning of Auchtavan is "the field of two kids," a throwback to the days when a pair of young goats was the rent paid by the tenant of Auchtavan to the laird of Invercauld. The view from the hills there can be incredibly beautiful, even more so at the tail-end of the year when I visited it, watching the great storm clouds drift and droop over the whitened corries of Lochnagar. Auchtavan is the highest farm in Glen Fearder, the "glen of the high water." The uppermost farm at one time was Auchnagymlinn, where there is said to be the grave of a giant, but this holding was swept away when the Great Flood of 1829 unleashed its fury on the Grampians.

12

Bealach Dearg

The second day of August, 1829, dawned clear and bright in the village of Braemar. Towards evening it began to rain and the following day there were heavy showers and strong gusts of wind from the north-west. By late afternoon the wind had risen to hurricane force. The first flash of lightning was seen, followed by a deafening peel of thunder, an explosion of sound that echoed over the hills "as if whole batteries of the pieces of Heaven's ordnance had been discharged in rapid succession." For the next two hours, while the rain fell and the rivers rose, the thunder rumbled on, and in the pitch-dark night that followed people felt the earth shaking and heard slates fall from the roofs of their houses. The "Muckle Spate" was on the move.

The events of that August were described by Sir Thomas Dick Lauder, in *The Moray Floods,* as "This awful admonition to a sinful land." The countryside both north and south of the Mounth was battered by a deluge that "poured down the furrowed side of the mountains." In Glenesk, the bridge at Tarf was carried away and the Rev. Peter Jolly's house at Loch Lee was flooded to a depth of three feet. At Gannochy Bridge, the flood rose to within a foot of the keystone, and a suburb of Brechin was flooded by the South Esk. North of the Grampian range the land between the Dee and the Don and along the banks of the Avon reeled under a torrent of water that swept everything before it. Not least affected was the remote and rugged region where the Bealach Dearg traced its path along the eastern edge of the Cairngorms, joining Glengairn with the broad plain of Strathavon and acting as a link in the historic route that ran from the Lowlands to the North of Scotland.

"The number of auld briggs which have stood, whilst new erections have been swept away, is rather a reproach to the boasted superiority of modern masons," commented Lauder. His tart remark could well have been aimed at the builder of the bridge at Ballater, which was destroyed in the flood. When the first two arches went the splash of the water was so great that it rose over the tops of nearby houses. Women screamed and waded for their lives. Every horse and vehicle was pressed into service. Many of those caught up in the holocaust had come to Deeside for the health-giving waters at Pannanich and one half-drowned visitor said wryly, "Call you this a watering place?"

The story I like best is that of Sir Thomas's conversation with Mr James Ogg and his wife, who owned the inn at Cambus-o'May, three miles from Ballater. They told him how they had lost corn and carts, whisky and rum, and "a deal o' oor furnitur'." "An' what think ye, sir?" said Mrs Ogg, "the very first thing I fand when we cam' back was a bit trootie in the plate-rack." Did they fry it, asked Sir Thomas. "Eh, na!" said Mr Ogg, "the poor beastie wasna dead; it was soomin' aboot among the dishes; she could nae hae fund in her heart tae harm it, sae I took it an' pat it into the reever again, an' it soomed awa'."

The Dee and the Avon tried to outdo each other in their fury. At the Linn of Dee the river rose three feet above the wooden bridge that spanned the gorge and at six different points of the Dee, the average breadth of which was 130 ft, the mean rise of the whole being from 15 ft to 16 ft. Away to the north the Avon was "like a vast moving lake" and in twelve hours forty gallons of rainwater poured through an 18 inch square hole in the roof of a Tomintoul house. The miller at Delnabo, where the Marquis of Huntly was captured by the Covenanters in 1647, was reported to have shaken his head in disbelief and remarked that it was "a'thegither ridiculous". Dick Lauder thought that it was a terrible judgement "sent by the Almighty Governor of the Universe for some great and beneficial purpose". John Cly, the meal miller at Tomore, who had suffered from severe flooding on a number of occasions, was more down to earth. He looked at his shattered property and said, "I took it frae the Awen—let the Awen hae her ain again".

Following the Avon south to Inchrory, you pass the Burn of Little Fergie, near Dalestie, where there was a landslide in the floods. Little Fergie marks the point where an old drove road went south-east by the Eag to Inchmore on the Inchrory-Corgarff road. Inchrory itself is over two miles to the south, where the river takes a curious U-bend after spilling out from the haugh below the Linn of Avon. This lovely spot was a crossroads for traffic coming down the Avon to Gairnside, to Braemar and the Cairnwell Pass by the Bealach Dearg, and east by Cock Bridge to Donside or Glen Fenzie. Here, where birch trees bow over the A'an waters—"the clearest and purest waters of all our kingdom", it was said—the drovers rested their herds as the reivers lurked in the hills. In the years following the '45 Rebellion, General Wade stationed patrols at Inchrory to stop cattle thieving. Their bothies were said to be on the slopes of Meall Gaineimh in Glen Builg, which would have been a suitable point from which to strike back at the raiders as they fled south through the Red Pass with their booty.

There is a different kind of hunting nowadays. When I passed Inchrory House, a large white shooting lodge with blue woodwork and blue chimneys, there were thirteen sets of antlers hanging on the fence in front of it. Only the day before I had seen unmounted antlers selling for £6 and £7 in a Braemar shop, so there was at least £80 worth of horn stuck on that fence. Inchrory is best seen from the road which climbs up behind it on the way to Corgarff, the route Queen Victoria took when coming up the Bealach Dearg from Loch Builg. Along this road lies Delnadamph Lodge, the 6700-acre estate bought by the Queen in 1977.

The main droving route, however, was from Inchrory

Inchrory House where the Bealach Dearg meets the Avon.

through the Bealach Dearg, south to Invercauld by Glen Builg. The path follows the Builg Burn until you drop down to the chilly waters of Loch Builg. It is a grey and gloomy loch, with a boathouse in the south-east corner that offers a draughty shelter in bad weather. "Welcome to the highest boat house in the country," someone had chalked on the wall. "Peace and love to you all." There was no boat, but a pair of oars in the rafters, and on the floor two mattresses, a shaky bench seat, a kettle, and a Glenfiddich whisky bottle—empty. Hanging from the roof by a string, encased in a plastic cover and a spider's web, was a visitor's book. The last entry was by a party of Scouts who were on their third visit in August, 1976. They or some other kindhearted wayfarer had done their good deed, for also hanging from the roof by a string was a woollen jersey. Across the front of it was written the word "Emergency."

Near the boathouse were the ruins of Lochbuilg Lodge, where Donald McHardy, a stalker, had once lived. It stood on

Loch Builg and its boathouse.

a knoll overlooking Lochan Feurach and Lochan Orr, two of the group of tiny lochans which mark the parting of the ways for the Bealach Dearg and the road to Gairnside by Corndavon. Behind it was the knotted brow of Ben A'an, which John Taylor saw with "a furr'd mist upon his snowie head."

Half a mile below Lochan Feurach the Bealach crosses the River Gairn and a branch cuts east between Culardoch and Monaltrie Moss to Inver on the main Deeside road. The main path goes due south between Carn Liath and Culardoch, changing to a shooting road where a wooden stable stands on the col. It is a trim little building with two stalls and, I believe, replaces an older structure that stood on the same spot, although whether or not it is still used as a stable I do not know. Anyway, you can look clear down to the church at Inver and the Dee and, descending to where the Allt Cul goes east to join the Fearder burn, you can see down the glen to the Royal shiel at Auchtavan. From the cluster of trees at Allt Cul you climb towards Meall Gorm, entering the woodlands of Invercauld on its west side. From there it is a pleasant

The stable on Bealach Dearg—the only shelter for a long stretch on this remote pass.

downhill walk to the road behind Invercauld House and along to Keiloch and the Invercauld bridge.

There is an alternative route to the Dee at Inver, crossing Craig Leek to the glen at Felagie. Striking off from the woodland south of Meall Gorm, you keep to the east side of Craig Leek on a high and windy area marked on the map "Am Bealach" (The Pass), which suggests that this itself was a recognised route joining up with the Red Pass. The hollow here was at one time cultivated and the ruins of old holdings run hard into the gut of Am Bealach. From the Craig Leek track you look down on little squares and stones marking sites where families once lived. The path runs from Craig Leek to what was the clachan of Middleton of Aberarder. Nothing remains but rubble.

On the opposite side of the Felagie valley a road connects Keiloch, on the Invercauld estate, with Inver, running parallel with the Deeside road. At one time it was well used in that part of Deeside, even being taken as an alternative to the main road in the early days of motoring. Earlier, in the second half of last century, it was repaired and linked up with the north route to the Gairn by Balnoe. The idea was to provide an alternative to the Bealach Dearg, avoiding the deer forests there, which gives an indication of the popularity of the old pass as a direct route to Strathdon and Speyside.

There are few Sunday trippers now, only estate workers and the occasional walker. And the deer. The first time I came through by Belagie it was mid-winter and a snow-storm was blowing itself out. Great storm clouds swirled and dropped over the whitened corries of Lochnagar and the Fearder Burn was frozen over, a white-breasted dipper hopping unhappily across the ice. In the fields at Balmore they were feeding hay to the sheep. Half-way along the road a stag rose from behind a ridge and, eyeing me warily, turned on its heels and trotted off to join the herd. They were at the Keiloch end of the glen, between 150 and 200 of them, foraging for food in the snow, and I watched them drift slowly towards the gap below Craig Leek.

A week later I was back at Felagie and saw the toll of that storm, the bodies of young deer calves lying pathetically in the heather. I had gone over to Craig Leek to look at the ruins of a holding on the face of the hill and as I came down the slope large herds of deer were spaced out along the valley. The snow had disappeared but a thin drizzle of rain spattered dismally through the glen. Then, in the distance, a Land Rover appeared and turned into a clearing near a cottage used as a summer retreat by Girl Guides. A moment later I could hear the loud blast of the vehicle's horn, repeated at regular intervals, and I could see the deer turn and move towards it. The driver was an estate worker on Invercauld, carrying a load of hay for the deer. He came there every morning to feed them. There were sixty or seventy stags around him and, farther off, a herd of hinds. Many of the stags were as close as thirty or forty feet.

Near Invercauld House another road comes in from the west to join the old pass. This was the route taken by travellers going north from Braemar, crossing the river at Inverchandlick, near Braemar Castle, almost opposite the point where the Allt an t-Slugain runs into the Dee. It was here, too, that the great cattle herds coming south by the Bealach Dearg shook themselves free of the chilling waters of that last river barrier and pushed on to the Cairnwell Pass. West of Inverchandlick the road on the north bank continues by Allanaquoich to the Linn of Dee and was probably used by drovers and other travellers coming through the Lairig Ghru by Glen Dee and Glen Derry and down the Lairig an Laoigh.

This road is also, in a sense, a dusty tailpiece to an unfulfilled dream, for if General Wade's plan to build a road through Glen Feshie had ever materialised this was the way it would have come, linked by a quartet of bridges over the Dee, the Lui, the Quoich and the Slugain. The road is well used to-day by hill walkers heading up by the Derry or by campers and holidaymakers going to Mar Lodge and the Linn of Dee. Near where it joins the Bealach Dearg at Invercauld House another path strikes north-west up Gleann an t-Slugain by Altdourie. I remember going through this glen on one occasion on my way to Beinn a' Bhuird and stopping for lunch at The Howff. This was a shelter built by climbers, who used great slabs of stone and a natural rock face to form the walls and roof, adding the luxury of a wooden door to complete their "hospice". The door was only four or five feet high and if you stayed too long you left with a permanent stoop, but it was welcome enough when the wind was snapping at your heels outside.

This is Farquharson country. There are various stories told of how the family came to be established on Mar, including a fanciful tale about the first Farquharson, a shepherd, being given permission to pasture his sheep in the haugh at Beinn a' Bhuird until the snow disappeared. He stayed for good, for you can always find snow on Beinn a' Bhuird. John Grant, in his "Legends of the Braes of Mar", has a different explanation. He tells how Findla Mor, the first Farquharson chieftain, who was killed at the Battle of Pinkie in 1547, played host to a stranger at Invercauld, feeding him and giving him "a few bumpers of the 'native'". Next morning he "accompanied him on his way a long distance, showing him how to attain Strathaven by the Bealach Dearg and Inchrory route". He later received a letter creating him Royal Standard-Bearer for Scotland and confirming the possession of all his property. This was in response to the hospitality shown to the king—the "stranger" Findlay had put on the right road through the Red Pass.

Thomas Pennant, the naturalist, was a guest at Invercauld when he visited the North-east of Scotland in 1769. In the days when travel was regarded as more of a penance than a pleasure, two of the earliest chroniclers on Deeside were Pennant and John Taylor. They blazed a tourist trail that was to be followed by countless thousands of visitors in the years to follow, and Pennant, in fact, claimed that after the publication of his *Tour of Scotland* in 1771 "the remotest part of North Britain" was inundated with southern visitors.

Both came over the Mounth to the Dee valley from the south and the records they left show that their passage across the Grampians was far from idyllic. But both, equally, fell in love with what Taylor poetically called the "sky-kissing mountains of the Braes of Mar". When those sky-kissing mountains were enveloped in rolling storm clouds they instilled in lesser souls a fear and foreboding that made the majority of travellers recoil from the mere thought of crossing them. The Water Poet, on the other hand, asked, "What braver object can man's eye-sight see?"

Pennant came out of the "dreary wastes" of Glen Tilt and looked with delight on the "verdant pyramids of pines" on upper Deeside. After the "wild, black, moory, melancholy" tract of the Tilt valley the views east of Braemar were "exceedingly romantic". He may not have been impressed with the village itself, where the houses seemed "like so many black mole-hills", but he enthused at length on the countryside around it, and particularly the scenery at Invercauld, where the silver birch trees, with their "long and pendant boughs, waving a vast height above the head, surpass the beauties of the weeping willow".

The mountains and forests south of the Dee were "pre-eminently magnificent", a vast theatre in which the pine trees thinned out and gave way to "naked summits of a surprising height, many of them topped with perpetual snow". Pennant the traveller found a wealth of material for his notebook and Pennant the naturalist revelled in the abundance of wild life all about him. There were stags ranging the hills, little roe bucks "perpetually bounding before us", swarms of grouse and ptarmigans, green plovers and whimbrels. There were eagles, peregrine falcons and goshawks; birds, wrote Pennant, that were proscribed, half a crown being given for an eagle, a shilling for a hawk. One wonders what his naturalist's mind thought of such a proscription, or what he might have said of the protection that the law would afford them nearly two hundred years later.

Pennant's host, Mr Farquharson, took him "into a magnificent forest of pines of many miles extent". This was the famous Ballochbuie Forest, the largest pine forest in Scotland, which tradition says was sold by a MacGregor of Ballochbuie to a Farquharson of Invercauld for a tartan plaid. The likelihood is that the plaid simply sealed the bargain, but just over a century after Pennant's visit, when Queen Victoria bought the forest, she erected a stone with the inscription, "The bonniest plaid in Scotland". Whatever the price paid in that long-forgotten transaction, Pennant was interested in the current value of the "bonniest plaid" being a tree planter himself. Mr Farquharson told him that for eight hundred trees he got "five and twenty shillings each".

Pennant entered Ballochbuie Forest by "a good stone bridge", the first Invercauld Bridge built in 1752 as part of the military road. This is more familiarly known as the old Brig o' Dee. The "new" Invercauld Bridge, carrying traffic up the A93 to Braemar, was built in 1859, when Prince Albert closed the Ballochbuie road to the public and the old bridge with it. It still allows pedestrian access and it is a favourite subject with artists, which is not surprising, for it straddles the Dee at one of the most picturesque corners of upper Deeside. The canvas here mixes the moody and magnificent with the gentler beauty of the Invercauld plain, where shaggy Highland cattle graze on the meadowland below Invercauld House. Between them, the old and new bridges have carried east-west traffic over the River Dee to Braemar and the Cairnwell Pass for more than two hundred years.

In the account of his visit to Invercauld, Pennant mentions "the great cataract of Garvalbourn, which foams amidst the dark forest, rushing from rock to rock to a vast distance". This was almost certainly the Falls of Garbh Allt, or Garrawalt, about a mile from Invercauld Bridge, which, as the naturalist remarked, made "a fine contrast to the scene" and which is still a spectacular attraction for present-day visitors. Queen Victoria saw them on her first ascent of Lochnagar. She thought they were "beautiful" and the rocks "very grand". I was there in mid-winter, when the beauty and grandeur was of a different kind, the ice forming weird patterns on the frozen burn and Victoria's "little bridge", the ornate iron foot-bridge over the Falls, standing out like some enormous iced cake above the dark pool into which the last of the Fall's three cascades plunges.

The Falls of Garbh Allt marked a "junction" from which travellers could make their way over the White Mounth to Glen Muick and Glen Clova or strike south-west by Carn an t-Sagairt Mor to Glen Callater and the Tolmounth. The Garbh Allt, the "rough burn", runs through the middle of Ballochbuie Forest, joining the Dee at the white suspension bridge which leads from the main Deeside road to the Danzig Shiel. From the shiel, which takes its name from a Danziger who ran a saw-mill which once stood there, paths link up with the one from Invercauld Bridge to the Falls. There was said to be an old right-of-way up the burn and over the hills to Glen Muick, following a route known as the "Smuggler's Shank", another echo of the days when whisky smuggling was rife on Deeside. From the Falls you can cross the bridge and reach Lochnagar by way of the Allt Lochan nan Eun and Sandy Loch, or, keeping to the west side of the Garbh Allt, follow the Feindallacher Burn. From the Feindallachar you can also cross to where a path runs down from Lochnagar to Loch Callater, providing access to the Tolmounth.

On his way from Braemar to Invercauld, Pennant passed the "ragged and broken" Craig Clunie, where he looked in wonder at "the melancholy green of the picturesque pine" growing out of the naked rock. He probably paused to view the enormous stone which lies in a field near Clunie Cottage, a little west of Invercauld Bridge. This is the "Meikle Stane of Clunie", and how it got there no one knows, although the popular theory is that it fell from Craig Clunie. The theory is suspect, for the crag itself is some distance away and if you have a fertile imagination you will probably think that more sinister forces were at work. It calls to mind other "meikle stanes" on Deeside; the Devil's Stone on Clochnaben and the Warlock's Stone at Craiglash. The Devil may not have set his cloven hoof on Invercauld, but the "Meikle Stane of Clunie" lies at a spot that was said to be a haunt of fairies. Whatever the answer, it was put to practical use by the local lairds, for it marked the dividing line between the Ballochbuie and Invercauld properties.

Had things been different, the traffic that chokes the Deeside roads in high summer might have followed the Bealach Dearg route on their way to Tomintoul instead of going by Gairnshiel and Corgarff. Caulfield's road-builders turned away from the thought of such a project, but in 1832 an Edinburgh civil engineer called James Flint actually drew up a plan which envisaged a new road being built over the Red Pass. The plan, which mapped out a route from Perth to Moray, proposed the building of a timber bridge across the Dee opposite Braemar Castle, probably on the line of the old ford. From the north side of the Dee, the new road would cross the Allt an t-Slugain by an existing bridge and strike towards Loch Builg, the Avon and Tomintoul, and from there to Craigellachie and Elgin.

The Flint road was a second Glen Feshie road; there was plenty of talk but no action, and to-day the ancient pass remains undisturbed by car-bound tourists.

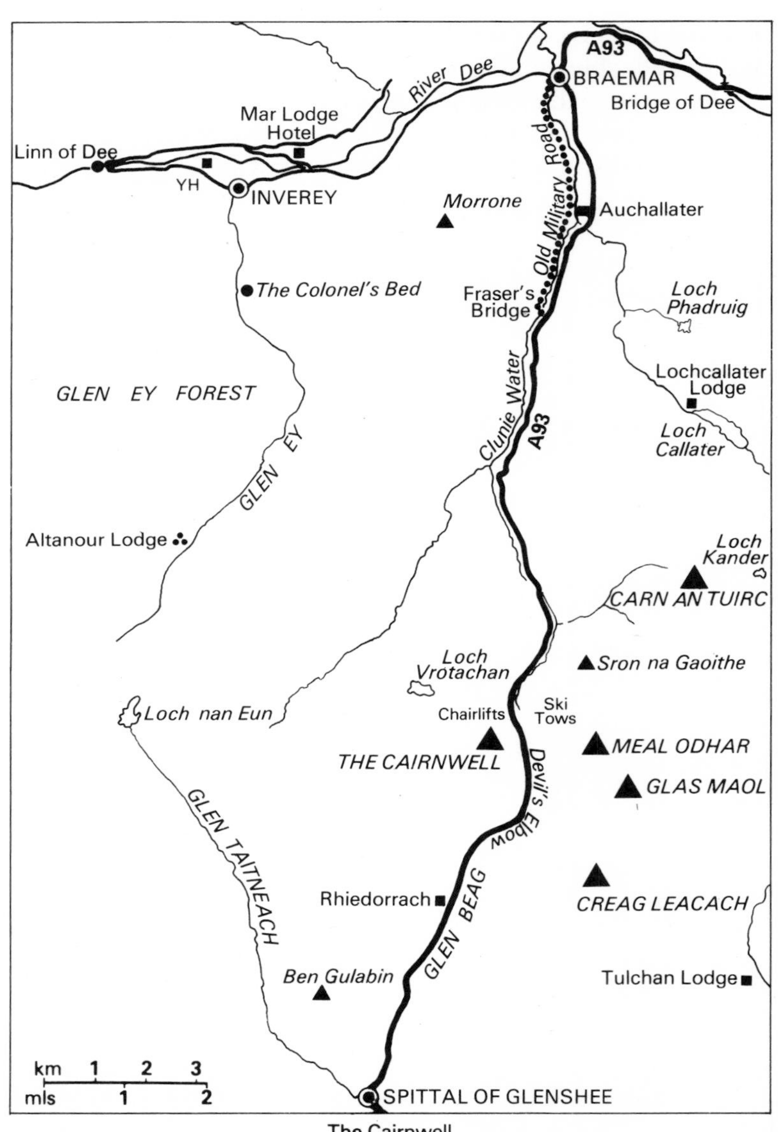

The Cairnwell

13

Cairnwell

They came over the hills to Braemar in the dying days of August. The first to arrive was John Erskine, the Earl of Mar, riding down the Cairnwell Pass by the Clunie Water, past the "black houses" and the barony courthouse and out of the village to the fire-gutted ruins of Braemar Castle, where he forded the River Dee and made his way to Invercauld House. The others came later, lords and lairds from a' the airts, names like Tullibardine and Athole, Huntly, Southesk and Traquair, the Lords Rollo and Ogilvie, men who held the destiny of Scotland in their hands. They were there ostensibly for the annual hunt, a traditional event on Deeside's calendar. Nearly a century before, John Taylor had come over the Mounth to take part in a similar hunt as the guest of an earlier Earl of Mar and had marvelled at this gathering of "the nobility and gentry of the kingdome". He had followed them as they chased the deer with "long bowes and forked arrowes, swords and harquebuses, muskets, dirks and Loquhabour axes", and had joined in a feast in which there was "such baking, boyling, roasting and stewing as if Cooke Ruffian had been there to have scaled the Devil in his feathers".

On the face of it, the gathering organised by John Erskine differed little from those held by his predecessors. The guests arrived at Invercauld to plan the hunt and on September 5th they were out in the Forest of Mar, split into companies to wait for the deer herds, two or three hundred strong, that were being driven down from the high tops. That night they feasted on the banks of the Quoich Water. Legend has it that the Earl brewed a great bowl of punch in a massive cup-like hollow in the river's rock formation. It is still there today, the Earl's

Punchbowl, conjuring up visions of an indelible moment in Scottish history. For the talk that day had little to do with deer and the result of the chase. The toast was to a bigger prize. On the following morning, September 6th, 1715, on a knoll in the Castleton of Braemar, the Earl of Mar raised the standard for James Francis Edward Stuart, the Old Pretender. On one side it carried the Royal arms of Scotland, the thistle of Scotland on the other, and across the streamers ran the defiant mottoes, "For our King and oppressed Country" and "For our Lives and Liberties."

There is a lingering irony in the fact that posterity has buried this ill-starred episode in Scotland's history beneath the clatter of tea cups and the chatter of tourists in the lounge of a Braemar hotel. This is the actual spot where the Earl of Mar raised the Royal standard in the '15 Rebellion. Outside the hotel a plaque erected by the Deeside Field Club commemorates the event. It was put there in 1953, which, as the wording on the plaque pointedly reminds us, was the Coronation Year of Elizabeth, Queen of Scots. September is still the month of the hunt on the Braes o' Mar, but now the "nobility and gentry of the kingdome" take fat fees for deer-shooting on the Deeside estates and many of the stalking tenants are wealthy visitors from Germany. The German carlies are still with us.

They still come over the Cairnwell and through the glens for a great September gathering, with the skirl of bagpipes echoing over Creag Choinnich and the bonnets and plaids bright and bonny in the village where "Bobbin' Jock" mustered his forces. On the first Saturday in September as many as 20,000 people descend on this tiny Deeside community to see the Braemar Gathering, an event which differs little from any other Highland Games but owes much of its popularity to the attendance of the Queen and other members of the Royal Family. Royal patronage goes back to Queen Victoria's first visit to the Gathering in 1848. In those early years, one of the highlights was a race up Creag Choinnich and Victoria thought "it looked very pretty to see them run off in their different coloured kilts." Pretty it may have been, but one of her ghillies was brought to her spitting blood. After that the hill race was discontinued.

Braemar sits between Creag Choinnich, east of the Water of Clunie, and Morrone (2,891 ft.) on the west. The latter, which takes its name from the Gaelic "Mor Sron," meaning Big Nose, is more popular with the tourists, partly because a hill indicator built there points the way to the mighty peaks of the Cairngorms. But lumpy little Creag Choinnich points the way to the past. It may not be the most impressive of hills, for it is only 1,764 ft. in height, but as I climbed up to where the wind had made skeletons of the trees around its bald pate I thought of how it had cradled so much history in its lap. Once, King Kenneth II had watched the hunt from this crag, and this was where the first hill race was held nine centuries ago, when Malcolm Canmore rewarded the winner with a purse of gold.

Down in that busy village the Old Pretender had cast the dice for "life and liberty" on that doomed September day in 1715, and on the slope below me, overlooking Braemar Castle and the haugh by the river, there was a reminder of the last and most famous of the Jacobite Risings. Here, in 1829, a cairn was built by the Redcoats to mark their long stay on Deeside after the defeat of Prince Charles, an occupation that lasted from 1748 to 1831. The cairn is crumbling now and the inscription on it barely readable—"Erected by Edwin Ethelston Ensgn 25 Regiment AD 1829." Perhaps, all those years ago, he had thought it would last for ever, for they had built it well, as tall as the tallest man in the regiment. Sitting there by the cairn, just as Ensign Ethelston did a century and a half ago, I could see a scattering of pygmy people moving about the grounds of the castle, visitors no doubt, mouths agape as they passed the yett at the entrance to the castle, or peered down into the Laird's Pit, or stared at the piece of plaid given by "Colonel Anne" to Prince Charles.

To the west of the castle I could see the kirkyard where old Dubrach was buried and I wondered what the oldest rebel would have said about it all. Peter Grant was 110 years old when he died and he remained an unrepentant rebel, declaring that if he had youth on his side and was wanted he would "fecht Culloden ower again." He was given a fitting farewell, for 300 people turned up for his funeral, although there were few present who could remember anything about the '45 Rebellion. That was five years before the Redcoats built their cairn. When they lowered Dubrach's coffin into the grave a piper played "Wha widna fecht for Charlie's richt?" It was a fine piece of Highland insolence.

Creag Choinnich is at the crossroads of Mounth passes on upper Deeside. The old ford and ferry road which took drovers and other travellers across the Dee is still there, adjoining the kirkyard, but it is heavily overgrown with grass and thistles and flotsam thrown up by the river. Curiously, it is still used as a ferry road, for the people who have Inverchandlick as a summer cottage cross from the north bank in a rubber dinghy, saving themselves a long trip by the Bridge of Dee or by Mar Lodge and Victoria Bridge. Near the ferry crossing you can still see the stepping stones where the ford was used by cattle and carts, and from Creag Choinnich[1] you can follow the line of their journey up the Bealach Dearg to the Avon and Tomintoul. On the west is the route to Glen Tilt, or up Glen Lui and Glen Derry to the Lairig Ghru and the Lairig an Laoigh, while from the east comes the A93, modern successor to Caulfield's military road.

Then there is the Cairnwell road itself, branching uphill away from the centre of the village, beyond the Invercauld Hotel, which stands where "Bobbin' Jock" raised the Standard. After the completion of Wade's road, building began on the road through Glen Clunie, starting at the historic heart of the village, by the Bridge of Clunie. The bridge marks the dividing line between the two hamlets which once existed separately and which now form the modern Braemar; Castleton on the east bank of the Clunie and Auchendryne on the west. The name of the former came from the ancient Castle of Kindrochit, which dominated the

[1] Kenneth's crag.

important Mounth route, as well as the other passes, just as Braemar Castle did in a later age.

What is left of the castle can be found on the east bank of the Clunie, near the bridge linking the two communities, but the only thing to distinguish it from any other derelict site is a flagpole which I was told was never used. I half expected to see one, for a Royal Standard flew there six centuries ago when Robert II sanctioned the building of a fortalice on Clunieside. It fell into disuse early in the 16th century, but the reasons are unclear, although one story has it that when plague broke out in the castle, cannons were taken over the Cairnwell from Atholl and turned on it until it crumbled into rubble and dust. By 1618 it had become a complete ruin and a decade later the Earl of Mar had started building Braemar Castle as a counter to the growing power of the Farquharsons. Some seventy years after that, in 1689, the Black Colonel, John Farquharson of Inverey, descended from Creag Choinnich and burned it to the ground. Both castles were of vital strategic importance, particularly for the traffic that came up Glen Clunie from the south, but in 1750 Major William Caulfield changed the approach to Braemar when he drove his military road up from Perth to Fort George.

To retrace Caulfield's road you have to start on the west bank of the Clunie, opposite the Castle of Kindrochit, and follow the course of the river to the golf course. Beyond the golf course it swings round the farm of Balintuim, but there are traces of the original track going up the back of the farm, past a ruined cottage and down to the river bank. After Balintuim the road clings closely to the Clunie, so that you are walking parallel with the traffic heading up the modern road on the other side of the river, passing Auchallater Farm, where a track goes south-east through Glen Callater to the Tolmounth. The old road links up with the A93 at Fraser's Bridge, a double-arched bridge spanning the Water of Clunie, shown on Taylor and Skinner's map simply as East Bridge.

The road ahead climbs up between the Cairnwell and the Glas Maol, both "Munro" mountains over 3,000 ft. high, lifting the ancient pass out of the haughlands of Mar and thrusting it down into the heart of Atholl. Long before the Hanoverians dreamed of a new highway to the north, long before John Erskine rode south with his "blue bonnets" and defiant streamers, this road was a major route over the Grampians. They called it Carnavalage, the name given to it by Sir James Balfour of Denmylne when he listed eleven main routes over the mountains from the River Tay to the River Dee. The relics of the martyred St Andrew came over this pass to be received by Angus I MacFergus, King of the Picts, who built a chapel to Scotland's patron saint in the Dee valley. The drovers used the route on their way to the markets in the south, while the caterans watched and waited in the hills. In a later age, a coach called "The Braes o' Mar" rattled up the Cairnwell pass on its way to Perth; then came the first spluttering, steaming motor car. To-day an endless conveyor belt of traffic streams over what is still the highest motor road in Britain.

The Cairnwell mountain gave its name to the pass, just as it now gives it to the ski centre which brings thousands of visitors to its slopes each winter, but in the process it has suffered, for it is not a place in which to look for solitude or beauty. During the summer, when the chair-lift goes churning up to the top, giving passing tourists a quick, ephemeral "taste" of the high places, it is even more tawdry. The road rises to a height of 2,199 ft. at the Cairnwell and cars still draw in at the car park to cool their protesting radiators after climbing up the steep gradient from the Devil's Elbow. The Elbow, a 1 in 5 double hairpin bend that once struck terror into the hearts of north-bound motorists, has long since been straightened out, but it is still a hard pull to the top.

Travelling south, the modern pass stretches away towards Glenshee and you come down out of the clouds like one of the hang-gliders that operate at the Cairnwell, dropping their rainbow colours onto a landing patch north of the chair-lift There are jigsaw pieces of old roads and new on both sides of the Cairnwell, some going back to the days when Caulfield's soldiers hacked their way over the Mounth. The old military road can be followed from the Allt a' Gharbh Choire on the Mar side of the Cairnwell. It runs south by the Cairnwell burn almost to the ski lift and from the car park goes down into the valley until it rises again beyond the point where the Elbow hairpin was sited. Farther on, it goes left again, passes under the remains of a single-arched bridge and swings back to the main road. The Wade roads were designed to bring peace to the Highlands and the darkening shadow of Meall Odhar, east of the Cairnwell, is a reminder of its most famous battle, the

The Wade bridge in the Cairnwell pass.

Battle of Cairnwell, fought between caterans from Argyll and men from Deeside and Glenshee. The people of Mar, Glenshee and Glenisla joined forces to destroy the intruders, but the Glenisla men brought shame on themselves by deciding it was "best to sleep with a hale skin" and keeping a safe distance on the slopes of Meall Odhar.

The caterans or reivers were a plague on the land. They were sometimes called "cleansers" because of the clean sweep they made on their raids, lifting anything from a single "nolt" to a complete herd. Early in the 17th century more than two and a half thousand cattle were driven off in a raid on Glenshee, Glenisla and Strathardle by raiders from Glen Garry, and the Cairnwell Pass was again the scene of a bitter clash between the caterans and their victims. There was little that the authorities could do about cateran activities because the clan chieftains were responsible for their tenants and seldom appeared to answer charges. The Earl of Argyll was charged in 1591 with raiding Glenisla, when his son "murthorit all the inhabitants they could lay hands on and took much spulzie (spoils), including a grit nowmor of nolt, schiep, etc." The records show that none of the accused appeared before the Privy Council, who pronounced them rebels.

The caterans travelled in the "silence of the night," coming out of the grey dawn armed to the teeth to look for "nolts" or spulzie. They were "lodden in form of war," carrying hagbuts, firelocks, targets and pistols. They came from the north and the west, from upper Argyll, Badenoch and Lochaber, riding through the gloomy passes of the Cairngorms or over the Mounth from Glen Garry. Those who looked for loot in Glenshee or Deeside or in Glenisla and the pastures farther east travelled up Glen Tilt and took a route cutting directly across the Mounth passes. This took them from the Tilt valley to Glen Lochsie, where they went over the northern shoulder of Ben Gulbeine or Gulabin, which stands above the Spital of Glenshee, to Rhidorrach, the highest shieling on the Cairnwell road. From Rhidorrach they crossed the eastern ridge into Glen Brighty, which opened the way by Tulchan to Glenisla.

This route, which was still known last century as the Caterans' Road, also touched Glen Taitneach, which branches off Glen Lochsie about a mile and a half from the Spittal of Glen Shee. Glen Taitneach was the home of Cam Ruadh (the lame red-haired man), a well-known archer called Grant, who played an important role in the Battle of the

Cairnwell. He had taken an oath not to shed blood for twenty-four hours and when the fighting got under way he was helpless, but the moment came when he was free of the oath and took a deadly toll of the caterans. The kinsmen of one of the cateran chiefs killed in the battle returned to Glen Taitneach a few weeks later to seek revenge. They asked the way of an old cattle herd, a half-witted loon wrapped in a ragged plaid, and offered to show him how to use a bow if he told them where to find Cam Ruadh. The herdsman fitted an arrow to the thong and announced "I am the Cam Ruadh!". The cateran fled.

It was in Glen Taitneach, too, that Donald Mor Campbell, the chief of the Lochaber caterans, was slain. For many years he and his men terrorised the people of Glenshee, Glenisla, Glen Clunie, Glen Prosen and Lintrathen, but time ran out for him in 1665, the year before the Battle of the Cairnwell. The Lochaber reivers were travelling home from raids on Lintrathen, Glen Prosen and Glenisla, driving their cattle through Glen Brighty and over Craig Leacach to Glen Beag. From there they went by Ben Gulabin to the foot of Glen Taitneach, halting at the foot of the fairies' burn, Coire Sidh. Here, a party of Ogilvies caught up with them, approaching their camp in the heavy morning mist. In the brief encounter that followed Donald Mor was slain. He was buried in the Spittal churchyard and the expenses of his funeral were paid by "Little Eppie", wife of the host at the Spittal Inn. She got her money back by selling Donald's clothes and silver buttons.

The old pass still saw spasmodic acts of violence after the reivers had vanished from the hills. The aftermath of Culloden brought two murders that became part of the Cairnwell legend. One was the killing of a Captain Millar, who was shot dead while going over the pass with his wife. The killer, Donald Dubh of Clan McKenzie, rode as far as Rhidorrach with the weeping widow and then disappeared into the hills. He was later captured and imprisoned in Braemar Castle, but escaped. The second murder, three years after Culloden, was that of a Sergeant Arthur Davies, who was in charge of a military post in Glen Dee. The sergeant and his men had arranged to meet the Spittal detachment at the head of Glen Clunie but on the way there Davies broke away on his own to stalk deer. He was never seen again.

This is a land of ghosts. The names come out of the past to haunt you. You can imagine the reivers riding by Rhidorrach on their way to Glen Brighty and the pastures of the Isla, and the fairy burn still glints and sparkles on its way past Ben Gulabin, where Donald Mor Campbell met his end. The cattle lift their heads to look at you just as they did when the caterans came "out of the cloud and silence of night" to spirit them away to the west. The sheep are still there, speckling the green-brown slopes and nibbling their way along the edge of the pass that once was a cart-track and is now a wide smooth highway to the south. Step away from it and you are back in a timeless world that had remained relatively undisturbed down through the years.

The sheep are a constant reminder of the old way of life and there are times when they stop the traffic and the clock with it. But some things have changed. The Rev. T. D. Miller, in *Tales of a Highland Parish,* told of a practice that disappeared many years ago, when women milked the ewes after the lambs had been taken from them and turned the milk into cheese.

Over two centuries ago any children in Glenbeg went for a month in summer to the moorland pastures, where the ewes grazed, to milk them. They carried all their supplies on the backs of ponies and lived in roughly-built shielings. They slept in bed-boxes which had mattresses filled with heather, and their staple diet was oatmeal porridge and ewes' milk. They also helped with the sheep-clipping.

The shepherds' principal market place was Lanark Moor and the journey from the Highlands to Lanark was done on foot. The flock-masters and their shepherds walked to Edinburgh from Glenshee, a distance of eighty miles, in two stages, and after spending a night there completed the final fifty-mile stage to the sales. Nowadays it seems an incredible

Tommy and his wife. Two of the sculptures near the summit of the Cairnwell pass.

journey, but the old herdsmen and shepherds literally took it in their stride, and it may be that in this idle-food-guzzling age, when no one can walk the length of a street without a car, there are lessons to be learned. Mr Miller thought it was "very conclusive proof" that plain fare contributes to length of life, and he quoted the example of Donald Ramsay, one of a family who lived at Cronaherie, in Glenshee, for several generations. Donald's maxim was "Drink little that you may drink long", and he was also a believer in the "early to bed" adage, for he turned in at nine o'clock at night and was up at five next morning. He died in 1842 at the age of ninety-two.

Donald Ramsay was born the year after Sergeant Davies disappeared. The date of the murder was 28th September, 1749, and in that same month Major William Caulfield reported that 300 men of General Guise's regiment of foot—Davies' regiment—had completed a stretch of the new military road from Braemar to the Spittal of Glenshee. Their aim was to link up with a party of Welch Fusiliers working north from Blairgowrie and they reached a point four miles south of the Spittal. Donald's father, who was born in 1710 and could remember seeing the Jacobites march down Glen Beag under the Earl of Mar in 1715, must have watched the Hanoverian road-building with mixed feelings, for his family had always supported the Stuart cause. He himself had defied the Government troops when they commandeered his hay and made him carry it across the river on a plank, the only method of crossing the water before the building of the bridge. Ramsay was followed across the plank by two or three soldiers and when he reached the bank he threw down the hay, jerked the plank into the air, and tumbled the King's men into the river. He is said to have escaped up Ben Gulabin, but what happened later is not recorded.

The old, arched bridge that replaced that plank is still there, quaintly out-of-place in the rush of traffic that spills down the brae from Glen Beag. Before coming to it I passed a sign just off the road, with its face turned away from the traffic, the reason being that it was a "Road Closed" sign used when winter snows block the Cairnwell Pass. There is a modern hotel to cater for you if this happens nowadays and it is the successor to the hospice or inn that sheltered travellers going over the Mounth many centuries ago. There was a hospice or hospital on both sides of the Cairnwell at one time, one in Glenshee and the other in Glen Clunie. A path at the south end of the bridge leads to Dalmunzie Hotel and Glen Lochsie, while a second path on the opposite side of the Shee Water strikes off to Glen Taitneach, the home of the Cam Ruadh.

The church and old kirkyard are also on the north side and on this site at one time there was a Chapel of Ease, where the Kirkmichael minister held a service once a month for Spittal folk who were unable to make the journey through the hills to the parish church. James Hogg, the Ettrick Shepherd, visited Glenshee at the beginning of last century and said he "never had seen a greater curiosity than the place of worship there." The door of the Chapel was locked, but Hogg stepped through one of the windows. The only seats were planks laid between a number of big stones; "things of great luxury," commented Hogg drily.

Mention of the Ettrick Shepherd's visit is made in *Tales of a Highland Parish,* but Hogg's description of the earthen floor was left out because it was "unpleasant and did not bear repetition." The floor, in fact, was covered with human bones, many of which had been gnawed by dogs. There were also hundreds of human teeth and in the north-west corner of the Chapel there was an open grave. The grave had apparently been dug for a man who had died in the Braes of Angus, but the mourners were unable to bring the corpse to the Chapel because of a violent storm. They buried him where he was and left the grave standing for the next corpse. The Chapel was pulled down when the church was built.

Across the road from the church a wooden bridge spans the Allt a' Ghlinne Bhig near the Old Spittal Farm. From here a path took me away from the stream and into the misty world of Celtic mythology. There was a stone circle on a high knoll on the left and, farther on, a deserted farmhouse below the Craig of Rinavey, turned its shuttered face towards Mount Blair. The farm is shown on some maps as Tomb Farm and the farmer was at one time called Fear Tulaich Diarmid, the laird of Diarmid's Hill. This is where Diarmid O'duine, the hero of one of the great Fingalian legends, is said to be buried.

The "military Road" follows the Shee Water past the farm of Finegand and, a little more than a mile ahead, a wood which hides the Clach-na-Coileach or Cock Stane. This is a massive stone standing on what is said to be the gathering place of the Clan MacThomas and the gate and path leading to it, along with an adjoining lay-by, were erected to the memory of Harold Edward McCombie of California, who died in 1968 at the age of seventy-three. The name McCombie is linked with the origins of the Cock Stane, for its story is said to go back to the time of John Mackintosh, McComie Mor, a legendary figure who owned Finegand. The Earl of Atholl's tax-gatherers had taken some poultry from a widow who lived near Finegand and when she complained to McComie he and his men pursued them, routed them, and took back the poultry. The cock immediately flew up on the stone and crowed triumphantly and the stone was known after that as Clach-na-Coileach. Clan MacThomas was connected with the 7th Laird of Mackintosh, who came to Glenshee from Badenoch in the 15th century.

Beyond the Cock Stane the road twists and dips past the B951, which leads round Mount Blair to the ruins of Forter Castle and Glenisla. South of Mount Blair the countryside softens and the brooding hills give way to farmland and woodland. The B950 branches off to Kirkmichael at Dalrulzion, which the Welch Fusiliers reached in 1749, when Guise's regiment took the military road down from Braemar to four miles below the Spittal. Four miles on is the Bridge of Cally and here, where the Black Water meets the River Ardle, Glenshee comes to an end. Together they form the River Ericht, which five miles farther south runs under the Brig o' Blair, linking Blairgowrie and Rattray. The two burghs became one in 1928 and to-day Rattray is a suburb of Blairgowrie, a town which sits on the hem of the Grampians.

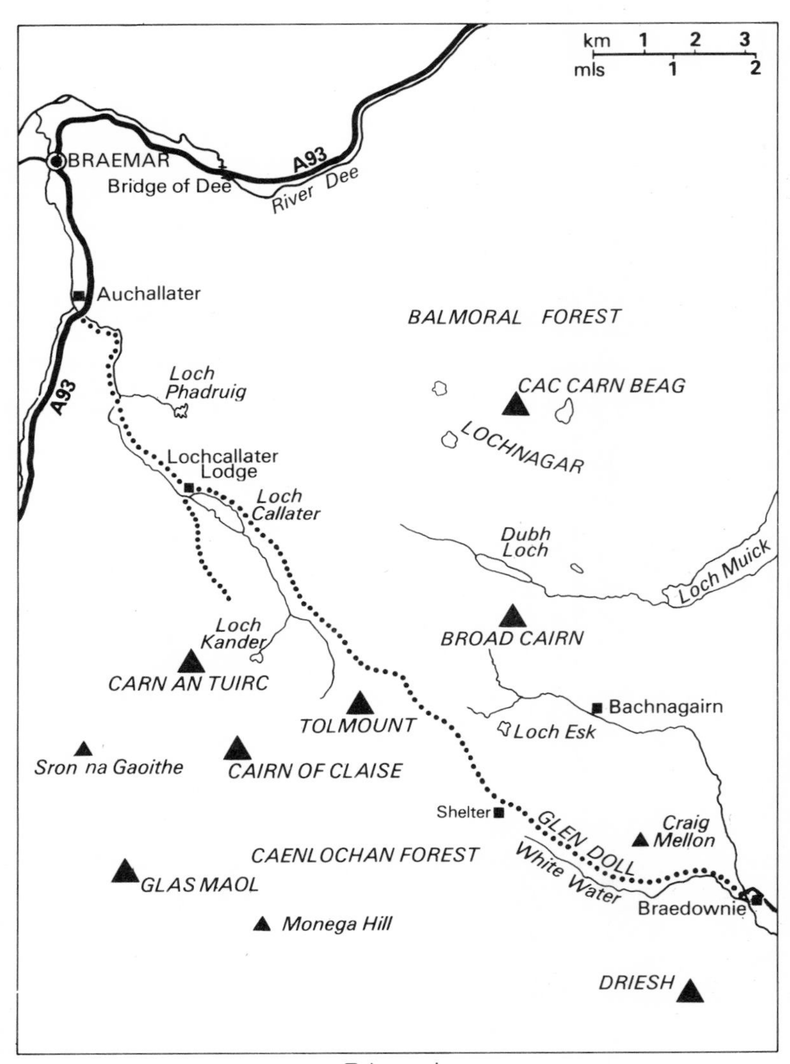
km 1 2 3
mls 1 2
BRAEMAR
A93
Bridge of Dee
River Dee
Auchallater
BALMORAL FOREST
Loch Phadruig
CAC CARN BEAG
LOCHNAGAR
Lochcallater Lodge
Loch Callater
Dubh Loch
Loch Muick
Loch Kander
BROAD CAIRN
CARN AN TUIRC
Bachnagairn
TOLMOUNT
Loch Esk
Sron na Gaoithe
CAIRN OF CLAISE
Shelter
GLEN DOLL
Craig Mellon
CAENLOCHAN FOREST
White Water
GLAS MAOL
Braedownie
Monega Hill
DRIESH

Tolmounth

14

Tolmounth

The Old Year died in a bitter bluster of wind and snow. On the first day of January, the five men strapped up their packs and set off from Braemar, heading up the Cairnwell Pass towards the sheep farm at Auchallater, where the Callater Burn disgorges itself into the Water of Clunie. That was their turning-off point, the start of a twelve-mile hike that was to take them along the icy rim of Loch Callater, up to the 3000 ft Tolmount, and across the barren plateau that led to Jock's Road and the descent to Glen Doll. For them, the reek and grime of the city were a long way off. They were all Clydeside men, members of the Universal Hiking Club in Glasgow, and they could see no better way to usher in the New Year than to breathe the clean air of the hills and feel the exultant sense of freedom that comes from being in the open spaces. Behind them, the radio crackled out a storm warning to climbers and skiers . . . .

Later that day the wind began to rise, blowing the dead leaves into great whorls on the outskirts of the village, rattling doors and windows, stirring the soft snow into a smoky veil on the slopes of Morrone. Higher up, where the old paths traced their fading lines across the Mounth, the gusts increased in force, and as daylight slipped away on the first day of the year a 70 mph gale was whipping the snow in the mountains into a near-impenetrable barrier. East of the Tolmount, the frozen footprints of the five hikers marked their route across the plateau, following a direct line to Jock's Road, then veering alarmingly off course. The men had lost their bearings.

Three days later, on January 4, searchers from Braemar

found their frozen footprints as they struggled across the plateau in the wake of the missing men, alerted by a friend who had arranged to pick them up at the youth hostel in Glen Doll. The searchers, lashed by blinding snow and a gale that cut through their heavy layers of clothing, came upon other signs of disaster, pieces of equipment discarded by the hikers as they fought desperately to reach the shelter of the climber's hut that stood at the south end of the plateau, almost on the edge of the descent to Glen Doll. Two large parties from Glen Clova were also out, searching the hillsides along Jock's Road, and a helicopter hovered over the area until forced away by the impossible conditions. They found the first body in a gully above Glen Doll, where the White Water drops down through precipitous ravines to the valley. By a cruel twist of fate, it lay only a few hundred yards from the climbers' hut. The other bodies were not recovered until later.

That was nearly twenty years ago, the first bleak days of January, 1959, but there are still grim echoes of the tragedy in the talk of hill-walkers who know and respect the moods of the Tolmounth Pass. It has never seemed to me to be a pass that you could dismiss lightly, and I cannot cross its windy, peat-strewn acres without seeing those frozen tell-tale footprints, stepping out ahead and then, suddenly, turning off the track and heading towards a path of no return. Long years ago, when the drovers herded their cattle through Glen Callater and over the Tolmounth to Angus, the Glen Clova poetess, Dorothea Maria Ogilvy, wrote a poem which carried a line that stuck in my memory. It was there when I set off from Braemar to cross this ancient Mounth pass. It filtered down through the years, down from the high peaks and the dark corries—"I daur ye gang yer lane till dark Glen Doll".

There is a gentle introduction to Glen Callater. You leave Glen Clunie at Auchallater Farm, following the bend of the Callater Burn into the widening valley, hemmed in by high hills and with little to relieve the grey-green monotony except the weird shapes of the river rock, jagged splinters of stone contrasting sharply with long, flat tabletops beaten smooth by the endless motion of the stream. They look as if they had been chipped by a sculptor whose chisel had run riot. Maybe the little people were responsible, for half-way up the glen there is supposed to be a green hillock inhabited by the "little folks". Professor William MacGillivray, the Aberdeen naturalist who roamed these hills and glens well over a century ago, reported in 1850 that a man still living had seen fairies dancing on the hillock, with a piper playing to them.

Myth, magic and miracles breed easily in these lonely straths. Near the little people's hillock a stream runs down to the Callater Burn from Loch Phadruig, which, like Creag Phadruig, takes its name from a priest called Patrick, who is also linked with Carn an t-Sagairt, or Cairn Taggart, a well-known landmark on the Callater approach to Lochnagar. Cairn Taggart is known as the Priest's Mountain, and if you see rain clouds looming over it as you make your way through Glen Callater you can blame Peter the Priest. Legend has it that at one time the Braemar district was held in the grip of a frost that lasted into May and the people, desperate for a thaw, called on Padruig to help. He led them to a holy well at the edge of Loch Callater and there he prayed until the ice melted and the water trickled from the well. Then, as he prayed on, clouds gathered over Carn an t-Sagairt, the frost loosened its hold on the land, and the thaw set in.

The Priest's Well is marked by a large boulder near Callater Lodge, which was once a keeper's house, and from there the route lies along the lochside towards the distant Tolmount. Loch Callater is about a mile long and covers about 70 acres. Its greatest depth is 30 ft. Nearly half of it is 10 ft deep and I have watched a great skein of geese drop down on to its frozen surface. Nan Shepherd, the Deeside authoress, wrote an article many years ago in which she described coming down from the Tolmount plateau to Loch Callater and seeing an 80-strong formation of geese flying low over the water. Her observant eye noticed how the leading birds bunched together when the first bird moved out of position, then a new leader moved up to take its place, a change that took place four

Loch Callater lodge.

times. "The birds faded into the clouds like an embodiment of mystery", wrote Miss Shepherd.

A raw wind blew down the loch as I set off from Loch Callater Lodge. Above me, on the left, two hill-walkers were pushing their way slowly up the path that led to Cairn Taggart. On the other side of the loch I could see a track that Queen Victoria had followed when she rode down the glen and over the hills to Caenlochan and the Cairnwell Pass. At the head of the loch the path went twisting through a flat expanse of wet and boggy terrain, sliced through at regular intervals by streams tumbling down from the Devil's Kitchen on Creag an Fhir-shaighde. The path, difficult to follow in places, rose above the Allt an Loch as it approached the mouth of Corrie Kander. High on the rim of the corrie I could see a clutter of stones which marked the ruin of an old shieling.

Beyond Loch Kander I stuck to the edge of the stream and about two miles from Loch Callater came upon a Scottish Rights of Way Society sign saying "Public Footpath to Glen

Doll by Jock's Road". Here the path cut away from the main stream, following a smaller stream uphill until it crossed it and struggled towards the west side of the Tolmount. There were a few small cairns marking the way and, near the top, a number of old metal fence posts that had been used as markers. Far behind and below I could see the glinting line of the Allt an Loch and the long stretch of Loch Callater. I rested there, watching the clouds swirling lazily around the Tolmount. In front of me was the trek over the plateau to Jock's Road and the downhill jog to Glen Doll.

As you head over the plateau the path keeps well up the slope on the left, away from the course of the White Water, and if you go to the top of the ridge you can see Loch Esk glittering in the hollow below, its waters going down to Bachnagairn and Glen Clova. Further over, unseen, is Loch Muick, guarded by the Broad Cairn and Lochnagar. Hill walkers coming up from Braedownie occasionally do a round trip by Bachnagairn or cut across to the Broad Cairn and go down to Deeside by Glenmuick. This is the flat roof of the Mounth, spreading westwards to the Cairnwell Pass.

It was while standing on the ridge that I looked across the White Water to Tom Buidhe and saw a dark mass spread across the hill as if a large part of it had been afforested. Then, like Shakespeare's Birnam Wood, it moved. Lifting my binoculars, I found myself gazing at the largest herd of deer I have ever seen, hundreds of them, moving up the hill in a tight mass, with a few stragglers taking up the rear. As they reached the top the leader turned and stood apart, surveying the scene like Landseer's Monarch of the Glen. They moved in an incredibly closely-knit formation, almost like a single unit, and I wondered if this was some defensive stratagem; or even, if you are to believe one 400-year-old theory, an offensive tactic.

The 16th century prelate and historian John Spottiswood recorded that Queen Mary "took the sport of hunting the deer in the forest of Mar and Atholl in the year 1563", and a contemporary report described how she was warned that a herd could come "as thick as possibly they could, and make their way over our bodies to the mountain that is behind us". The Queen, not surprisingly, was a little alarmed, and shortly afterwards was given a frightening taste of what could happen when a large herd stampeded towards a party of hunters.

The leading deer in the herd they were watching was startled by a Royal dog and the whole herd took flight, heading towards a line of Highlanders. They, it was said, knew "the power of this close phalanx of deer, and at speed", and the only way they could save their lives was to fall flat on the ground and let the herd run over them. Many were injured and the Queen was told that "two or three had been trampled to death". The death of a few Highlanders was obviously not considered important enough to halt the Royal sport. The chase went on and it was reported that "three hundred and sixty deer were killed, five wolves, and some roes, and the Queen and her party returned to Blair delighted with the sport".

The toll seems immense, but it becomes more acceptable if you are prepared to believe the fact that before the great hunt two thousand Highlanders were sent out to gather the deer from Mar, Badenoch, Moray and Atholl. They spent several weeks driving the deer—"besides roes, does and other game"—to the "appointed glen", and when Queen Mary and the "great concourse of the nobility, gentry and people" were assembled two thousand animals were ready for the slaughter. There is little doubt that these ancient deer hunts were mammoth affairs, but the Queen Mary "shoot" strained even the credulity of William Scrope, author of *Days of Deer-Stalking in the Scottish Highlands* (1894), a writer who could never have been described as a master of under-statement. He was highly sceptical of the claim that 2000 men could muster 2000 deer in the mountains, but he grudgingly accepted the toll of 360 deer. "If a hundred couple of fierce and swift dogs were let loose, which we are told was not unusual, they must have pulled down a great many hinds and calves, though probably but few harts". Unusual or not, the thought of 400 dogs descending on 2000 red deer is enough to stretch imagination to breaking point.

There is little doubt that dogs played an important part in the old deer hunts. More than 200 years before Scrope's work was published, John Taylor wrote about the use of "a hundred couple of strong Irish greyhounds" at a hunt given by the Earl of Mar in 1618. They were "let loose as occasion serves upon the heard of deere". Here again are statistics to stagger us; fourteen or fifteen hundred men and horses, five or six hundred men and horses, five or six hundred of Tinchels or beaters driving the deer towards the hunters in herds of two, three or four hundred, and a two-hour tally of "fourscore fat deere". As well as dogs, the hunters used guns, arrows, dirks and daggers to dispatch their unfortunate quarry.

Taylor liked this sort of sport so much that he composed two sonnets about it.

> Through heather, moss, 'mongst frogs, and
> bogs, and fogs,
> 'Mongst craggy cliffs, and thunder-battered hills,
> Hares, hinds, bucks, roes, are chased by
> men and dogs,
> Where two hours hunting four score fat deer kills.

This sort of carnage gave way to a more gentlemanly slaughter in later years. Scrope reported that in Victorian times the deer in the Forest of Mar were "for the most part killed by stalking, and not by driving them to passes, or coursing them with dogs, except when wounded".

The excitement of the deer-hunt, as well as the taste of that costly delicacy, venison, to-day brings an ever-growing army of overseas visitors willing to pay for the privilege of shooting on the estates of Scottish nobles and lairds. Scrope himself regularly sent venison to Sir Walter Scott and on one occasion the reply came in a letter carrying the lines—

> Thanks, dear Sir, for your venison, for
> finer or fatter
> Never roam'd in a forest, or smoked
> in a platter.

The long bows and forked arrows, the harquebusses and Lochaber axes, have gone . . . now Land Rovers carry the eager sportsmen to the high tops, travelling on bulldozed tracks which scar the hillsides. Those who once owned these immense acres jealously guarded their property and it took long and complicated legal argument to establish the right of ordinary people to cross the Mount by the old paths. I would not have been walking the Tolmounth had it not been for a lawsuit in 1888 between the Scottish Rights of Way Society and Duncan Macpherson of Glen Doll. It was fought in the Court of Session and in the House of Lords and it finally established the Glendoll Right of Way.

In the end, Nature has a way of asserting itself. It takes something like the Tolmounth tragedy of 1976 to remind us that the rights of passage often lie elsewhere. When I stood on the ridge above Loch Esk I was looking down on a scene where the last act was played out in a drama that began when three Dundee University students, one a girl, set out from Braedownie to cross the Tolmounth to Braemar in March, 1976. The alarm was raised when one of them, turning back for help, staggered into the youth hostel at Glen Doll. High on the plateau a blizzard obliterated the tracks of his companions and the hopes of the searchers. The missing couple, who were to be married later that year, were finally found huddled together in a single survival bag, covered by six inches of snow, 30 yards from where their rucksacks had been found earlier in the week.

Farther on, just before the path dipped down by Jock's Road to Glen Doll, I came upon a large stone on which a metal plaque had been fixed. It carried a simple message, R.I.P., and had been put there by the Universal Hiking Club of Glasgow in memory of the five members of the club who had died there early in 1959. Close to it was a climbers' bothy made from stones, beams, turn and corrugated iron. It was the successor to the wooden hut near which the body of the first hiker had been found by the rescue party from Glen Doll. As I stood there, with the sun shining out of a clear blue sky, it

The bothy on Jock's Road, successor to the wooden hut near which the Glasgow hillwalkers perished.

was difficult to imagine the nightmare of wind and snow that had struck them down as they crossed the plateau. Nevertheless, not far back along that path I had unwittenly taken the same steps that had probably led them to disaster.

Half-way across the Tolmounth, between Tom Buidhe and Loch Esk, the track becomes difficult to follow and at one point I had strayed down from the ridge to the course of the White Water. The few cairns that mark the route brought me back to the path, but in bad weather they would be difficult to follow. Hill walkers coming up from Braedownie use the stream as a guide to the Tolmount in thick weather, but experts warn against using this route in reverse during the winter or in misty conditions. The danger is that you will follow the course of the stream down into the ravines that lie below Craig Maud.

Even sticking to the path there is a temptation to veer towards the stream, for the recognised way, as you approach it, seems to lead to a dead-end. In fact, it curves round to cross a side stream and swings back towards the White Water before heading straight downhill. The first of the Glasgow walkers was found on the slope to the right of the climbers' bothy, and it is believed that he took the wrong turn. Two of my newspaper colleagues, David King, former assistant news editor of the "Evening Express", Aberdeen, and Gordon Bisset, the picture editor, were covering the story of that grim search twenty years ago and both have vivid memories of how they climbed up Jock's Road with the search party, lashed by snow and wind, and came upon the first body. Steps had to be cut in the snow to get it out of the gully and Gordon Bisset still has the stark picture of the rescuers making their way down the hill to Glen Doll.

David remembers that the RAF mountain rescue team set a cracking pace. Snow was falling, the wind was in their faces and when a call went out for volunteers to haul the stretcher sled Gordon took one of the early stages, with David carrying his camera case, and then they swopped over. The snow was lying six to eight inches deep on the higher ground and, because of the steepness of the path, the wind and the snow, another newspaper reporter from Dundee passed out. They had what David called "three gut-wrenching miles" up the hill to the hut and when they got there someone gave him a piece of chocolate and he had to go outside and to be sick. This is how he remembers the events that followed—

"I was wearing a tweed sports jacket over the top of a windcheater. The snow had melted on it and then frozen into beads on the individual hairs. On my feet I had ankle-length rubber boots and the deep snow had poured in and melted, so that I was sloshing about in the water inside the boots. Word went up that they had found one of the bodies and we went out to give them a hand. It was the body of the youngest and least experienced member of the group and ironically he had almost made it. He was within a few hundred yards of the hut. His body had been found face down in the snow, with his left hand thrown up under his face, as if he had just lain down to sleep. Most of his gear seemed in place but his face was frost-blackened.

"I don't remember them actually cutting the steps down into the gully where the body lay. I do remember the biting cold and the snow showers sweeping over. It was the first time that the phrase 'chilled to the bone' took on real meaning for me. On the way down the stretcher sled threatened to develop a life of its own on the steep downhill stretches and it was a surprisingly slow, awkward business getting it down to base. Nowadays we would have seen very little of the action. The helicopter would have been in and out before we got there.

"It was claimed later that the party had set out despite a warning from the warden of the Braemar hostel about the weather, but it was said that they had been anxious to get through and meet up with the wife of one of the men. I was back down later when another body was found. One of the RAF mountain rescue men told me then that they had back-tracked along the trail of jettisoned gear, which seemed to me the most moving testimony of the desperation of their efforts to reach shelter. But the last of the bodies was not recovered until the snows had melted well into the spring. I've never been back to the Glen Doll area."

Jack Nicoll, a former journalist and now director of Leisure and Recreation for the Grampian area, wrote an article following the 1959 tragedy which examined the suggestion that all hiking and climbing should be banned. He admitted that he himself had been foolhardy on the same route, travelling from Glen Doll to Braemar, and he recounted his experience to show "that youth with half a reason will walk into the jaws of danger without a thought." It happened in April, 1951, with a good deal of snow on the ground after a long winter, and it began at Glen Doll Youth Hostel, where he had planned to set out with Bob McLeod, an experienced hill walker from Monifieth.

Ten minutes before they were due to leave heavy snow began to fall and McLeod refused to go, finally agreeing reluctantly when Jack said he would go on his own. They set off in the teeth of a bitter wind, snow falling thickly and lying up to 3 ft deep on the track. Once on the plateau they found the snow and wind unbearable and, after consulting map and compass, decided to veer right down Glenmuick rather than continue into the face of the storm. Having seen that awesome expanse of wilderness in fair weather, I marvel that they made it at all, but they finally reached the shores of Loch Muick and got into Ballater in the early evening. Now, in retrospect, he believed that he had been stupid, but he could understand why people did it, escaping from the monotony of the desk, facing the challenge of the unknown.

So, as he said, you have to make your own decisions, but standing by the bothy, not far from where the White Water tempts you to destruction, I couldn't help thinking the odds are on the mountains in this grim game. Inside the bothy, a snow shovel was perched against the wall, a last reminder that, before long, the winds would be rising again over the naked plateau and the first flakes of snow would come drifting down to cover the long, uncertain finger of the Tolmounth track. I ducked under the door and made my way towards the point where that sad cortege had made its way to the safety of the valley nearly twenty years before. In a few minutes the plateau was out of sight and I was looking south-east into the heart of "dark Glen Doll", where the great forest lands lie in the lap of the corries above Braedownie.

Jock's Road is the comparatively short length of track that curves away by the White Water tributary and acts as a loop between the main path and the plateau, but the whole of the route over the Tolmounth has become known by the name. There has never been any explanation of how it got it name, or if, in fact, there was ever a Jock at all. From the bothy it is an easy jog down to the edge of the forest, through a gate and on to the woodland path that takes you past a sign-post which says "Jock's Road—Braemar 14 miles". Soon you pass the Youth Hostel, a beautiful old house with yellow-ochre woodwork and white walls, and a little beyond it is Acharn, where another road goes west to Kilbo and Glen Prosen.

Then you are at Braedownie, lying in the shadow of the Scorrie of Dreish. Here is the end of the Tolmounth trail, and on the opposite side of the White Water, across from the picnic spot and camp site that brings scores of week-end trippers to the edge of the Mounth, the Capel path comes down from Moulzie, forming a junction for the routes that took travellers over the hills from Ballater and Braemar.

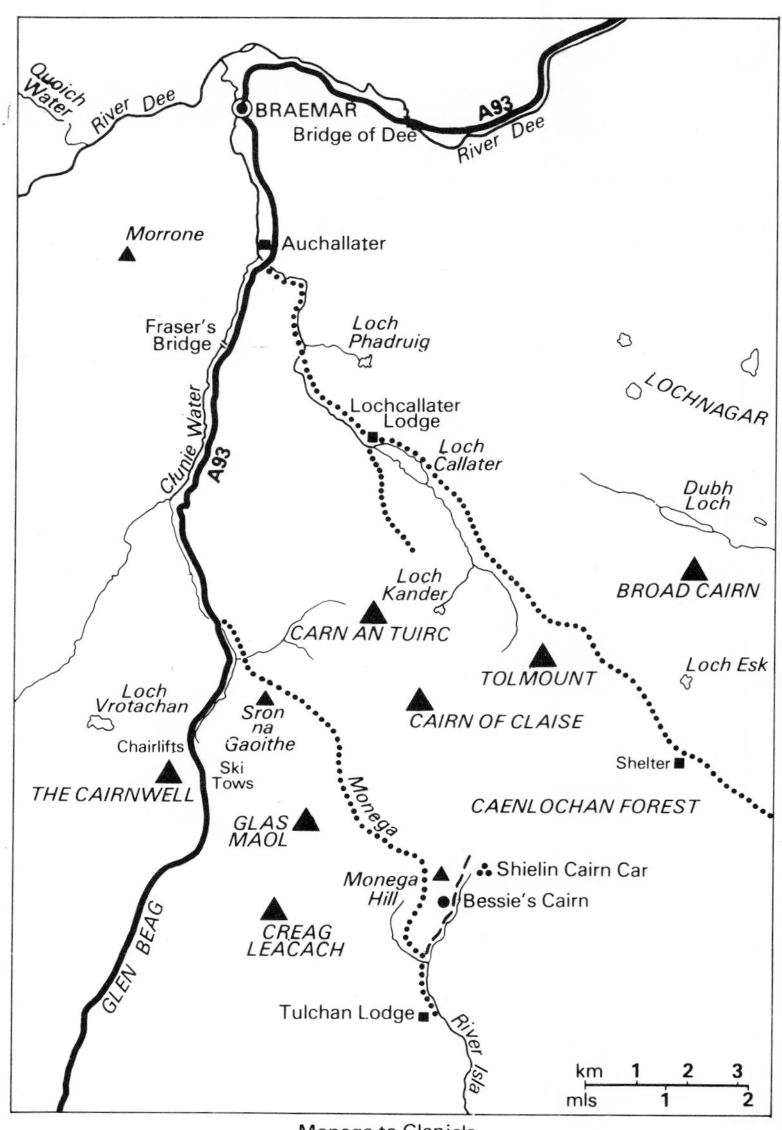

Monega to Glenisla

15

Monega

The old brig spanning the Cairnwell Burn below the rocky snout of Sron na Gaoithe leads to nowhere except the past. It marks the junction of two Mounth passes, one the road which Sir James Balfour of Denmylne said "layes from Glenshie to Castletoun in Brae of Mar", the other the Monega Pass, which crosses the Glas Maol at over 3000 ft and drops down into Strathmore. The old brig is known as the Seann Spittal Bridge, for at one time a hospice stood there, serving travellers going over the Mounth. "Ther was an Hospittal at Cairnwall (called Shean-Spittal or Old Hospital)", said the *View of the Diocese of Aberdeen*, "wher ther is a road over the Grampian hills. 'Tis said ther were several other such hospitals for poor travellers passing over Granzbin". To-day the only indication that the Monega Pass exists or did exist is a faded Scottish Rights of Way Society sign on the east side of the modern bridge less than half a mile away, where the headstreams of the Cluny Water meet and go north to Braemar, seven miles away.

The little-used road on which the sign stands runs parallel with the main road but goes only as far as the old brig, where the Allt Coire Fionn joins the Cairnwell Burn. From there the route lies through the heather, up the rough face of Sron na Gaoithe and round the eastern shoulder of the hill. As you climb away from the Seann Spittal Bridge the world below shrivels into insignificance and once on top you are walking on what is said to be the highest public path in the country. From the summit of Sron na Gaoithe a thinning track goes over the plateau on what would have been the line of the ancient pass. There are small cairns marking the way, many of them formed

The old bridge near the start of Monega pass.

from quartz stones. Cairn na Tuirc is on the left, separated from Sron na Gaoithe by the Allt a'Gharbh-choire, and Meall Odhar on the right, overlooking the Cairnwell.

The plateau I was on was only one corner of a tableland stretching away to Caenlochan Glen, east to Cairn of Claise and Corrie Kander, to Callater and Loch Muick, and over the Tolmount to Glen Doll and Glen Clova. The Monega Pass is a slender thread in this immense tapestry. It runs south-west over the spine of Sron na Gaoithe before turning towards the northern corrie of the Glas Maol, where a sharp, white crescent of snow lingers long after winter has eased its grip on the hills. It was near here that I met a lone hill-walker who had risen with the dawn to do a circuit from the Seann Spittal, climbing up to Carn an Tuirc and walking from there to Cairn of Claise and back by the Glas Maol. Three of the old counties—Aberdeen, Angus and Perth—meet at the Glas Maol, and the boundary line is marked by a dyke coming down from Cairn of Claise.

Beyond it, the ground slopes down to the northern corrie of Caenlochan Glen, which opens up in front as if someone had ripped the land apart to form a bowl for the source of the Isla. It is a deceptively gentle slope, for at the edge of the corrie the drop is deep and forbidding. I stood on the edge of it, looking down on its "hanging gardens", and thought of that remarkable man, Professor William MacGillivray, Professor of Natural History at Aberdeen's Marischal College, whose botanical explorations led him to Caenlochan in the early and mid-years of last century. He was the author of *The Natural History of Deeside and Braemar*, which was regarded as a valuable contribution to the natural history of the Cairngorms and the Grampians, but for me the fascination lay with the man, not the botanist.

He loved the hills. Even when he was in his fifties he could walk his students "into limp helplessness" when he led them on to the high peaks in search of rare plants, and there were few of his pupils who could have emulated his marathon hike to London in 1819. He was twenty-three years old, driven by a burning desire to see the precious bird collection in the British Museum but lacking the money to take him there. So he walked. He had ten pounds sterling in his pocket and with little else covered 500 miles in the first thirty days, taking a roundabout route by way of Braemar, Fort William and Inveraray. He reached London six weeks after setting out and he recorded that his trousers were ragged, his shoes worn down, and his stockings "fairly finished". He was on the doorstep of the British Museum the following day.

His "Natural History of Deeside and Braemar" was the record of a journey in the autumn of 1850 into what he called "the central Highlands of Braemar". It is regarded as a classic of its kind, but its interest goes well beyond its botanical references, for it lets us see the hills through the eyes of an early pioneer of hill-walking, one of those Victorian gentlemen who set off for the high tops as casually as if they were going for a Sunday stroll. I remember seeing some old photographs of Victorian naturalists on an outing, and they wore their bowlers, waistcoats and "Alberts" with suitable dignity. One even wore a top hat.

I like to think of Professor MacGillivray standing on the corrie of Caenlochan wearing a top hat and consulting his timepiece, but it is an improbable picture. Nevertheless, it was an intriguing thought that he probably stood near where I stood, looking out over that vast panorama of hill and valley—"a superb view all round", he wrote. He could see the peaks of Perthshire and, ranging northward and eastward, "the great mountains of Cairntoul, Braeriach, Ben-na-muic-dhui, Bennabuird, Benaun, and others". Closer at hand, he could see Lochnagar, which made "no great figure" from the Glas Maol viewpoint, and to the south and east lay Glenesk and the Clova hills, "their valleys beautifully verdant". He thought these hills contrasted strongly with the stony summits of the Aberdeenshire mountains, and he would have been aghast if he could have looked down on the Cairnwell to see the ugly scarring that marks its summit to-day.

There was another Victorian image in my mind on Monega. One of the illustrations in "Leaves from the Journal of Our Life in the Highlands" shows Queen Victoria and Prince Albert lunching at Caenlochan during an expedition to the glen in October, 1861. The napkins are spread, the hamper opened, and one member of the party appears to be opening a bottle of Scotch; the Queen liked her dram with a meal. The sketch shows them on what appears to be a plateau, with the mountains behind them, and an entry in the Queen's diary suggests that the picnic spot was on the edge of the north corrie. "We sat on a very precipitous place", she wrote, "which made one dread any one's moving backwards". It would never have done if her Majesty had stepped backwards and vanished into oblivion.

Like Professor MacGillivray ten years before, Victoria noted all the peaks she could see, marvelling at "the wonderful panorama which lay stretched out before us". She would no doubt have shared the Professor's view that he who finds no pleasure in gazing on the fair face of nature has a soul deadened to all that is capable of conferring true happiness.

Professor MacGillivray ignored the Monega Pass on his way up to the Glas Maol; his manuscript shows that he went "to the highest part of the glen, whence we could see down Glenshee, and then ascended the hill eastward". This would make his starting point at the Cairnwell on the main road, where the ski lift is now sited. There is a path from the Glenshee centre to Meall Odhar, from which you can climb up by Glas Maol to the Monega plateau. Queen Victoria, who admitted that "my head is so very ungeographical that I cannot describe it", came up from Loch Callater but returned by the route I had taken from the Seann Spittal.

The Queen got Duncan, her ghillie, to write the names down. It appears that the Royal party turned for home at Canness, on the east side of Caenlochan, and went over by Cairn Claise to Gharbh Choire. After crossing the "Month Eigie Road" to Glas Maol they went down to the Seann Spittal Bridge by "Fian Chory", which would have been Coire Fionn. The "Month Eigie Road" was clearly the Monega Road, but it raises interesting speculation on the origin of the word. The Gaelic "eag" means "notch" (there is an Eag Mhor or "big cleft" in the Braes of Abernethy) and Victoria's "Eigie" could well have been the Mounth or Mountain of the Cleft, which is a fairly accurate description of Monega Hill and the great notch of Caenlochan Glen.

Princess Helena was delighted with the trip, for, said Victoria, "it was the only really great expedition in which she accompanied us". When it was all over the Queen made the entry in her diary: "Alas! I fear our last great one!" Her words were prophetic, for two months later Prince Albert was dead and there were no more expeditions together. For that reason, the Monega expedition may have lain closest to her heart. She would always remember that bright, frosty morning when she rode along the path to Loch Callater on her pony, "Fyvie", the Prince Consort at her side, John Brown leading. When they reached the loch they cut south into the hills towards Carn an Tuirc, looking back over their shoulders to see the massive peaks of the Cairngorms clear and sharp against the cloudless sky. Below them, to the east, lay Loch Kander, "very wild and dark".

It was this remote mountain loch and its corrie that first drew me to the hills above Loch Callater. "Lonely, lonely, dark Loch Candor", it was called. The spelling has changed over the years, but the original was probably Loch Ceannmore and there was a theory that it came from Malcolm Canmore's connection with Braemar. The track leading to it leaves Loch Callater soon after crossing the bridge at the lodge, and as you climb uphill the view becomes incredibly beautiful. Behind me I could see Ben A'an, the first of the winter snow powdering its peaks and above them grey rolling banks of cloud that were soon to be chasing me across the Kander plateau. The village of Braemar was in a bowl of sunshine and Loch Phadruig came out of its hiding place above the glen.

To the west a Land Rover made its way slowly along a track that led to Glen Clunie, finally stopping on the long ridge of the hill to disgorge its party of grouse shooters at a line of gun butts. Directly ahead, tiny figures were silhouetted on top of the steep slope that reached up to the Kander plateau. There were a dozen or more, and then they disappeared. Away to the right, Cairnwell came into view. Behind me, the storm clouds were moving in fast from Ben A'an, blotting out Braemar, filtering into Glen Callater. The rim of the corrie came into sight, and then the dark blot of Kander itself, and as I reached the ruin that sits high above the loch the first bite of hailstones beat against my back. Moments later, a grey swirl of mist swept in over the corrie and I huddled down in the old shieling and waited for the storm to pass.

This old shepherd's bothy was "a very neat hut" when Professor MacGillivray visited Loch Kander and he mentioned that it had a place for a small fire, two stone benches and two recesses in a wall for pipes and other articles. One of the benches is still there and it was while sitting on it that I noticed the hole in the wall in which the pipes were stored. When the storm had passed I left my roofless but-and-ben and went outside to have a look at Corrie Kander, this "recess in the bosom of a mountain," as the Professor described it. The loch is over 2000 ft above sea level and Professor MacGillivray estimated that the depth of the corrie was about 800 ft. From my bird's eye perch I could see far down into the valley, where the path from Loch Callater began its climb to Jock's Road, and on the right was the summit of the Tolmount, marking the route of another Mounth pass. Away to the north-west were the snow-mantled Cairngorms and to the south the broad tableland that led by Carn an Tuirc and Cairn of Claise to the edge of the corrie at Caenlochan.

Queen Victoria went over this plateau—so flat, she said, that you could drive on it—until she reached Caenlochan; "a bonnie place," she recorded. There were patches of snow in the hollows when I crossed Cairn Tuirc. The Royal party made the journey at the same time of the year but it must have been colder, for they found ice thicker than a shilling. John Brown took it in his hand but failed to melt it. It was somewhere on this mountain rooftop that Prince Albert wrote on a bit of paper that they had lunched there, put it into a water-bottle, and stuck it into the ground. I wondered if it had ever been found, or whether it was still there, a Royal message cast adrift on what Victoria once described as "these seas of mountains."

The "Month Eigie Road," as Queen Victoria called it, crosses the county march and goes up the east side of the Glas Maol, keeping well away from the rocky western face of Caenlochan until it descends to the top of a deep gully at the foot of Little Glas Maol. Near here there is a small wooden hut used as a shelter. Beyond the hut the path is never far from the precipitous drop on the left. I could see it stretching away in front as I crossed Monega Hill and I could see, too, the distant glint of the Isla beyond the woods of Tulchan. The track downhill is boggy in places and it meets the road to the Linns and Dalhally a little to the north of a right-of-way sign pointing to the Monega Pass. This is probably where the path originally branched off the glen road. There is also a wooden

The wooden hut used by hillwalkers crossing the Monega.

sign with the faded lettering, "Footpath to Braemar by White ----," the last word being unreadable. It is probably White *Strone,* the hill on the opposite bank of the Isla. It faces directly on to the traveller going through the glen from the Linns and might have indicated a way over the hills by Cannes, at the top of the Glen.

Caenlochan is almost as impressive from the bottom as it is from the top. There is a cairn called Bessie's Cairn, said to mark the spot where someone's favourite dog was buried in 1852, and farther on is the ruin of a sheiling that once stood between the Caenlochan and Cannes streams. The building was always known as "The Sheilin" and it is a reminder of the days when cattle were driven up to this lush corner of the valley for the summer grazing. There are still signs in many glens of bothies or shiels built by herdsmen for their annual migration to the hills.

The Isla ripples through a history deeply entrenched in war and violence. The Romans are said to have passed the foot of the glen on their way north and there are traces of a Roman

Caenlochan from the Monega.

iter crossing the mountains from Blairgowrie by way of Mount Blair, which links the Isla and the Shee. The Roman route went by Braemar through Glen Gairn to Speyside. When Queen Victoria was returning from her trip to Caenlochan, she looked back on the distant hills above Glenisla and noted that this was "Lord Airlie's country." The Ogilvy who took the title of 1st Earl of Airlie received it from Charles I when he rode south with a troop to join the king at York after civil war broke out in England in 1639.

This was not only the start of a memorable chapter in Ogilvy history, but also the culmination of a bitter feud between the Ogilvys and the Campbells. Airlie's son, Lord James Ogilvy, staunchly Royalist like his father, refused to sign the National Covenant in the Earl's absence and the scene was set for a head-on confrontation between the Ogilvys and the Earl of Argyll, who was granted a commission of fire and sword by the the Committee of Estates.

Before it came, the figure of James Graham, Marquis of Montrose, was to pass fleetingly across the stage. Then a leading supporter of the Covenant, but with both his convictions and authority diminishing, he arrived at the gates of Airlie Castle to demand its surrender. His intentions may have been honest enough; indeed it was said that he was acting on the instruction of the Committee of Estates, but there was a feeling in Protestant circles that it was a ploy to save James Ogilvy, who had been a fellow-student at St Andrews. The castle was handed over to Montrose and he wrote to Argyll telling him he need not bother with Airlie. The letter was ignored. King Campbell's men, who had been cleaving a destructive path through Badenoch and Mar, marched on the castle and brought it to the ground before despoiling Ogilvy lands at Alyth, Lintrathen, Glenisla and Cortachy.

Following the Isla from the Linns, past Crandart, where McComie Mhor lived three centuries ago, the road divides on either side of the river and on the right bank a ruined castle faces down the glen. This is Forter Castle, built strategically where the passes to Monega and Glenshee strike north and west, and it was here, if one version of an old story is to be believed, that the young Lady Helen Ogilvy looked "o'er the high castle wa'" and saw Argyll's men approach to wreak the same havoc inflicted on Airlie Castle. They were led by Dougal Campbell of Inverawe, whose instructions from MacCailein Mhor were to "demolishe my Lord Ogilvy's house of Forther," and to "cast off the irone yettis and windows, and tak doon the roof." This they did and Forter stands to-day as it was after that vengeful assault on it in the summer of 1640.

Four years later the Earl of Airlie and his sons gave their arms and their loyalty to the man who first sought their surrender at Airlie Castle. The Marquis of Montrose, his Covenanting coat discarded, had raised the colours for Charles I and embarked on what was to become known as "The Year of Miracles." If Montrose's campaign was a heartbeat of hope to a withering Royalist cause, its arteries were the old passes of the Mounth. Through them, Graham led his Highland army to a series of victories that won him the reputation of military genius, and always, across the hills, the

Forter Castle.

brooding, thin-lipped Earl of Argyll waited for the day of reckoning. When it came after the Battle of Philiphaugh, the Marquis returned to the Grampian hills, seeking forlornly to raise fresh recruits in Mar and Angus, but on May 19th, 1646, while on Speyside, he received a letter from Charles: "You must disband your forces and go into France." Montrose broke camp and marched to Glenshee and at the end of July crossed the hills to Glenisla. At Rattray, Blairgowrie, while his soldiers wept, he said farewell to them and the old warlord, Airlie, and went into exile.

From Forter I took the route that Montrose had followed with what remained of his army, soldiers who, according to the Marquis' biographer George Wishart, were concerned only with "the fate that awaited their brave, successful and beloved general, torn from his king and country, from themselves and all true men." The way lay ahead by Brewlands Bridge to the Kirkton of Glenisla, where pony trekkers were heading out for the hills and youngsters were practising on dry ski slopes in preparation for the winter ahead. On the way to Dykends I passed, on the opposite side of the Isla, the farm of Peathaugh, once the home of James Winter, who won a measure of mortality in his fight with the caterans at the Water of Saughs. At the Dykends fork one road runs to the Loch of Lintrathen, but I went on a detour by the Bridge of Craigisla to look at the Reekie Linn, whose thundering waters can be heard long before you reach this well-known beauty spot. Here the Isla plunges through a narrow gorge and, dropping through another fall called the Slug of Achrannie, goes dancing past the rocky base of Airlie Castle.

The castle lies about half a mile west of a road which crosses the Melgam Water as it comes down from the Loch of Lintrathen to join the Isla. The hamlet Bridgend of Lintrathen slumbers on the edge of the great loch, undisturbed by the traffic which grumbles along the Kirriemuir road on the north side of the water. Yet it was a busy enough place at one time, marking the old route through Glenisla and housing an annual market that brought drovers and dealers over the Monega Pass from as far away as Badenoch and Strathspey. The market was moved to the Kirkton and disappeared from Bridgend towards the end of the 17th century. The road south follows the Melgam until it swings right towards Airlie Castle. The "bonnie house" was rebuilt in 1792 and is again the residence of the Earl of Airlie. East of it, a side road dips down the Brae of Airlie to a quiet backwater where travellers once stopped to refresh themselves on their way over the Mounth.

The Kirkton of Airlie lies in the hollow of the Brae, so that when you go down into it you feel as if you were dropping out of the present and into the past. It lies halfway between Kirriemuir and Alyth, nestling beside a burn which passes near the old church. In the kirkyard I found stones going back to the 16th and 17th centuries, the Latin lettering worn and unreadable. Past the church was a building with its back to the road, its roof falling in and its tiny windows no more than gaping holes. This was Cleikheim, once a drovers' inn, now a ruinous memory of the days when the great cattle herds came down from Deeside. From the Brae of Airlie the road turned east by the farm of Muirhouses and across the moor from which it took its name, to Kirriemuir.

There was also a market at Ellit, or Alyth, and if you took the direct route south from the Bridge of Craigisla you passed Barry Hill, where Queen Guinevere, wife of King Arthur, was said to be imprisoned after having a romance with a Pictish prince. Rattray, where the Marquis of Montrose disbanded his army, is about six miles to the west of Alyth, an unassuming little town which also has a link with the Covenanting years. It was there that General George Monck's troops captured leading members of the Committee of Estates during Cromwell's invasion of Scotland. Sir James Balfour of Denmylne, in his "Annales of Scotland", gives the date of this as August 28, 1651. "The Committee of Estaits, convened at Ellet, in Angus, wer betrayed to the Englishe", he recorded, "and surpryssed by 500 horsse commandit by Colonell Aldride, one Thursday in the morning, the 28 of August. They wer taken, stript of all they had and carried to Brughtie, and ther shipped for England".

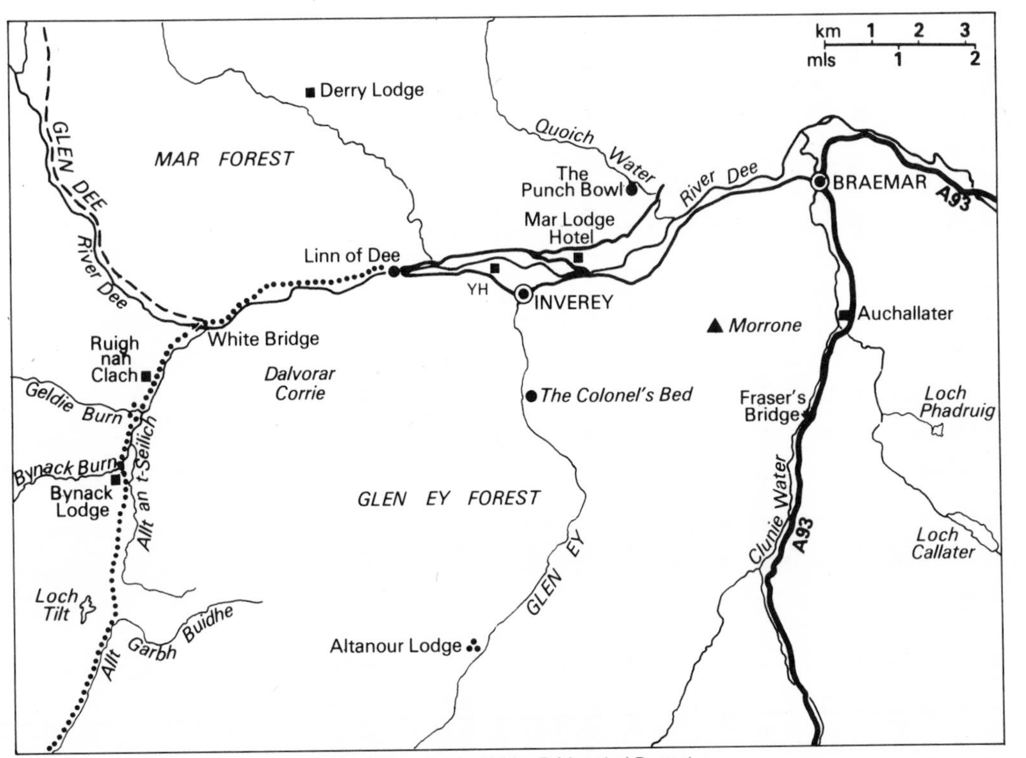

Glen Tilt — by the White Bridge and Bynack

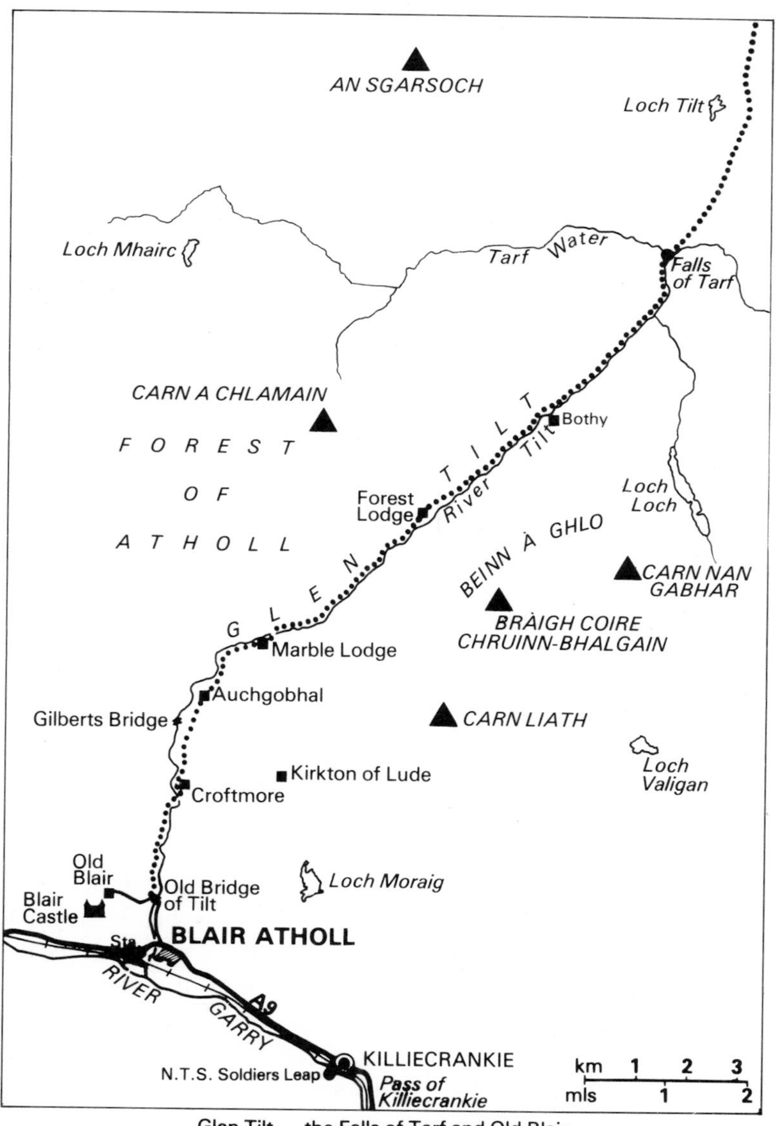

Glen Tilt — the Falls of Tarf and Old Blair

16

Glen Tilt

On that blustery October morning, climbing up from Inverey on Deeside, the sound of the rut was a roaring echo on the hills. Near Cairn Bhithir a small herd of hinds moved over the ridge as a great, bull-chested stag, its coat black from the peat hags, pounded across the heather towards them. There was another stag on the banks of the Connie, but it lifted its head, sniffing danger, and moved off along the valley. Higher up, where the track petered out, groups of hinds nuzzled the heather for food while the stags circled them, moving in on hind ground for the rut. When it was over they would be dismissed. The hinds would fall back on their own company. But now they were behind me and I was up on the plateau, looking down into the belly of the glen and the long road to Blair.

I had climbed Carn Liath to get a bird's eye view of one of the ancient passes across the Mounth from Deeside to Atholl. I could see the road coming up from the Linn of Dee and beyond it the track through Glen Lui to Derry Lodge and the Cairngorms. The Dee spun like a bright thread below the Geusachan face of the Devil's Point, swirling down to meet the Geldie at the White Bridge. Here was the meeting place of two passes which together opened up a route from Rothiemurchus to Blair. One was the Lairig Ghru, the Gloomy Pass, the other was Glen Tilt. From the ridge west of the main cairn on Carn Liath I saw the red-roofed bothy on the banks of the Geldie and the thin outline of the footbridge that I was to cross later on my way to Bynack. The distance from Aviemore to Braemar by the Lairig is twenty-eight miles and from Blair Atholl to Braemar by Glen Tilt twenty-seven miles. H. V. Morton likened the Lairig Ghru to "an early Italian painter's idea of hell" and Thomas Pennant described Glen Tilt as "the most dangerous and most horrible I have ever travelled." But there is a marked contrast between the two and the same contrast can be found travelling west to Atholl from Braemar, following the Dee through scenery softened by birch and pine, catching glimpses of red deer feeding at the riverside. I once tracked down an eagle's nest just west of the Linn of Dee and I remember thinking how odd it was that the eagle had made its home within half a mile of picnic parties and tourist buses. It had come to the edge of the wilderness. The moors and mountains to the west were its hunting territory.

The bridge at the Linn was opened by Queen Victoria in September, 1857. The Queen and Prince Albert, dressed in Royal Stuart, rode through a triumphal arch and drank whisky in a toast, "Prosperity to the bridge." Four years later the Royal carriage rattled over the bridge carrying the Queen back to Balmoral at the end of an expedition which had taken her to Glen Feshie, Dalwhinnie and Blair Atholl, and north through Pennant's "horrible" Glen Tilt.

The road from Inverey crosses the bridge at the Linn of Dee and, once over this deep and dangerous gorge, does a U-turn on the north side as if shying away from the wilderness on the west. The way to the west leads to Athol and the Cairngorms, and is bare and bleak. About a mile from the Linn the ruins of Dalvorar can be seen on the south side of the river. Here, where the Dalvorar Burn runs into the Dee, Viscount Dundee is said to have camped with his troops fourteen days before the Battle of Killiecrankie. Here, too, the swollen Dee raged across the valley in the floods of 1829, sweeping round the farm-house at Dalvorar so quickly that the farmer, his wife and seven children barely had time to make their escape. They waded away from their home and tramped through the storm to Inverey.

After the 1745 Rising, Dubrach, the home of Peter Grant (the oldest rebel) was used to quarter a detachment of

Hanoverian soldiers, and the man in charge was Sergeant Arthur Davies, whose disappearance led to a murder trial which fascinated Sir Walter Scott. About a mile farther on, where the River Geldie joins the Dee, is the White Bridge, junction of a trio of passes that lead to the Lairig Ghru, to Braemar, and south to Glen Tilt and Atholl. There is nothing white about the White Bridge, although it was said to be painted that colour at one time, but despite the fact that it spans the Dee it probably takes its name from the Geldie.[1]

This is where the Mounth parts company with the Dee. For over sixty miles, from the coast at Aberdeen, the Grampian barrier stretches along the Dee valley, broken by glens like Esk and Clova, Tanar and Muick, the old, traditional passes to the south, but above the White Bridge the Monadh Ruadh, the red mountains, claim the river as their own. Beyond the line of Glen Dee, where the river comes down from its source on Braeriach, the Mounth pushes westward by Loch Tilt and An Sgarsoch, and on to Gaick and the Pass of Drumochter. This was where my travels on the Mounth would finally end, but now I was going south, turning my back on the forbidding face of the Devil's Point and the giants of the Cairngorms. My way lay across the White Bridge towards the "wild, black, moory, melancholy tract" through which Thomas Pennant passed on his way to Braemar.

The Geldie was on my left, a fenced-off forest plantation on my right, and less than a mile on a style went over the fence to a crumbling ruin well back from the path. This was the remains of the Ruigh nan Clach. The word "ruigh" means a summer pasture, and it was here that cattle came for the summer grazing. The shieling was probably also used by drovers coming through the Lairig Ghru and the Lairig an Laoigh on their way south, heading for Blair Atholl or by Glen Fernate to Kirkmichael, and perhaps by the droving traffic from Glen Feshie. The route from Speyside to Deeside by Glen Feshie and Glen Geldie was a well beaten path and An Sgarsoch, where the Geldie rises, was said to be the site of

[1] Gaelic geal dheidh—White Dee.

one of the old cattle trysts. It succeeded a cattle market held in Glen Feshie and was the forerunner of the famous Falkirk Tryst.

Half a mile from the Ruigh nan Clach the Geldie comes bouncing and bubbling in from the west. The track I was on turns up the glen past the lower Glen Geldie cottage and stables, to follow the burn past the ruin of Geldie Lodge, three miles up on the opposite side of the stream. Here it branches off to meet up with the Feshie, marching on through Glen Feshie to Speyside. Follow that path and you are walking in the shadow of a dream that began with General Wade in the 18th century and has haunted planners ever since. Wade saw it as a road link between Braemar and Ruthven Barracks and his 20th century successors have had blueprints in their minds of a fast tourist highway from east to west. The cost of such a project to-day would be immense and it is unlikely that it will ever be more than a tantalising thought. There are many who will be happy to leave it at that.

Going south, the Geldie is crossed by a ford or by a wooden footbridge near the stables and the height of water banished any idea of using stepping-stones, so I munched my sandwiches in the bothy while considering the alternative. The stables and their stalls are still largely intact but the cottage is little more than a ruin. The usual graffiti showed that the majority of travellers using it had been making for Aviemore. The bridge was in a state of advanced dilapidation. There were four spans. One section lay at the river's edge; another, badly damaged, lurched dangerously towards the water. The remaining two, one also tilting alarmingly, were still usable. Before I climbed on to the bridge, clutching uneasily at the wire above me, I noticed the message someone had cut on a board: "Extreme care. Temporary repairs". I was glad I hadn't arrived before the repairs.

On the other side of the water the ground was soft and boggy and a narrow path ran alongside the Bynack Burn, a tributary of the Geldie, towards Bynack Lodge, less than a mile ahead. Looking back, I saw four Land Rovers ford the

The broken footbridge on the Geldie near Bynack lodge. Behind are the bothy and stables.

Geldie and Bynack and follow the east bank of the burn to the lodge, where they drew in on the wooded knoll and halted in a line facing south. They carried stalkers and ghillies out with a party of grouse-shooting Germans from Mar Lodge, and they had arranged to meet the hunters at Bynack before covering the hills down to the Tilt. Later, the stalkers passed me on the track, stepping out smartly in their heather-coloured suits and deer-stalker hats. They were a friendly lot, or so I thought, but there was another traveller at Bynack who had a different opinion.

He was a hiker from Kent, heading through the Lairig Ghru for Aviemore. He had come north from Pitlochry by Enochdhu and Glen Fearnach, branching off by Loch Loch to come out on the Tilt below the Falls of Tarf, and had pitched his tent by the ruined walls of the lodge. For some reason or other he felt that the chief stalker had resented his presence there and his observation on the Germans was that this part of the world was becoming full of foreigners. "Even Englishmen!" I joked. Whether his complaint was justified I do not know, but the older breed of stalker in the Highlands still tends to treat hill-walkers with faintly-disguised suspicion. They are still very much the Laird's men, quick in defence of his person and property. The majority, on the other hand, rarely bother you if you stick to the rules.

The camper from Kent had kept his tongue in check because he wasn't sure if the pass was a right-of-way, but there was nowhere he could have stood firmer on his rights than in Glen Tilt. Back in the year 1847, Professor J. Hutton Balfour, Professor of Botany at Edinburgh University, came face-to-face "wi' gillies four" when he attempted to lead a party of botany students through the glen. The botanists' aim was innocent enough, for, as Sir Douglas Maclagan crisply put it in "The Ballad of Glen Tilt"—

"Twas a' to poo
Some gerse that grew
That ne'er a coo
Would care to pit her mouth till".

The Duke of Atholl, who was in charge of the ghillies, was less concerned about his grass and cows than he was about the intruders frightening away his deer, and when "the Sassenachs cam' doon to Blair" they found the glen closed to them and the Duke glowering through the yet (gate), telling them "twas trespass clear." The Professor had other ideas—

Balfour he had a mind as weel
As ony Duke could hae, man,
Quo' he, "There's ne'er a kilted chiel
Shall drive us back this day, man.
It's justice and it's public richt,
We'll pass Glen Tilt afore the nicht,
For Dukes shall we
Care a'e bawbee?
The road's as free
To you and me
As to his Grace himself, man.

The incident led to a famous legal action brought by the Scottish Rights of Way Society and the result, as I told my Kent friend, was that today "the road's as free to you and me" as to anyone. There were certainly no closed gates or frowning ghillies when Queen Victoria was at Bynack in October, 1861. It was nearly dark when the Queen's party reached Bainoch, as she called it, and as they approached the shiel the two pipers out in front struck up the tune "Athole Highlanders." Lady Fife was waiting at Bynack to give them tea and then they all climbed into their carriages and said goodbye to the Duke of Atholl.

The Queen regarded the journey by "the good Duke of Athole" back to Blair in the darkness as "rather a hazardous proceeding, at least an adventurous one, considering the night, and that there was no moon—and what the road was!" The road, or at least that stretch from Bynack to the Falls of Tarf, has changed little if at all, and travelling on it even in day time is something of an adventure. The path is narrow but easy enough to follow, keeping fairly high to avoid the bog and marshland on the floor of the valley. The hill ahead hides the waters of Loch Tilt and you pass it without seeing it, but from it comes a tiny stream that, farther south, goes surging through the heart of Atholl as the mighty Tilt. Thomas Pennant dined on the side of Loch Tilt on his way through the glen. He said it was "swarming with Trouts."

The path, clinging to the hill, takes you down to a gap by the foot of Sron a' Bhoididh, into a pleasant haugh where a stream comes gurgling in on the left to join the Allt Garbh Buidhe as it runs down to the meeting of the Tilt and Tarf. From some distance away I saw a herd of deer grazing at the edge of this grassy oasis, where everything was so much in contrast to the "wild, black, moory" terrain around it. There was another herd on the hill overlooking Loch Tilt but, almost in the flicker of an eyelid, they had picked up my scent and were gone. They were a reminder that it was in Glen Tilt that many of the great deer hunts of a few centuries ago took place. When James V was there in 1529 he lived in "a fair palace of green timber" and was treated to "all manner of meats, drinks and delicates." The gluttonous feast was washed down with ale, beer, wine . . . "malvasy, muskadel, hippocras and aquavitas."

There were no signs of feasting in the haugh below Loch Tilt when I was there, only the blackened embers of fires where hill-walkers had brewed up their tea on their way up the pass. From there I crossed the stream coming down from the loch and looked ahead to the wedge of hills where the Allt Garbh Buidhe and the path thrust through a long ravine to the Falls of Tarf. The ravine is called the Garrabuie and a handbook for travellers published at the end of last century described it as "like a gigantic canal-cutting." The path lifts away from the stream on the way through the ravine and drops back to it before reaching the Falls.

The Tarf Water, plunging through a deep, rocky gorge to join the Tilt, is a reminder that Sir James Balfour of Denmylne called the route through Glen Tilt the Potarffe pass. "Ye cheiffe passage from Castletoune in ye Brae Mar to ye Castle of Blare in Athole is called Potarffe and contains 18 miles of Mounthe." It is more than likely that he meant Polltarffe, commonly spelt Poll Tarf. The Gaelic word "poll" means a pool or a pit. This refers to the dangerous ford that had at one time to be crossed at this spot and it was here that an 18-year-old English visitor, Francis Bedford, was swept away and drowned in August, 1879. The present Bedford Bridge was built by the Scottish Rights of Way Society in 1886 from funds raised by his friends following the tragedy.

Queen Victoria had to splash through "the celebrated ford of the Tarff (Poll Tarff it is called)" when she travelled from Blair to Deeside in 1861. She noted in her Journal that it was very deep and after heavy rain almost impassable. "To all appearance the ford of the Tarff was not deeper than other fords, but once in it the men were above their knees—and suddenly in the middle, where the current from the fine, high, full falls is very strong, it was nearly up to the men's waists." There was an illustration in early editions of the Royal Journal showing the party "Fording the Poll Tarf," and it looks at first sight as if the artist had carried artistic licence too far. The Queen sits sedately on her pony while in front, up to their middles in water, two Royal pipers blow stoically away on their bagpipes. It was no exaggeration. "The two pipers went first", recorded Victoria, "playing all the time".

The satirist of to-day would make a feast of such material, but Victoria's Great Expeditions would have been incomplete without the piping. Whether it was at Victoria's request or on the Duke of Atholl's instructions, they had come up all the way from Forest Lodge with the pipers puffing on the bagpipes at the head of the Royal procession. They played alternately the whole time, said the Queen, and it "had a most cheerful effect". "The wild strains sounded so softly amid those noble hills; and our caravan winding along—our people and the Duke's all in kilts, and the ponies, made altogether a most picturesque scene".

The Queen and her party stopped for lunch at "a place called Dalcronachie". This would have been Dail Chruineachd", which, as Victoria noted, "looked up a glen towards Loch Loch"—the route taken by the Kent camper I had met at Bynack. It was south of here that I had my own lunch, at a spot described in one old guide book as "one of the grandest bits in the glen". Here the River Tilt is fed by the Allt a' Chrochaidh, dropping to the valley through an enormous waterfall, and on the opposite bank by the Allt Fheannach. There was, according to the guide book, a shepherd's foot-bridge leading to the left bank and the ascent of Beinn a' Ghlo, but now a more solid wooden bridge takes you across. The remains of a wooden bothy lie near the Fheannach. There are a number of old bridges or what remains of them along the glen, including one at Dail an Eas on the north side of Forest Lodge. It was used to take sheep and shepherds on to the hills but it had been washed away. It was known as the Black Bridge, and it is said that there was a fine pool for poaching salmon under it.

Near the Chrochaidh waterfall, one of many feeding the

Tilt, there were the remains of one of the old shielings, which were scattered along the upper reaches of the glen. The crude type of shieling that existed two centuries ago was seen by Pennant when he followed the Tilt north in 1769, stopping at one to refresh himself with goat's whey. He described it as "a cottage made of turf, the dairy-house, where the Highland shepherds, or graziers, live with their herds and flocks, and during the fine season make butter and cheese. Their whole furniture consists of a few hornspoons, their milking utensils, a couch formed of sods to lie on, and a rug to cover them. Their food oat-cakes, butter or cheese, and often the coagulated blood of their cattle spread on their bannocks. Their drink milk, whey, and sometimes, by way of indulgence, whisky".

I found it curious that Pennant should be so critical of Glen Tilt as a whole. He contrasted its "dreary wastes" with the "rich vale, plenteous in corn and grass", that he found on Deeside. Yet in the journey between the Linn of Dee and Blair Atholl the two halves north and south of the Falls of Tarf provide a contrast that is no less striking. Passing through the Garrabuie ravine you move from bleak and forbidding terrain that has the scowl of the Larig Ghru on it to where the Tilt bounces boisterously towards the Garry through one of the loveliest glens in Scotland. Pennant's soul remained unmoved by the sight of "the great hill of Ben y glo". All that he could say about the mountains was that they made excellent sheep-walks.

It may be that our 18th century traveller got off to a bad start, for the road from Blair was not what it is to-day. It was so rugged, according to Pennant, that horses had often to cross their legs to find a secure place for their feet. Nor was he impressed by the fact that he looked down from his horse's back on a precipitous drop which ended where a black torrent roared and rolled through a great bed of rock. There are still spots on the Tilt track where you pass deep drops and black torrents, but the road from Forest Lodge to Blair is now wide enough to take a Land Rover. The track crosses the Tilt by

Gaw's Bridge, named after the mason who built it, and not far from it is Marble Lodge, a modest little dwelling-house which Queen Victoria mentioned as a keeper's cottage. There was a good deal of marble in Glen Tilt at one time, which is how the lodge got its name.

The road runs on to the farm of Auchgobhal (pronounced Auchgowl) and Gilbert's Bridge and here there is a parting of the ways. From the bridge one road climbs up the hill by Blairuachdar and ends at Old Blair, while a second route, sticking to the Tilt, emerges west of the Old Bridge of Tilt. These are the well-travelled ways up the Tilt valley to-day, but the old, traditional road pulls away from the main road a short distance before Auchgobhal, passing close to the farm and above Croftmore. This ancient track takes you high above the river on its eastern side, travelling along the face of Meall Gruaim and through woodland until it passes Kincraigie and joins the road to Fenderbridge. Where the Kincraigie path meets the Fenderbridge road there is a Scottish Rights of Way Society sign indicating the route to Deeside and a second sign near the Old Bridge of Tilt, pointing the way by the west bank road. These signs seemed to provide the last word in that long-forgotten dispute in which Balfour had declared that he would "pass Glen Tilt afore the nicht." Well, I had passed Glen Tilt, seen the "gillies four" go marching past at Bynack, and had emerged unscathed.

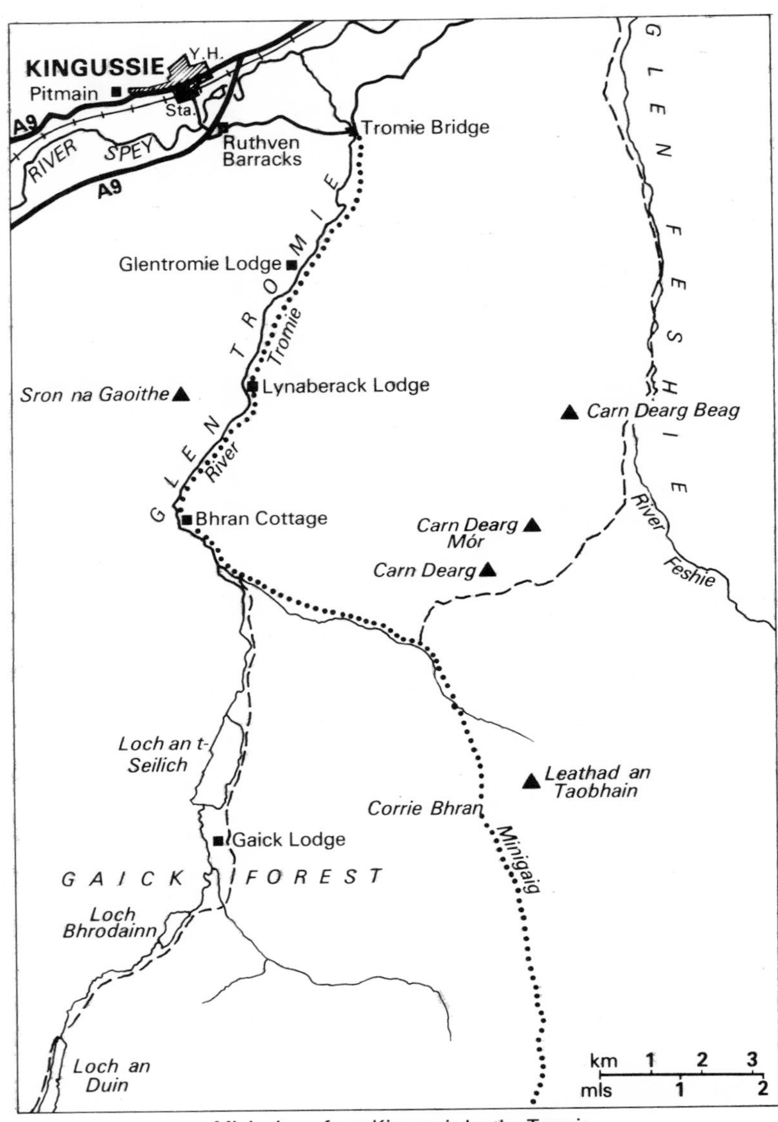

Minigaig — from Kingussie by the Tromie

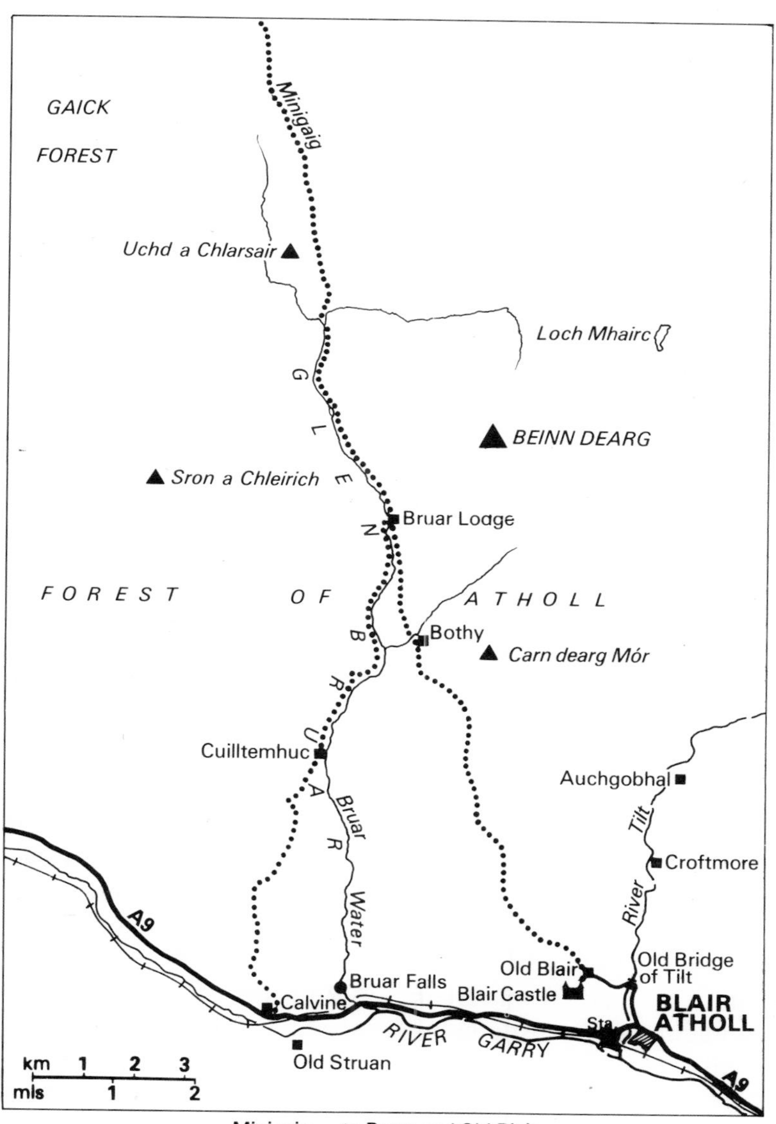

Minigaig — to Bruar and Old Blair

17

Minigaig Pass

The dream of a Great North Road was in the minds of men long before General George Wade cut his way through the gloomy Pass of Drumochter to the back-door of Badenoch. It was there when the Lords of Badenoch, the "wild Cumyns", sat in their frontier fortress at Ruthven, where the marshlands cling wetly to the long sweep of the River Spey. There was a Comyn's Road over the Grampians in the 13th century, but it is uncertain who built it, although some say it was John Comyn, 3rd Earl of Badenoch, son of the Red Comyn. The more likely theory is that it was Walter Comyn, Earl of Menteith, who received a charter from Alexander II granting him the lordship of Badenoch and Lochaber. It is Walter who figures in the legendary tales about the origin of the road from Badenoch to Atholl.

This ancient route over the Mounth is paved with a mixture of fact and fantasy. Tradition has it that Walter Comyn and his wife stopped at an inn at Kilmaveonaig on their way through Atholl and, finding the beer to their taste, asked about its ingredients. The malt, they were told, was from Perth and the water from a small stream nearby called the Aldnehearlain. Comyn decided that he would build a road from Blair to Ruthven to take the ingredients to his castle home on the Spey and he mapped out a line from Kilmaveonaig to Ruichlachrie and through the Gaick hills to Ruthven. There are, in fact, records of a "way" from Blair to Ruthven "for carts to pass with wine". There was also, according to William Scrope, a great precipice called Cum na feur or the Cart's Precipice", which appears to have been just north of the Grampian ridge, where

Comyn's Road ran down to Abhainn Gharbh Ghaig, south of Gaick Lodge.

The Cart's Precipice would have taken its name from the gruesome happenings which, if legend is to be believed, marked the building of Comyn's Road and led to Walter Comyn's death. This Comyn had an appetite for women as well as wine and had ordered all females between the ages of twelve and thirty to work naked in the fields of Ruthven, but on the day before this was due to take place he rode south to Atholl to inspect work on his new road. He never returned. When dusk was falling his horse galloped up to the courtyard of Ruthven Castle with one of its master's legs dangling from the stirrup. Fragments of his clothes and pieces of bone and flesh were found in a narrow valley in the Gaick wilderness.

The likelihood is that he met his death in an accident, for an old record on the "way of wane wheills" says that the Cumming who built it "ended miserablie being torne in pieces with a hors in Badenoch, whair falling from his horse, his fute stak in the styrrop and ane of his thighs stiking in the styrrop was brocht to Blair be the said hors". But there was no room for a rational explanation in that superstitious age. The blame was laid at the doorsteps of two witches, one at Ard Ghaoith in Moulin and the other in Cnoc Barrodh, a small village nearby. They took the form of eagles and put Comyn's men to flight, drove the horses and oxen over Cart's Precipice, and then, turning on Comyn himself, tore his body from his horse and stripped his flesh until nothing remained but that one ghastly foot. The witches were said to be mothers of two of the girls ordered to reap stark naked at Ruthven. Whether you believe the story depends on your imagination, but there is little doubt that Comyn's road existed, for there are still traces of it to-day.

The place where Walter Comyn met his death, the original Cart's Precipice mentioned by Scrope, is also known as Leum nam Fiann, or the Fingalian's Leap, and it was a Macpherson from Ruthven who, in the 18th century, breathed new life into the poems of the Gaelic bard Ossian, son of Fingal, and set a style for the Romantic movement in poetry. The fair-haired lad who came to be known as "Ossian" or "Fingal" Macpherson was born at Invertromie, a mile east of Ruthven Barracks, in 1736. His father, Andrew, was a farmer but James studied for the church and then became a teacher, serving for a time in the little school at Ruthven, the thriving hamlet which lay at the foot of the great mound from which the barracks surveyed the surrounding countryside. Ruthven was the gateway to the south, not by the vanished Comyn road but by the Minigaig Pass, which roughly followed the same route, and it may be that it was here, on these old trails, that the young Macpherson was fired by thoughts of the ancient Celtic heroes whose deeds had rung down through the centuries on the tongues of the bards. His translations from the works of Ossian brought him instant success—and a thundering controversy that raged on for years. His most fiery critic was Dr Samuel Johnson, who said that Macpherson's failure to produce the originals showed "a degree of insolence with which the world is not yet acquainted." He believed that the Ruthven schoolmaster had merely translated "some wandering ballads."

James Macpherson was a boy of ten when the Jacobites attacked Ruthven Barracks in August, 1745, and it is more than likely that he often saw the burly, red-faced figure of Sergeant Terence Molloy, the Irishman who faced the Highlanders with a force of only fourteen privates. He almost certainly knew and may even have been related to Mrs McPherson, the Barrack-wife, mentioned in Sergeant Molloy's report to Lieut.-General Sir John Cope. "There appeared in the little town of Ruthven about 300 men of the enemy," wrote Molloy, "and sent proposals to me to surrender this redoubt." When the Sergeant refused the Jacobites attacked with about 150 men but two hours later, after parleying, carried off their dead and wounded. The next morning they went west to "their grand camp at Dalwhinny." The sergeant was given an immediate commission for his bravery, but some five months later the Jacobites attacked the barracks again, this time using cannon, and Lieutenant Molloy was forced to surrender. The barracks and stable were burned.

These were the last military acts in a violent story going back to the days of the Comyns, and perhaps even before that, for there is thought to have been a broch there at one time. The barracks were never to rise again from the ashes of the Rebellion and for over two centuries the ruin of the building has looked across the Spey to Kingussie. With the decline of Ruthven there came a change in road travel. The Wade road, pushing up through the Drumochter Pass, had already replaced the Minigaig Pass as the main route to Atholl and there was no longer a fortress to act as a gateway to the hills of Gaick.

Monadh Miongaig—the "wild Month and hills of Myngegg"—was used as a route over the Grampians as far back as the 16th century, although there is no clear indication of when it replaced Comyn's Road. Early maps show it as a road to Badenoch long before the appearance of the Drumochter Pass, which would probably have been little more than a footpath when the Minigaig was in full use. The drovers used it, coming south to Kingussie and fording the Spey near where the present bridge spans the river. The start of the Minigaig Pass lay opposite the town of Ruthven and this route, going south by Braeruthven and over Beinn Bhuide, can still be traced two miles to Glen Tromie Lodge, where it crosses the Tromie to join the present track.

In the Highland Folk Museum at Kingussie I saw a 1719 "Plan of the Barrack at Ruthven in Badenoch" which showed a large number of houses west of the barracks, around what is now Ruthven Farm. There was a road to the west marked "Road to Killewhiman[1] and Fort William" and one going in the opposite direction "to Strath Spay and Bremar," the latter being the forerunner of the "back road" to Aviemore or to Feshiebridge and through Glen Feshie to Deeside. There was no Kingussie on the map, but a road was shown running

[1] Now Fort Augustus.

down to the Spey and coming to an end on the opposite bank.

The houses at Ruthven looked on to the "Foot Road to Blair of Athol" and the fact that it was shown as a foot road may have indicated that early in the 18th century it was losing its importance. Other maps of that period described the Minigaig as a "Summer Road to Ruthven," suggesting a seasonal restriction on its use, but despite these points to disuse, it continued to carry droving traffic well into the 19th century.

I began my own journey through the Minigaig Pass, not at Ruthven, but a mile and a half to the east, not far from the farm at Invertromie, where "Ossian" Macpherson was born. Here, where the River Tromie rushes through a rocky gorge on its way to the Spey, the Minigaig Pass leaves the road "to Strath Spay and Bremar" and cuts sharply south from the picturesque, single-arch Tromie Bridge, passing Killiehuntly, its name a reminder of the days when the Earls of Huntly ruled in Badenoch. The first few miles of the "Summer Road" are pleasantly wooded and two miles from Tromie Bridge a small, wooden bridge crosses the river to the old Braeruthven path, passing Glentromie Lodge.

Farther on, beyond some smart, modern estate workers' houses, the glen opens up where Lynaberack Lodge shelters under the rocky slopes of Croidh-la. This ultra-modern shooting lodge is in sharp contrast to the disused, red-roofed cottage that stands a short distance in front of it. This is all that is left of the old Lynaberack, a tiny community which, a keeper told me, once had a hundred people and a schoolhouse. There are the remains of a number of similar settlements in the glen and the one at Lynaberack was still occupied at the end of last century. The building is surrounded by the ruins of other dwelling houses and inside, on one of its walls, was the inscription, "John Stewart was born in this village of Lynabiorach in 1862. Inscribed by his great-grand-daughter Betty Stewart August 1950".

The hill rising from the Tromie on the west bank, directly opposite Lynaberack, is Sron na Gaoithe. The old Comyn's

The only house remaining in deserted Lynaberack, once a thriving community.

Road crossed the shoulder of Sron na Gaoithe and forded the river farther south before Bhran Cottage. This desolate building, with its porch falling down and its doors and windows boarded-up, is about half a mile from where the path parts company with the Tromie and goes south-east on the line of the stream from which the cottage takes its name, the Allt Bhran. Less than half-a-mile ahead is Bhran Bridge. From here, one route lay through the Gaick hills and the Edendon valley to Dalnacardoch, the other swinging east by the Minigaig Pass to Blair-in-Atholl.

There was, at one time, a Scottish Rights of Way Society sign at Bhran pointing the way to Struan by the Minigaig Pass, but it was taken down more than half a century ago. The only sign now is at Tromie Bridge and it indicates a public footpath to Atholl by the Gaick Pass, itself an indication that the Minigaig has been consigned to the history books. Whatever the Minigaig's importance in the past, it is Gaick that beckons

Where the Minigaig and Gaick tracks part.

to-day, its long, wide track snaking away through the valley to the lofty hills and the waters of Loch an t-Seilich, Loch Bhrodain and Loch an Duin. This is Gleann Tromaigh nan Siantan, the Glen of the Stormy Blasts. Comyn's Road lay that way, turning east by Allt Gharbh Ghaig towards the Bruar Water and Blair, and it was in Gaick that Captain John Macpherson of Ballachroan, the "Black Officer", died with four companions in an avalanche in January, 1800. They called it the "Loss of Gaick", and it was said that Macpherson had a pact with the Devil.

The Gaick Pass draws you south, pitching you out at Atholl on the new north road, but the Minigaig hides itself in the heather and discourages travellers. At first, I could find no sign of it, and then I picked it up just before the Bhran Bridge, a thin line of trodden earth creeping east above the Allt Bhran, becoming clearer as I followed it along the lower slopes of Meallach Mhor. There was a bulldozed track on the south side of the stream, but this led only to a weir about three-quarters of a mile up, and from there you have to cross the Bhran and join the old path. It sticks close to the water, climbing up by Coire Bhran, with Leathad an Taobhain on the left, until it crosses the old county march to the summit at Uchd a'Chlarsair. There is a stream called the Cauchan Lub on the plateau and it was here that the drovers rested their herds on their way over the Minigaig Pass, which they used to avoid the tolls at Dalnacardoch. Cauchan Lub, or Kichan na Lub as it was anciently called, was also used for summer grazing.

From Uchd a' Chlarsair the path runs down to meet the Bruar Water and joins the road to Bruar Lodge, which, dwarfed by mighty Beinn Dearg, sits at the foot of a wooded slope where the river goes through a series of snake-like wriggles before straightening out and pressing down the glen to the Garry. The lodge was at one time farther up the glen but was rebuilt on its present site and on a larger scale in 1789. The normal route from Bruar Lodge is by the estate road on the west bank of the river to Calvine, for there is little to indicate the existence of the Minigaig. The road to Calvine and Struan was used by drovers going to the Falkirk Tryst. It reaches Calvine about a mile west of Bruar, where the river drops into the Garry. The Falls of Bruar are a favourite haunt of tourists, largely because, to use his own words, "Poet Burns cam by" in 1787. He looked at the bare slopes above the turbulent falls and addressed the "Humble Petition of Bruar Water" to the Duke of Atholl.

> Would then my noble master please
> To grant my highest wishes,
> He'll shade my banks wi' towering trees,
> And bonnie spreading bushes.

The Duke acted on Burns' advice. To-day, the woodlands of Bruar are green and lovely, and, as Rab forecast, many a grateful bird returns his tuneful thanks.

Back at Bruar Lodge, the old Minigaig Pass, once followed

by drovers going to Perth by Blair and the Tay, branches away from the east bank of the river and heads south to Druim Dubh ridge. There is not much of the track left, but you can pick up traces of it and there is a quite recognisable stretch on top of the ridge. From there it drops down to Allt Sheicheachan, on the south side of which it becomes a bull-dozed road, rising up the side of Meall Tionail.

There is a fine, stone bothy on the edge of the Sheicheachan, owned by the Atholl Estates but maintained by the Mountain Bothies Association as an overnight shelter. One of the entries in the visitors' book was by a J. B. Hart, who in August, 1977, was on his way to Kingussie. "Happiness is a hot bothy", he wrote. "This bothy is cold". With snow drifts piled high on the banks of the Sheicheachan outside, I shared the view of the next visitor, Fergus McAlpine, who thought that Mr Hart "oughtn't to look a gift bothy in the mouth". The man who was looking after the Allt Scheicheachan Bothy, or the Druim Dubh, as it is sometimes called, was David Dixon, of Musselburgh, who recorded that in July, 1977, he came over from Ruigh-aiteachain in Glen Feshie to check on the bothy. "Good track all the way", he wrote. "Joined the old Comyn's Road half-way over (ancient route from Badenoch to Atholl, which passes bothy)". The road was the Minigaig, not Comyn's Road, and the Glenfeshie track comes in from the east about three miles from Bhran Bridge.

The Minigaig Pass runs from Allt Scheicheachan in a slightly south-easterly direction, curving away from Meall Dubh, crossing the Allt an t-Seapail by a modern bridge and going on to cross the Allt na Moine Baine. Here there is a concrete crossing a few yards from the remains of an old, high bridge and beyond it a large cairn, one of many which dot the hills in this area. One, the Carn Mhic or Mac Shimi, commemorates a fight between the Murrays of Atholl and a raiding party of Frasers. As well as cairns, milestones mark the route from Druim Dubh to Old Blair, but how old they are I do not know.

The dry arch bridge at Old Blair.

From the cairn near the Moine Baine the road sloped down into Glen Banvie. Where the stream joined the Banvie Burn I could see the old Comyn Road on the far side of the water. It comes in from the west, branching off the Bruar-Calvine track at Cuilltemhuc, where it crosses the Bruar Water. Originally, the pass ran through the Gaick hills to Cuilltemhuc and Ruidhchlachrie and along the south bank of the Banvie to Old Blair. The present track faithfully follows the line through a woodland known as the Whim Plantation. Less than half-way through the wood there is a bridge linking the two tracks, so that the Minigaig and Comyn's Road come together at the end of their long journey from Ruthven and race each other along the Banvie on the last leg.

The two ancient routes end on either side of Old Blair. The Minigaig Road, or what seemed to me to be the line of it, went through a nursery garden to join up with a quaint, hump-backed bridge spanning the road which goes through Old Blair to Blair Castle. The alternative was to stick to the track until it joined this road, which was once known as Minigaig Street. There was, until fairly recently, a street sign carrying the name. The picturesque cluster of houses that make up the old Castleton lie north of the castle, well away from the traffic which shatters the peace of its successor, Blair Atholl. Yet Old Blair itself was at one time the gateway to the Minigaig and later a link in the new road built by General Wade. It was this road, ironically, that was to thrust the Minigaig into obscurity.

The inn at Old Blair, which was a popular halting place for travellers heading north, is still there, although to-day it is an attractive dwelling-house. Elizabeth Grant of Rothiemurchus, author of *Memoirs of a Highland Lady,* stayed there on her way to Speyside in 1812. "The old inn at Blair," she wrote, "was high up on the hill, overlooking the Park, the wall of which was just opposite the windows. We used to watch through the trunks of the trees for the antlered herds of deer, and walk to a point from whence we could see the Castle far down below, beside the river, a large, plain, very ugly building now, that very likely looked grander before its battlements were levelled by order of the Government after the rebellion."

There was another well-known guest at the Inn of Blair in the early years of the 18th century. Wade's road cut through the estate, passing Old Blair and turning down towards Baluain. The General stayed at the Inn during the work on this section of the road and it may be that he walked in the woods there, dreaming his dream of a great new highway to the north. He could never have foreseen that the day would come when the road that he had built would be a historical irrelevancy, a dusty piece of history swept aside by the planners who followed him.

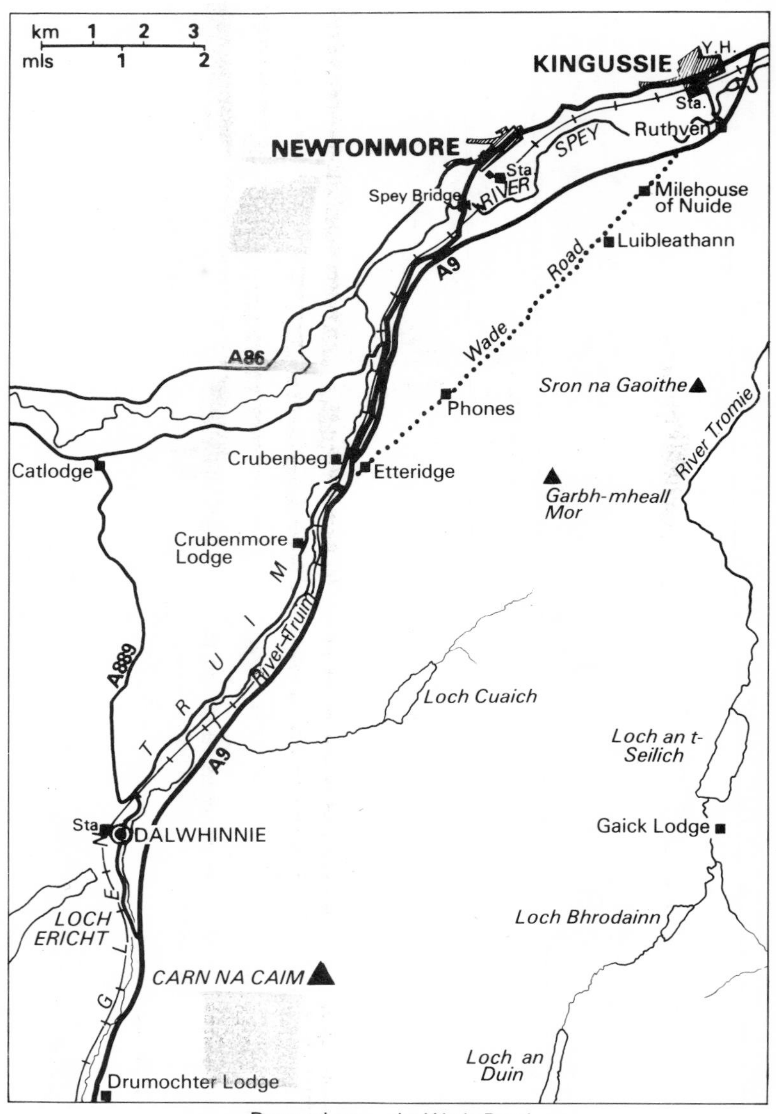

Drumochter — the Wade Road

18

Pass of Drumochter

The rain clouds rolled in ominous banks over the Pass of Drumochter, chased by an icy wind along the ragged line of the Mounth. I could see the new trunk road curving up from Glen Garry, the rail track from Dalnaspidal keeping it company as it arced past the Boar of Badenoch. Behind me were the Grampians, stretching across the country from the Mearns to Mar, to the valley of the Tilt and the Forest of Atholl, and, finally, to Glen Truim and Drumochter. This was where the Mounth met Drumalban, the watershed of Scotland, a mountain spine running from Ben Hope in Sutherland to Ben Lomond.

Nearly two and a half centuries ago, General George Wade, seeking "short and speedy communication" between Perth and Inverness, rejected as a possible route north the Minigaig Pass, already used by his soldiers on their way to Ruthven in Badenoch. He decided, instead, that his way lay through the "barren country" of Drumochter, a choice that may have been influenced by the possibility of opening up another route to Fort Augustus through the wild Corrieyairack Pass. Whatever the reason, he turned a rough and little-used track into a highway that is still one of Scotland's main arterial roads.

Drumochter Pass, lying between Glen Garry and Glen Truim, crosses the Mounth at 1500 ft, near the point at which the two great mountain ridges meet. The road over the pass was redesigned by Thomas Telford in 1829 and another reconstruction took place in 1926-28. Today, progress still marches on, for in 1973 plans were drawn up for what was described as the toughest civil engineering project Scotland had ever seen—the building of a new road from Perth to the north shore of the Cromarty Firth, a distance of 137 miles. Wade's vision of "short and speedy communication" was to be fulfilled in a way that would have been incomprehensible to 18th century planners.

Nevertheless, Wade faced problems that were just as formidable to his time as those faced by road-builders two hundred years later, and he must have looked at the desolate country around him and wondered if he would ever carve a new pass to peace out of this hostile terrain. The land and the people were against him. Many, as Neil Munro put it in *The New Road,* believed that the Road was going to be a rut that, once hammered deep enough, would be the poor Gael's grave. "Never was penitent banished into a more barren desert, to suffer for his sins, than what you have suffered in since your confinement to Drumochter", wrote the Lord Advocate, Duncan Forbes of Culloden.

Wade's commitment was "the good settlement of that part of the Kingdom", but he must have known that it had implications far beyond the pacification of the Highlands. "The Grampians, like ramparts, stood between two ages", wrote Neil Munro. In *The New Road,* Alan-Iain-Alain Og, uncle of the hero, Aeneas MacMaster, watches "Geordie's shovellin' brigade" at work and foresees the commercial possibilities. With vessels weather-bound among the isles or "staggering round Cape Wrath" it had always been difficult to get goods to Inverness in winter; now he saw a chance of opening communication by the Corrieyairack on a route "as safe as the King's highway to London". "It may be a sodger's road", he cries to Aeneas, "but it's just the very thing for merchant wagons".

Not everyone thought it "just the very thing". Seventy years after the opening of the road from Dunkeld to Inverness, Thomas Telford reported: "The Military Roads, having been laid out with other views than promoting Commerce and Industry, are generally in such directions and so inconveniently steep as to be nearly unfit for the purposes of Civil Life". Private travel was a nightmare and broken axles were as common then as punctures are to-day. Lord Lovat, travelling from Inverness to Edinburgh with his two daughters in 1740, had so little confidence in road conditions that he took his own wheelwright with him as far as Aviemore. It did him little good. He was eight miles from Aviemore when his back-axle broke in two and his daughters had to ride bare-back behind the footmen until they got to Ruthven. "I got an English wheelwright and a smith, who wrought two days mending my chariot . . . and I was not gone four miles from Ruthven when it broke again, so that I was in a miserable condition till I came to Dalnakeardach".

Ruthven Castle near Kingussie.

Ruthven was still the main stopping place for travellers at that time. General Wade's road turned off the present line of the A9 at Etteridge, five miles north of Dalwhinnie, and went by Phones and Milehouse of Nuide to the Boat of Kingussie at

Ruthven, skirting Kingussie on the opposite bank of the Spey as it pushed on to Inverness. It was on a forgotten stretch of the military road at Dunachton, four miles north-east of Kingussie, that my journey over the last of the Mounth passes really began, for it was on this ancient estate that I picked up the trail of Aeneas MacMaster and Ninian Campbell, the main characters in Neil Munro's novel. It was here, near Loch Insch, "a swelling of the Spey where wild-fowl thronged", that the two adventurers and Ninian's daughter Janet were stranded while on their way home from their exploits in the North.

They were pressing on to Dalwhinnie, "over a wild unfinished weal of road", when their coach, meeting the same fate as Lord Lovat's carriage, broke an axle on the slope of Monadh Liath. The coachman had to go to Dalwhinnie for a blacksmith and the two men lit a fire and passed the time fishing. "They were among a concourse of the hills whose scarps were glistening in the sun that gave the air at noon a blandness, though some snow was on the bends. The river linked through crags and roared at linns; all rusty-red and gold the breckans burned about them; still came like incense from the gale-sprig perfume. They sat, these two young people, by the fire, demure and blate at first, to find themselves alone. From where they sat they could perceive down to the south the wrecks of Comyn fortresses; the Road still red and new was like a raw wound on the heather, ugly to the gaze, although it took them home. Apart from it, and higher on the slope, a drove-track ran, bright green, with here and there on it bleached stones worn by the feet of by-past generations. They saw them both—the Old Road and the New—twine far down through the valley into Badenoch, and melt into the vapours of the noon".

It was fascinating to stand there and match Munro's prose to both the past and the future. The New Road, creeping quietly down through Craigbui Wood, was no longer new; it had long since been replaced by that torment of tarmacadam below, a roaring, over-burdened highway with a number instead of a name. Now it, too, would soon give way to another highway, wider and faster, carving its way through to Cromarty with scant attention for the land that carried it. Suddenly, like Aeneas, I doubted if the new ways of the world were better than the old, and I could share his quick longing for Corrieyairack and the wilds of Badenoch, far better than "this humdrum track on which was only that tame pleasure, comfort".

There are no bright green drove tracks now, but this is how they came on their way to the Trysts at Falkirk and Crieff, down from Inverness to the Spey valley and on over the Mounth by Drumochter Pass. The alternative route lay by the Cairngorms, whose mist-blue peaks I could see from Dunachton, either by the Lairig Ghru or the Lairig an Laoigh, the Pass of the Calves. Those that went by Badenoch linked up farther south with cattle driven over the Corrieyairack Pass from the West. During the 18th and early 19th centuries an endless flow of droving traffic moved through Glen Truim and Glen Garry and in 1723 Bishop Robert Forbes reported seeing a drove a mile long in the Pass of Drumochter and eight droves, totalling 1200 cattle, at Dalwhinnie.

Those footprints of lost generations, marked by the bleached stones that Aeneas and Janet Campbell saw when they looked down the valley, may still be there, if not in the old drove tracks at least in the remains of the road that was once Wade's pride. The wrecks of the Comyn fortresses will not be found by the passing tourist, except at Ruthven and on the waters of Loch an Eilean, whose ruined castle is all that is left of earlier strongholds built by the Wolf of Badenoch and, before that, by the Comyns. Dunachton House, near the point where the Wade road joins the A9, stands on the site of Dunachton Castle, once the seat of the chiefs of the MacNiven clan. It was destroyed by fire in 1869. Three miles south, above Lynchat, the Cave of Raitts marks the scene of a massacre of the MacNivens after some of them had ill-treated a daughter of a Macpherson.

There is another bloodthirsty legend around the Castle of

Raitts, a Comyn fortress which stood about a mile away. The Mackintosh clan, who held Dunachton Castle after the MacNivens, were invited to dine with the Comyns at Raitt's Castle and the appearance of a boar's head on a dish was to be the signal for each Comyn to slay a Mackintosh. The guests, however, had been warned of the plot and when the boar's head appeared each Mackintosh slew a Comyn. The ancient castle has disappeared and in its place is a striking building, originally designed by Robert Adam, which was the home of the man who, born on a farm on the other side of the Spey, won fame and fortune as "Ossian" Macpherson.

Dr Johnson may not have approved, but James Macpherson's translation of Ossian's poems, authentic or not, brought him wealth and social standing, although some of his money is said to have come from the Nabob of Arcot, for whom he was agent in 1779. He was described as "a great man from London and the Court, bedizened with rings, gold seals and furs", but, living in his grand house at Balavil, or Belleville, he never forgot his roots, and he was regarded by most people as a generous and kindly man. There is a private burial ground for the Macphersons of Balavil, the graves surrounding an obelisk erected in memory of this famous son of Badenoch, who died in 1796 at the age of fifty-nine. But "Ossian" Macpherson sleeps elsewhere; he is buried in the Poets' Corner of Westminster Abbey.

From Balavil I followed the road into Kingussie, which, over the years, has become trapped in the bedlam of the A9. Now it is being thrust back into the obscurity from which it came, for the last time I was there work was well ahead on the new north road, bypassing the town. This, in many ways, is full cycle, for when General Wade took his military road up the Spey valley it skirted the village after crossing the river and went north-east by Kerrow.

The town of Ruthven grew around the mound on which the castle was built; the town of Kingussie was centred on another mound, Tom a' Mhoid, the mound of the court, on the north side of the Spey. Its name is from the Gaelic "ceann-naghiubhsaich", the end of the fir wood, and its origins go back to the time of St Columba, who founded a chapel on the banks of the Gynack burn. It was the dominant community in church affairs, but it stood on the side roads of history while Ruthven became the focal point of change, its brooding castle walls guarding the men who moulded the future. The somersault came after the 1745 Rising, when Ruthven's importance diminished and Kingussie grew in stature as a centre of agriculture and commerce. The leap over the Spey was complete when the parish school and the Baron Bailie Court were transferred from Ruthven to Kingussie.

Nevertheless, Kingussie has always been ill at ease with progress; it was never meant to be a booming burgh and it will do nicely now that the tourist traffic has turned aside from the old A9. Queen Victoria, passing through it in 1861 on her way to Blair Atholl, found it "a very straggling place with very few cottages". There had been little change in the half century that had passed since Elizabeth Grant of Rothiemurchus, then a girl of fifteen, came upon "indications of a village" when she arrived at Kingussie in 1812 on her way to the Doune, near Aviemore. The impression she was left with was of "a few very untidy-looking slated stone houses each side of a road, the bare heather on each side of the Spey, the bare mountains on each side of the heather".

Elizabeth was one of two women named Grant who put this corner of the Highlands on the map through their writings in the 19th century. Mrs Anne Grant, poetess, essayist, and friend of Sir Walter Scott and other prominent men, including James Macpherson, was the wife of the minister at Laggan. It may be that she found some of her inspiration from the works of the Ossian translator, who, she said, was "now moving like a bright meteor over his native hills". Macpherson had "given a ball to the ladies, and made other exhibitions of wealth and liberality", and it is likely that Mrs Grant of Laggan was one of those who paid court at Belleville. In 1802 she published a volume of poems and the following year *Letters from the Mountains,* brought her instant success.

Elizabeth Grant was a year-old baby when *Letters from the Mountains* appeared in print and, some ten years later, she came to know about her namesake through another Mrs Grant, also a minister's wife, who had similar literary ambitions. Her husband was the Rev. Peter Grant, minister of the united parishes of Duthil and Rothiemurchus, and she was, says Elizabeth, dignified, literary—and a blue-stocking. "She had one aim in life—to rival the fame of Mrs Grant of Laggan. She began by two volumes of letters, full of heather and sunsets, grey clouds and mists". But she never made it; the two volumes were a failure, "though the Clan stood to her and bought half of the edition".

Young Elizabeth, who was more interested in sketching and writing at that age, could never have imagined that many years later she would write her own memoirs. She met and married an Irish officer, Colonel Smith, in India, brought up a family, and completed her memoirs in 1867. She died at the age of 89 in 1885 and thirteen years after her death *Memoirs of a Highland Lady* was published. It was written for her children, but it reached a wide and responsive audience, for it painted a vivid and authentic picture of life in the Spey valley in the century spanned by *Letters from the Mountains* and *Memoirs*.

Mrs Grant of Laggan knew "Ossian" Macpherson, but Elizabeth Grant of Rothiemurchus knew the son, "our Belleville", who was "thoroughly a gentleman". He had also been in India and returned to take possession of his Highland property about the year 1800.

For me, the way south to Drumochter lay over a memory trail followed all those years ago by the young Elizabeth Grant. She knew "every mountain, every hill, every bank, fence, path, tree", and when she came as a child to her home at the Doune, Inverdruie, near Aviemore, it was "in a perfect fever of happiness". She watched the eagles rise from their nest on the ruined Comyn castle at Loch-an-Eilean, where the fir trees "ran far up among the bare rocky crags of the Grampians". There was said to be a zig-zag causeway beneath the water, from the door of the old castle to the shore, the secret of which was always known to three persons only, but Elizabeth never found it. She knew the shepherds who lived in bothies in the hills, their only food a bag of meal with which to make a pot of brose. It did them no harm, for, wrote Elizabeth, when they came down from their high ground to attend the kirk sometimes they had "such looks as put to shame the luxurious dwellers in the smoky huts with their hot porridge and other delicacies".

The road that climbed over the Mounth from Blair to Badenoch was as familiar to her as the streets of London when she lived at Lincoln's Inn Fields. On her way north, she often stopped at the old inn at Blair, and once over the Mounth and into Badenoch slept a night at Pitmain, the last stage of the journey. "We never see such inns now; no carpets on the floors, no cushions in the chairs, no curtains to the windows. Of course, polished tables, or even clean ones, were unknown".

Pitmain is half a mile from Kingussie, but there is no sign of an inn now, only the farm of that name. Yet at one time it was known to travellers far and wide; firstly, because it was the main coaching halt between Inverness and Perth, and, secondly, because of the Pitmain Tryst. These smaller trysts were held so that cattle could be brought to a central point to be sold and collected into droves for the long journey south to the bigger trysts. There were usually anything from 100 to 300 beasts in a drove, with one drover to about sixty of them, but dealers at the more important local trysts gathered much larger droves, such as the mile-long drove seen by Bishop Forbes in the Pass of Drumochter. It was probably coming from Pitmain, which was one of the bigger trysts, serving drovers going to the Falkirk Tryst.

Elizabeth Grant knew all about these great cattle treks. She would have seen their long dark lines stirring up the dust as they lumbered south by Rothiemurchus and her father, a lawyer, had dabbled in the business, buying "a large drove of fine young black cattle for no small penny". They were sent south under the care of two Highland drovers, but the herd, a hundred head in all, was decimated by food poisoning. The Tryst of Pitmain was held every September on the moor between Kingussie and Pitmain and it was as much a social occasion as a business one. The Glorious Twelfth, the Pitmain Tryst, and the Inverness Meeting were the main ingredients of the "season", along with dinners and dances and expeditions to the lochs and glens. "A merrier shooting season was never passed", said Elizabeth of one of them.

On the day of the Tryst the bare moor above the Spey became alive with noise and colour. The drovers reminded Elizabeth Grant of the characters in Walter Scott's "Rob Roy". The air rang with greetings and bargains struck and the lowing of cattle. "Ossian's" son may not have had his father's turn of phrase, but he knew a good beast when he saw one and in the end he generally got the top price at the Tryst. "Belleville had a hundred cows, thus he had every year a hundred stots, sold generally from £7 to £8 a piece. If any died during their period of growth he made up his number by buying from the cottar farmers, the only way these little bodies had of disposing of their single beast".

Pitmain was a magnet for cattle men, rich and poor, long before Elizabeth's day. I remember seeing an exhibition of pictures in the Landmark at Carrbridge, which told the story of Alastair Grant, who lived beside the River Spey between 1670 and 1720. Every autumn he sold two of his cows to a drover at the Tryst of Pitmain, or at a market on the Moor of Ballintomb, to the north. If prices were good he would get £3 for his beasts. It was the only money he received all year and £1.15 of it had to be paid to Patrick Grant of Muckrach Castle. His cattle joined a drove going to Crieff and in the second week of October were sold to a dealer from England. Alastair Grant had six children. Three died in infancy and two more died of famine in 1697-98, and in the same year three of his eight cows were stolen by caterans.

Early in the 19th century, the Pitmain Tryst was rounded off with a dinner attended by drovers, farmers and lairds, followed by a dance. Lord Huntly presided and sent a stag from Gaick forest for the feast. Elizabeth Grant and the rest of the ladies were invited "to shine on the assemblage", but there was no question of invading the male preserve; they were barred from the dinner but allowed "to prepare tea in another room". Miss Grant obviously regarded it as right and proper that the female sex should be kept in their place. Moreover, despite the fact that she was to become known as a woman of decided opinions, she shows thinly-disguised approval of the snobbery which marked the ball. It was, she wrote in her *Memoirs*, "so consonant to the spirit of feudalism still cherished throughout our mountains", and she thought that "the manners of the higher portion of the company had a sensible effect on the lower". Later, she was to regret that "all this is over" and that "the few grandees shut themselves up rigorously in their proud exclusiveness".

The following day the cattle were on the move, strung out in bellowing black lines along the road to Drumochter by Dalwhinnie. Dalwhinnie is the apex of a rough triangle formed by both old and new roads, the routes from Spean Bridge and Fort Augustus coming in from the west, the Inverness road by Kingussie from the north-east, with the River Spey on the line of the top leg. From Kingussie, the A9 whips you down by the River Truim to Dalwhinnie, but I sought out the Wade road, on the south side of the Spey, branching off about a mile from Ruthven Barracks.

The old track cuts away from the B970 at Knappach, but it had been swallowed up in a great conglomeration of road works. I picked it up a mile farther on, by the Milton Burn at Inverton, and as I climbed up the hill towards it I could see the new road well to the south. It was something that was to follow me all the way to Blair, a parallel running of the old and the new, the Wade road, the A9, and the motorway of the future. The stones of the Milehouse of Nuide were a reminder that this rough track that I walked on had once held a promise of change and progress. I crossed the Milton Burn by a wooden bridge at a bothy at Luibleathann and went on past Lochan Odhar, which is almost on its doorstep.

There was another bridge farther on, a near perfect specimen of a Wade bridge. Beyond that was the soggy mass of Nuide Moss and then a dammed lochan before a grassy track reached Phones. The house of Phones, pronounced Fo-ness, is a large, imposing mansion which was shuttered up when I passed, but Rory, a young golden Labrador, came out from the neighbouring farm to greet me, followed by two youngsters, Michael and Julie. The road ran on past Loch Ettridge to Ettridge Farm, where a farm track cut down to the A9.

The road from Kingussie to Dalwhinnie by the main road is faster but a good deal less interesting. About a mile out of Kingussie you pass the farm of Ballachroan, home of the notorious "Black Officer", Captain John Macpherson, who came to a sticky end in the forest of Gaick, and another mile on is Newtonmore. Newtonmore, like Kingussie, gives the impression of being one main street, a passage for traffic and little else, but when you wander off the street you realise why it is so popular with tourists. It is fringed on the south side by an 18-hole golf course and it is on these pastures that the drovers coming over the Corrieyairack Pass for the Pitmain Tryst grazed their herds before driving them to market.

The Laggan Junction, where the Macpherson Museum is sited, marks the point at which the road to the Pass of Drumochter begins to shake itself free from the Spey and turn south. The road to the right sticks to the line of the river, heading west towards Loch Laggan and the Corrieyairack Pass. The road from Newtonmore, breaking away at the Laggan junction and crossing the Spey near Ralia Lodge, passes the back road to Glenmore and two miles on meets the Wade road from Ruthven at Ettridge. From there the way south is by the new dual-carriageway or through the bleak moorland to Dalwhinnie.

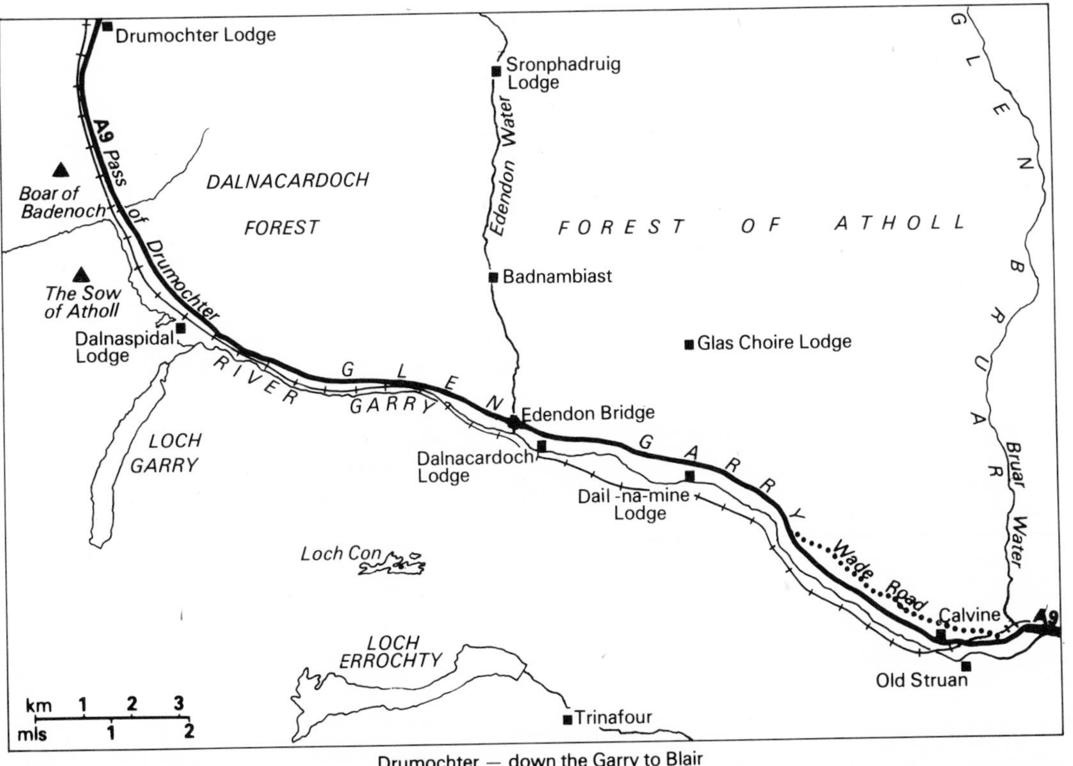

Drumochter — down the Garry to Blair

19

Road to Atholl

> Land of bens and glens and corries,
> Headlong rivers, ocean floods,
> Have we lived to see this outrage
> On your haughty solitudes?

The great iron engine, snuffing and snorting, drew away from the huddle of houses at Dalnaspidal, once a halting place for drovers on the way south, now one of a chain of stations linking the new railway line from Perth to Inverness. From the window of his carriage, John Campbell Shairp, poet, critic, and Professor of Latin at St Andrew's University, could see the twin rail tracks pushing ahead towards the Sow of Atholl. The long shriek of the engine's whistle rose and died on the mountain air as the train gathered speed for the climb over the Pass of Drumochter. Only a few months before, on September 9, 1863, the Highland Railway had been officially opened and a new chapter in Highland travel begun, but John Shairp shared little of the enthusiasm that marked this momentous event. Now, travelling for the first time on the newly-opened railway, he pondered on what it would mean. The Ironsides of Cromwell had marched up this ancient pass, but here was an Iron Monster whose invasion was stronger on the mountain-barriered land than Cromwell, bloody Cumberland, or any that had gone before.

Shairp, who was to become Principal of the United College at St Andrew's in 1868, four years after his trip on the north train, regarded the introduction of the Highland Railway as an outrage. He wrote an epic poem which cast a mournful and nostalgic eye over the route of the new railway, from the

Garry, "cribbed with mound and rampart", to "grisly, storm-resounding Badenoch", along the Spey to Rothiemurchus, with its forests of primeval pine, and up past "dark Glen More and cloven Glen Feschie". The title of the poem was "A Cry from Craig-ellachie", and the call that Principal Shairp sounded was "Stand fast, Craig-Ellachie", the war-cry of Clan Grant. It was too late. The Principal knew that the iron horses were on the rampage—

> Northward still the iron horses!
> Naught may stay their destined path
> Till they snort by Pentland surges,
> Stun the cliffs of far Cape Wrath.

Principal Shairp took twenty-one verses to say what some people are still saying to-day: what price progress? There was an underlying fear that opening up the country would mean an end to all that was good and beautiful in the lonely places, and if the professor had lived a century later he would have been appalled at the changes brought about by new and faster forms of transport. Geordie's shovellin' brigade started it all when they dug their way over the Mounth two and a half centuries ago. Wade's road left a good deal to be desired. Elizabeth Grant wrote in her *Memoirs* of a "narrow precipitous pathway tracked out by General Wade, up and down which one could scarcely be made to believe a carriage, with people sitting in it, had ever attempted to pass". Nevertheless, the 2,000 or so miles of roadway that the General built were the foundation of to-day's road system in Scotland.

Ninian Campbell, in Neil Munro's *The New Road*, talked of the changes it would bring. "The road is cut already through from Crieff to nearly Lovat's country", he said. "I trudged a bit o' the lower part o' it myself last summer; most deplorable!—the look o' things completely spoiled, and walkin' levelled to a thing that even cripples could enjoy. A body might as well be on the streets!" Munro's character was a conservationist before his time, but Principal Shairp was concerned with more than just "the look o' things", although he, too, regretted the rape of the "haughty solitudes". Whatever benefits progress brings, something is lost. Ninian Campbell described the Road as a rut that would be the poor Gael's grave; Principal Shairp saw those shining railway tracks pointing the way to the disappearance of the ancient Gael.

Ah! you say, it little recketh;
Let the ancient manners go:
Heaven will work, through their destroying,
Some end greater than you know.

Be it so, but will Invention,
With her smooth mechanic arts,
Bid arise the old Highland warriors,
Beat again warm Highland hearts?

Nay! whate'er of good they herald,
Whereso' comes that hideous roar,
The old charm is disenchanted,
The old Highlands are no more.

Forty years before that poem was written, Joseph Mitchell, a young engineer from Forres, went to work for the famous Thomas Telford. His father, John Mitchell, was Telford's Chief Inspector of Highland Roads, and when he died in 1824 Joseph succeeded to the title at the age of 21. That year the roads in the Highlands were nearing completion, travel was becoming more sophisticated, and there was a slow transition from horseback to gig. The last of the "riders", as they were called, were the commercial travellers, and Mitchell was to recall in later years how he saw them in the inns on the way north, portly old gentlemen with rubicund faces, wearing top-boots, blue coats with brass buttons, and carrying large, heavy whips. They rode good horses, did their business in no hurry, and had saddle-bags behind them for their cloths and patterns.

Mitchell quickly made a name for himself under Telford, but his eyes were fixed on new horizons. The future would be built on railways, not roads, and he visualised a network of tracks spreading across the Highlands like a spider's web. One of the schemes he had in mind was for a line going over the Mounth by the Pass of Drumochter, linking Perth and Inverness. The idea of a railway crossing the Grampians was greeted with derision. The Great North of Scotland Railway opposed the plan and at a Parliamentary inquiry in April, 1846, William Austin, a barrister for the opposition, declared with caustic wit that ascending a 1,580 ft summit was very unprecedented and that Mr Mitchell was the greatest mountain climber he had ever heard of. He beat Napoleon outright, sneered Austin, and he quite eclipsed Hannibal.

Austin went on to say that he had read a book of several hundred pages describing how Hannibal had crossed the Alps, but if this line was passed no doubt quartos would be written about Mr Mitchell. The plan was rejected, but the barrister's jibe was to boomerang on him, for quartos *were* written about Joseph Mitchell. Seventeen years later the first train went over the Grampians by the Pass of Drumochter.

One of the strongest opponents of the scheme was the Duke of Atholl and Mitchell met him at Blair Castle to try to win him over. They dined with three stalwart Highlanders waiting on them in full Highland dress and Mitchell remarked that he had met the Duke's grandfather thirty-six years before in the same room. "Ah! how odd", the Duke said. "Your father built the Tilt bridge and made the new road below the castle, and now you are to make the railway". Mitchell converted the Duke to his cause and often stayed as a guest at the castle. On the eve of the opening of the line the Duke, who was seriously ill with cancer of the throat, was given a special trip from the Pass of Drumochter to Pitlochry. "He seemed to enjoy the rapid motion in descending from the County March at the rate of fifty miles an hour—rather a dangerous speed on a new-made line", said Mitchell. At 10.18 am on September 9, 1863, a long train started from Inverness with the names "York, Euston Square and King's Cross" marked on the carriages. Another train started from Perth for the North in the middle of the night. The first of the "iron horse" invaders had stormed the Mounth.

The Principal, peering disapprovingly from his train at Dalwhinnie, clung to one faint hope. He believed that there were still countless glens undesecrated, still unnumbered lochans "where no human roar yet travels". As his train pulled away from the platform at Dalwhinnie station and swung north-east through Glen Truim he could see on his left a road coming down through the hills from the north. If he had followed it he would have eventually found his unknown corries and dark rocks where "the white foam flings". This was the road that General Wade had built to bring his troops from Fort Augustus over the wild Corrieyairack Pass and down to Dalwhinnie on their way south.

I have never tramped the whole of the Corrieyairack Pass but I have been half-way across it, north of Loch Spey, somewhere near the point where the Marquis of Montrose turned down Glen Roy on his famous march to Inverlochy. But the figure who steps out of history on this savage, wind-swept pass is that of Charles Edward Stuart, the Young Pretender, for it was on his way through the Corrieyairack that he sent Sir John Cope and his troops scurrying north to Inverness and the events which were to spark off the mocking lines of Adam Skirving's ballad—

> Hey, Johnnie Cope, are ye waukin' yet?
> Or are your drums a-beating yet?

History has been kinder to Sir John Cope than the balladeers, for he was a brave and competent soldier. The Board of General Officers who investigated his behaviour at the Corrieyairack debacle found it "unblameable". Curiously, the board was presided over by Marshal Wade, as he had then become, and it was Wade's road-building that allowed Sir John to make a speedy march north to Dalwhinnie when he heard that Prince Charles had landed in Scotland. On his arrival at Dalwhinnie, Sir John learned that Prince Charles' forces had moved east from Invergarry and seized the

Corrieyairack Pass. There were 2500 Jacobites in the pass, armed with twenty small cannon, whereas General Cope had only 1400 ill-trained soldiers. Sir John decided to march on to Inverness—and the way to the south was opened up for Prince Charles and his followers.

The strength of the Jacobite army was only one factor in Johnnie Cope's decision. The bigger enemy was the formidable Corrieyairack itself. "The South Side of the Corriarrick", said the Report of the Board of Officers, "is so very sharp an Ascent that the Road traverses the whole Breadth of the Hill seventeen times before it arrives at the Top. The Road, in descending on the North Side is flank'd for a considerable Space by a Wood, and is crossed by a large Hollow, which is the Bed of a Torrent, and whose Banks are so extremely steep, that it is not passable but by a Bridge, which was possessed by the Rebels, and could have been broken down in a very short time, if they had found it necessary. From this description it is plain that a very small Force, who were Masters of this Hill, were capable of stopping or even defeating a considerable Army that should attempt to dislodge them".

Sir John said that the rebels had planned to meet the King's army "at the several passes above Snugborough, a place at the north side of the Corrieyairack over which lay the direct road to Fort Augustus". In his book "In Scotland Again", H. V. Morton told of going over the Corrieyairack and of his search for Snugborough. "I looked everywhere for the unlikely word Snugborough", he wrote, "but could find no trace of it".

The name Snugborough was, in fact, invented by Wade's men in the way that soldiers give their own names to the places they find themselves in. They probably thought it anything but snug, stuck as it was in the fastnesses of the Corrieyairack, far from home and the comfort of a good billet. A celebration held to mark both the King's birthday and the completion of "the great road for wheel-carriages between Fort Augustus and Ruthven" took place in "a little glen among the hills called Laggan a Vannah, but now by the soldiers Snugburgh". There is no Laggan a Vannah on the map, but west of Corrieyairack mountain the Wade road passes Lagan a' Bhainne. This spot, so near the end of the pass, would have been a suitable place to pitch camp and celebrate their labours.

There is also an account of a journey across the Corrieyairack by coach in 1798, in which the writer, the Hon. Mrs Murray, describes the first seven miles of the pass and then says, "It is not till after the crossing the bridge over the river Tarff, at the hollow, called in Gaelic Laga-ne-biene, the hollow of milk, that the base of Corriyarrick begins". She mentions that there were "two or three huts at Laga-na-veine". The road crosses the Allt Coire Uchdachan, a tributary of the Tarff, at Lagan a' Bhainne, which is clearly the same place. Moreover, there were summer shielings at Lagan a' Bhainne.

The conditions under which the Hanoverian soldiers worked were pictured vividly in "The New Road". "Seven miles were yet to cut and build to Fort Augustus and Leggat hounded on his soldiery as if they had been slaves of Carolina. As yet the winds of autumn breathed, the floods had not yet begun, but days were shortening, and he meant to have the Pass accomplished ere the winter burst upon the land and took possession till the spring. His soldiers' sixpence extra pay each day was earned in sweat. The mattock and the spade were in their hands at daybreak; often through the night they wrought prodigiously by torchlight or the flare of brushwood fires, stemming the course of new-born torrents from the hills, strengthening the bridges, shattering or burying enormous boulders, patching up the damage done at times by natives, who, since the Road had come across Dalwhinnie, loathed it like a pest".

The road through the Corrieyairack, which Edmund Burt, Wade's chief surveyor, claimed was "more easy for Wheel Carriages than Highgate Hill", has no fine coaches rattling over it in the 20th century. It has been given back to the wilderness. When I was there the latest thing in Corrieyairack transport was being unloaded from a Land Rover at Drummin.

This was a miniature "buggy" which a keeper was using to recover a stag shot in the hills some distance away, and I left him and climbed up the stony track by the Allt Yairack. It was difficult to believe that this was once the main road between Fort Augustus and Laggan, only twenty-five miles in length, yet a place which even the boldest traveller faced with reluctance, sobered by the thought of its fearsome storms and other unseen dangers. Mrs Grant of Laggan, in her *Letters from the Mountains*, said that the country people devoutly believed that an evil spirit dwelt there. "This awful mountain", she called the Corrieyairack.

The road pulls itself out of the wilderness east of Drummin, following the Spey to Garva or Garbha Bridge, a double-arched bridge which takes you over the river and down to Garvamore, a former kings-house or inn, where Prince Charles stopped in 1745. There is another Wade bridge about two miles on, but it has been set aside from its original use by the development of waterworks. Sherramore and Sherrabeg are passed and at the east end of the Spey dam a bridge crosses the river, but the military road keeps to the south bank. It passes Dalcholly House, now called Dalchully Farm, and curves round to the Spean Bridge-Newtonmore road, crossing another Wade bridge over the Mashie Burn. From there it goes straight on to emerge farther east than the present farm road. It was at Dalcholly House that Sir John Cope did the turn-about that gave him an unenviable place in the history of the '45 Rising.

The Wade road was on the line of the A86 to Cat Lodge, where there was once an inn, and it was here that the link road from Ruthven joined the main route to the Corrieyairack Pass. Taylor and Skinner's map of 1775 shows it as "Catleack", showing the name derives from Gaelic leac, a hillside. From Cat Lodge whose stone cats are a reminder of the Clan Chattan motto, "Touch not the cat bot a glove", the military road follows the Bruthach Druim an Lagain[1], the A889, to Dalwhinnie.

[1] Ascent of the Laggan ridge.

On the Bruthach Druim an Lagain, above the railway line which carried Principal Shairp on his journey over the Pass of Drumochter, it was hard to accept, even a century later, that what the Principal said was true and that "grisly, storm-resounding Badenoch is a wilderness no more". The railway cut the shackles of isolation, but not much has really changed. It is still, as Sir Archibald Geikie, the noted Scottish geologist said, "by far the wildest scene through which any railway passes in this country". Away to the south-west lay the long sweep of Loch Ericht, its waters tumbling by a miracle of modern engineering down into Loch Rannoch, and my mind chased the memories of earlier years when I followed a stone-strewn track from Rannoch to its twin loch in the north. This was Shairp country again—

There o'er the abyss by long Loch Ericht cloven
Ben-Aulder, huge, broad-breasted—the heavens bowed
To meet him—hides great shoulders in dark-woven
And solemn tabernacle of moveless cloud.

There is not much in Dalwhinnie to hold you; it has been thrust even farther into the background by the new north road. There is the railway station, and the distillery, and a hotel that has spent the last hundred years trying to live down the reputation Queen Victoria left it with when she stayed a night on her way to Blair. "There was hardly anything to eat", she complained, "and there was only tea, and two miserable starved Highland chickens, without any potatoes! No pudding and no *fun;* no little maid (the two there not wishing to come in), nor our two people—who were wet and drying our and their things—to wait on us. It was not a nice supper; and the evening was wet".

Rail and road keep each other company down through the Pass of Drumochter, or Druimuachdar, as the sign by the rail track spells it; then on past the Boar of Badenoch and the Sow of Atholl to Dalnaspidal. You can still retreat into the past and follow the old military road where it hasn't been gobbled up by the bulldozers. Dalnaspidal means "the field of the spital or hospice", which suggests that its use by travellers goes well back over the centuries. It was certainly used as a halting place by drovers, who followed an old drove route down the west side of Loch Garry to Kinloch Rannoch. When the Highland Railway opened it became an important link in the service over Drumochter to Speyside.

The Wade Stone, a large marking stone said to have been erected by the General in 1729, is (or was) some three miles south of Dalnaspidal, but it had been temporarily removed while the road developments went ahead. There is a story that Wade put a golden guinea on top of the stone and found it still there a year later. About a mile and half below the stone the Edendon Water runs into the Garry and it is here that the old path from the Gaick hills creeps out of the woods at Dalnacardoch and joins the new roadway. Dalnacardoch is the last of the three main "dals" or fields. There was an inn there at one time and the road coming in from the south by Trinafour was the main route from Stirling to Inverness. General Wade planned his road across the Grampians from his "Hutt at Dalnacardoch".

Across what Elizabeth Grant of Rothiemurchus called "the dreary moor to Dalnacardoch" lies Calvine, where the Minigaig route by the Bruar Water comes in from the north and the modern B847 goes west by the Errochty Water to join the Trinafour road to Rannoch. The Bruar joins the Garry a mile east of Calvine and it was there, at Pitagowan, that Wade's military road turned slightly north-west and followed a line above the route of its modern successor, the A9, emerging south of Dail-na-mine Lodge. There is not much trace of it from Pitagowan to Calvine, but west of that there is a splendid stretch that must be virtually unchanged since the day it was built. It crosses the Allt a' Chrom Buidh by a magnificent Wade bridge, which for some curious reason was known as "The Eye of the Window". It was beyond this bridge that I heard a great explosion, the sound of blasting, a reminder of the new era of road-building, and from where I stood I could encompass in a glance more than two centuries

The Wade bridge known as 'The Eye of the Window' near Calvine.

of progress. There was the Wade road itself, the dying A9, the new road of the 1980s, and, through the trees, a glimpse of the railway which Principal Shairp had disliked so much.

Walking along it, I could see, too, the Struan road going away to Kinloch Rannoch. This is Struan country and in the Clan Donnachaidh Museum and Centre at Bruar there is a map of the Barony of Struan, or Strowan as it was known, dating back to 1756. The map is a copy of one in Register House in Edinburgh, made by John Leslie surveyor, for the Government's Commissioners for the Forfeited estates to show the extent of Struan's lands confiscated after the '45 Rising. There is a line on the map which reads, "The Military Road from Augustus by Daalnakeardoch", and near the Brower (Bruar) bridge are the words "a sergeant's command here". There is a ferry marked near "Brower Bridge", also a Boat House, "but it is indicated on the River Garry, 'A bridgeway necessary'". The museum, a superbly laid-out building, is run by Alex MacRae, who was a garage owner in Blair before taking charge of the museum when it opened in 1969. If you seek information, the inevitable answer is, "Ask Alec MacRae". Rightly, he is regarded as an authority on local history.

From Pitagowan it was only a mile or two to Blair Atholl, following the Garry, the river that Pennant called "an outrageous stream, whose ravages have greatly deformed the valley". Queen Victoria looked on it more kindly when she passed that way in 1844, for she recorded in her Journal that she thought the Garry "very fine". She visited Blair on her Third Great Expedition through Glenfeshie and south by Dalwhinnie to Atholl in 1861 and in 1863 she made a return journey that was saddened by memories of Prince Albert. "To think of the contrast of the time two years ago when my darling was so well and I so happy with him", she wrote. The Duke of Atholl asked permission for his men, "the same who had gone with us through that glen on that happy day two years ago", to give the Queen a cheer. "Oh! it was so dreadfully sad", said Victoria.

For me, however, another figure strode across the pages of history when I was at Blair-in-Atholl. Talking to Alec MacRae at the Clan Donnachaidh Museum, I noticed two volumes of Napier's *Montrose* in the book-case. It turned out that Alec shared my admiration for the hero of "The Year of Miracles", and he took me to the door of the museum and pointed away down Glen Garry to where James Graham had raised the Royal Standard on that fateful day in 1644. The actual spot was a mile north of Lude House, where Montrose had spent the night. Alec said there had been some sort of memorial there at one time but all that was left was the base.

The Great Montrose had been with me from the very start of my journey over the Grampian passes. He had been at Tollohill, overlooking the old Causey Mounth, as I looked down on the grey glitter of Aberdeen. He had stirred a breath of romance under "the Baron's old grey towers" at Crathes Castle and had ridden with me across the ancient Cryne's

Cross Mounth to what became the land of Burns and Grassic Gibbon. I had thought of him among the dead stones of Ruthven in Badenoch and when I tramped through the Gaick hills to Atholl. He had taken me on his road to defeat down Glen Isla and past the broken walls of Forter Castle. Blair Castle was where it all began for James Graham, 1st Marquis of Montrose. For me, it was the end of my pilgrimage over the Mounth.

Blair Castle.

Bibliography

Allen, David Elliston, The Naturalist in Britain.
Balfour, Sir James, The Historical Works of Sir James Balfour of Denmylne and Kinnaird.
Barbour, John, The Bruce.
Brown, P. Hume, Early Travellers in Scotland.
Buchan, John, Montrose.
Dinnie, Robert, An Account of the Parish of Birse.
Fraser, G. M., The Old Deeside Road.
Gibbon, Lewis Grassic, a Scots Quair.
Gordon, Patrick of Ruthven, A Short Abridgement of Britanes Distemper from the years MOCXXXIX MDCXLIX.
Gordon, Seton, Highways and Byways in the Central Highlands.
Graham, Cuthbert, Portrait of Aberdeen and Deeside.
Graham, Henry Grey, The Social Life of Scotland in the Eighteenth Century.
Grant, Anne, Letters from the Mountains.
Grant, Elizabeth, Memoirs of a Highland Lady.
Grant, John, Memorandum Book, 1771.
Grant, John, Legends of the Braes of Mar.
Gough, Henry, Itinerary of King Edward I 1272-1307.
Haldane, A.R.B., The Drove Roads of Scotland.
Hardyng, John, The Chronical of John Hardyng.
Jervise, Andrew, Land of the Lindsays.
Johnson, Samuel, Journey to the Western Islands of Scotland.
Keith, Alexander, A Thousand Years of Aberdeen.
Kirk, Thomas, An Account of a Tour in Scotland.
Laing, Alexander, The Caledonian Itinerary.
Lauder, Sir Thomas Dick, The Moray Floods.
Michie, Rev. J. G., Deeside Tales and History of Loch Kinnord.
Miller, Rev. J. T., Tales of a Highland Parish (Glenshee).
Milne, John C., Poems.
Mitchell, Joseph, Reminiscences of My Life in the Highlands.
Mollyson, Charles A., The Parish of Fordoun.
Morton, H. V., In Scotland Again.
McConnochie, A. I., Deeside *and* Lochnagar.
Mackintosh, John, History of the Valley of the Dee.